KINGDOM OF SWEDEN
Stockholm
St. PETERSBURG
MOSCOW
RUSSIAN EMPIRE
penhagen
PRUSSIA
Berlin
Warsaw
KINGDOM OF POLAND
Vienna
RO-HUNGARIAN EMPIRE
SEBASTAPOL
BLACK SEA
CONSTANTINOPLE
OTTOMAN EMPIRE
ples
KINGDOM OF THE TWO SICILLIES
Athens
ALTA
CRETE

A VICTORIAN RSM

From India to the Crimea

A VICTORIAN RSM

From India to the Crimea

George Loy Smith

COSTELLO

First published 1987

Enquiries to:
D J Costello (Publishers) Ltd.
43 High Street
Tunbridge Wells TN1 1XL

British Library Cataloguing in Publication Data
Smith, George Loy
A Victorian RSM : from India to the Crimea.
1. Great Britain. *Army. Prince Albert's Own Hussars, 11th*—History 2. Great Britain. *Army*—Military life
I. Title
357'.1'0941 UA659.P/

ISBN 0-7104-3022-1

Typeset by Composing Operations Ltd., Southborough
Printed by Billings & Sons Ltd., Worcester

CONTENTS

Part One—1833–35 Enlistment—Selected for India—Aboard the Herefordshire—Arrival at Fort William 7

Part Two—1836–38 Meerut and Kānpur—Famine in India—Victoria ascends the throne—Lord Cardigan takes command—Return to England 27

Part Three—1839–53 'Prince Albert's Own Hussars'—The Queen's Duty—Appointed sergeant—In aid of civil power in Ireland—England and return to Ireland 55

Part Four—1853–54 War declared with Russia—A long sea voyage—Arrival at Varna—Enemy encounters at the Almá—Arrival at Balaclava 77

Part Five—Wednesday 25th October 1854 The Charge of the Light Brigade 125

Part Six—26th October 1854–26th January 1855 After the Charge 149

Part Seven—1855–56 Winter in the Crimea—Discharge from the Army—Return to Old England 175

Part Eight—Appendix and Evidence from the Charge 213

PART ONE

1833–35

Enlistment—Selected for India—Aboard the Herefordshire—Arrival at Fort William

It was on a bright May morning in 1833 that the Headquarters of a cavalry regiment marched into a pretty country town and formed up in the market-place directly opposite my master's shop. What I was doing at the time I cannot now call to mind, perhaps making pills or mixing medicine, this being my daily occupation, having been apprenticed about six months previously to a chemist and druggist. This was the first time I had seen a regiment of cavalry with their mounted band and I became enchanted with them, particularly when I thought of what a glorious life theirs must be to mine, they marching from town to town and seeing the world, and appearing so light-hearted, and I, condemned to stand behind a counter from Monday morning to Saturday night. Even on Sunday we were not free, the shop only being closed during divine service, I attending to it one Sunday, the other apprentice the next.

The following morning they again paraded in the same place before marching off. I cannot describe my feelings when I heard the last strains of the band, and the rear-guard fast receding from sight. What would I have given to go with them! You will not be surprised at this when I tell you that I belonged to a family that had seen service both by sea and land—a love of adventure was therefore natural to me. My grandfather served under the Duke of York in Flanders, was present at the Siege of Dunkirk and N....?—at the latter place he was wounded in the head by the bursting of a shell. My father served in the Peninsula; one uncle wore the Gold Medal for Leipsic and the

Waterloo Medal, having served in the Rocket troop; another uncle lost his right arm in boarding a French man-of-war in the Mediterranean and saw much service— so that I think you will forgive me for wishing to follow in their footsteps.

On 10 June 1833, less than one month later, I took the oath of allegiance to serve the King, his heirs and successors in the 11th Light Dragoons. Being but 16 years and 2 months old, I was enlisted by special authority, consequently the first year and ten months did not count for service. Colonel Brotherton commanded the Maidstone Garrison at this time, which consisted of the riding establishment: viz. two men from each cavalry regiment, and depots of the four regiments in India: viz. the 4th, 11th and 13th Light Dragoons and the 16th Lancers.

It was the custom at this time for all recruits to be placed in hospital till their uniforms were made. In a few days mine was fitted, and I was told off to a room by Sergeant-Major James, in which were 12 men, most of them belonging to the 11th. This room, without exception, contained the roughest set of men I ever met with. The ringleader's name was Dungate, he was a terror to most of us. In a few days, the sergeant-major removed me to the adjoining room where the men were altogether of a different stamp, more quiet and orderly, and I was much pleased with the change.

A friendship now sprang up between me and a young fellow of the name of Dodsworth, the son of a surgeon of Leeds. Opposite me at table sat another young fellow who was conspicuous for his ill-looks and vulgar demeanour: he would say 'Jack or Bill, throw me a handfull of salt'. He, at this time wore a round white piece of cloth, about the size of a five shilling piece, sewn on his right arm which denoted that he was confined to barracks. This man was called Billy Taylor. He went to India about a fortnight after this. On arriving at Kānpur, the colonel of the 16th Lancers sent for him, when he became his guest. The detachment proceeded to Meerut without him, and he was sent back to England. We afterwards heard that he was the son of an English nobleman. ['Lord Exmouth' crossed out].

I was now placed in a squad to learn the foot drill, Sergeant-Major Anson was our instructor. After our first lesson, he asked me if I had ever drilled before, I replied, 'No.'

At this season, we attended foot drill before breakfast, riding drill after, and foot drill again in the afternoon. Our uniform was: scarlet jacket with buff facings, dark grey overalls with yellow stripes, shakos with white plumes. One day I saw a sergeant-major in a different uniform to any I had before seen; he wore a blue jacket with buff facings and a cap with a peak. I was told that he was the regimental sergeant-major of the 11th and that he had just returned from India to be discharged, he having completed his service. His name was Widows.

There were many orchards not far from the barracks, and the apples now looked very tempting, this being the middle of September, so a party of half a dozen was formed to go on a pillaging expedition, amongst them being this Dungate and a man by the name of Chapgate of the 4th Dragoon Guards who were to take the lead in this affair. It was arranged that, if we were attacked, we were to defend ourselves and stick together; it was likewise arranged that some of us should empty the straw out of our pillow cases to carry the apples in, I being one to do this. As soon as it was dark, we proceeded to the orchard and were busy picking away, when two men and a dog suddenly came rushing through the gate. Our leaders, instead of doing as they had proposed, were the first to decamp. We all managed to get clear away, however and heard nothing more of the affair, but I made up my mind that I would never again go on such an expedition.

MEERUT
Delhi
New Delhi
THE GREAT
N
KANNAUJ
Agra
Lucknow
GANGES
KĀNPUR
GAGARA
Gwalior
YAMUNA
ALLAHABAD
INDIA
THE PLAINS OF THE GANGES
DELHI
CALCUTTA
MADRAS

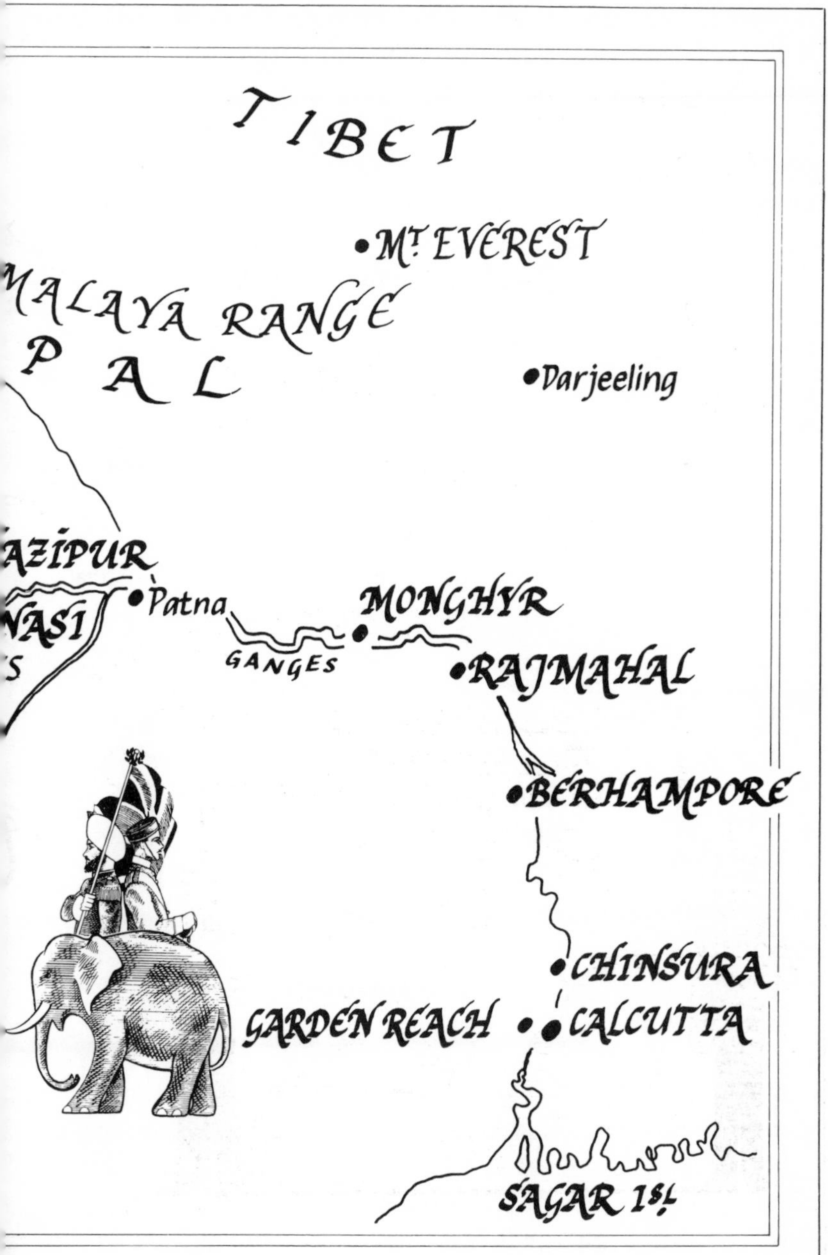

TIBET

• MT. EVEREST

MALAYA RANGE

P A L

• Darjeeling

AZIPUR

• Patna

NASI

S

MONGHYR

GANGES

• RAJMAHAL

• BERHAMPORE

• CHINSURA

GARDEN REACH • • CALCUTTA

SAGAR ISL

Shortly after this a man, (I do not now remember which regiment he belonged to), was brought into barracks by another man who had with him a little dog; he had been taken in the act of robbing this man's orchard. Colonel Brotherton ordered a general parade, the soldier was marched a prisoner between a file of the guard. Colonel Brotherton then beckoned to the man, who came forward with his little dog. He then addressed us, at the same time looking at the man with contempt, saying, 'This soldier allowed this old man and this little dog to bring him into barracks a prisoner.' He then awarded him a heavy punishment, but we all understood it was more for allowing himself to be taken than for stealing the apples. Desertion was a crime so rare in the army at this time, that not more than two or three cases occurred annually in the whole garrison.

There is a saying in the Army, 'Still improving like Joshua Brooks,' the saying originating in this way: Brooks was a soldier's son. When a boy, he was placed with the garrison armourer to learn the trade, who had to send in a weekly report to the commandant, which was read by him after church parade, with reports of other boys who were learning trades. The report attached to Joshua's name was invariably 'Still improving.' Brooks, when I joined, was a sergeant in the 4th Dragoon Guards and an instructor in the Riding School; he drilled the ride I belonged to. He was an exceedingly smart fellow and a first-rate drill.

Flogging in the army at this time was suspended in consequence of a man of the Greys having been, as the country considered, unjustly flogged. Had it not been so, Private W Bayldon of the 11th would certainly have been awarded corporal punishment. The story is this: Bayldon was at kit drill with others under the charge of a corporal, when he halted, unbuckled his kit, threw it down in the centre of the barrack yard, and positively refused to carry it. The crime was considered so serious that it was at once reported to the commandant, Colonel Brotherton, who came out of his quarters and walked across the barrack yard to where Bayldon was standing by the side of his kit. In a loud tone of voice he gave the word of command 'Attention!' Bayldon took no notice. All who witnessed this stood aghast, for a man to refuse to do what he was ordered, at this time was unheard of. Colonel Brotherton ordered a drum-head court-martial to assemble immediately. They were not long. The trumpets then sounded 'Turn out the whole' and every man immediately ran out into the barrack yard and fell in, as he was. The court-martial was at once read, and Bayldon was awarded thirty days' imprisonment with hard labour. In less than ten minutes more, he was lodged in Maidstone Jail.

Captain Myer, a German, was the Riding Master. Learning to ride at this time was a long and tedious affair. I do not remember ever having been put back, and nothing was allowed to prevent us attending every day; still, when I had been 12 months at drill, although I could ride well by balance, I could not ride with stirrups for I had only had a little practice—the entire lesson generally being given without, as the following incident will prove:

> In consequence of four detachments having been sent to India in the following June, I, being one of the most efficient men in the garrison at this time, was ordered to turn out in Review Order to carry a dispatch to Chatham (rate seven miles per hour). I started at a trot but kept losing my stirrups, and was much embarrassed for some distance. Before arriving at Chatham, I got on much better, but lost one spur and my plume tube broke, so that I was obliged to take my plume out and put it in my holster—and I rode into Chatham garrison with one spur like a butcher's boy.

On 25 June 1834, a draught of the 11th embarked for India. I was much dissatisfied at not being selected to go, especially as many were sent who had joined after I did. I was foolish enough out of vexation to apply to resign my rank as corporal, which was permitted. In about three months after this, I was dismissed, with a ride consisting of one officer and 11 non-commissioned officers and men, having learned during the 15 months the use of the lance, sword, carbine and pistol (mounted), also infantry sword exercise and gun drill.

There was an order at this time that, as soon as possible after a recruit joined, before leaving hospital, the Articles of War should be read to him. This was a duty Sergeant-Major James generally selected me for. Many of the recruits at this time could not read and numbers could not sign their names whilst at the same time there was a sprinkling of moderately educated men.

On 10 December following, I was again appointed full corporal. About this time, a recruit was placed in my room, by name, Thomas Silver. He had been a lieutenant in the 77th Regiment, but we did not know it at the time. Many years afterwards, when we were sergeant-majors together, he told me his history. In 1858, he left the regiment as lieutenant on half pay.

The month of June 1835 having now arrived (this being the month that the draught invariably embarked for the regiments in Bengal), we were all constantly on the alert for the trumpet to sound 'Orders' in the morning—a sound we never heard at this time, except for the draughts to prepare to march early the following morning. No man knew who was going until the sergeant-majors had been to the office and the men selected. The eventful morning at length came [on] 25th June. Orders-sounded, all hearts beat high. I was very anxious to go, but serious thoughts flashed across my mind: how many thousands of men had left the garrison for India never to return?—but still I wished to see the world.

Shortly the parade trumpet sounded for the 11th and 16th. Mine was the second name callèd, being the second senior corporal on the list, 26 in all being selected. Rigby, being senior to me, was appointed acting sergeant and to take charge of the detachment. I was also appointed acting sergeant, but we both had to resign our rank as full corporals, now being placed on private's pay. The remainder of the day was spent in packing up.

The following morning we paraded early with 60 of the 16th Lancers and the garrison band. Colonel Brotherton inspected us, then marched us off. The band struck up *The Girl I Left Behind Me*, we gave three cheers, and so left Maidstone, I having been there a little over two years. There were many who had joined but a few weeks.

The band played merry tunes as far as Sandling, then left us to proceed on our way to Northfleet, where we arrived about midday and at once embarked on board the ship *Herefordshire* (1350 tones, Captain Wolf commander).

We found on board a strong detachment of the 9th Regiment, consisting of several officers, 159 non-commissioned officers and men, 16 women and 27 children. We likewise had one woman, and the 16th Lancers, four, but no children. We (the 26 men of the 11th) had the midships on the holop deck appointed to us, between the sailors and the 16th Lancers, the infantry occupying the lower deck. Each detachment was now divided into three watches, so that there was always one-third of the soldiers on deck during the night and in fine weather all remained on deck during the day.

Two days after we weighed anchor and dropped down the river with the tide, some of the sails being set, but unfortunately as soon as we got clear of the river, a strong head wind set in, so that we were obliged to tack frequently to make any headway. It was full a week before we arrived off Portsmouth.

All this time I was dreadfully seasick and ate little or nothing, and the water was so bad and the tea worse being made of it, that I suffered very much. After leaving Portsmouth, the wind abated and became more favourable so that I soon recovered from my seasickness and was not again troubled with it during the voyage.

We touched at Madeira but did not cast anchor. The weather now became warmer as we neared the line. The sunsets were so beautiful that to describe them is far beyond my power. We stood and gazed at them with wonder and admiration. As the sun neared the horizon, the colours changed every moment; then he disappeared and it was soon dark, till the moon rose; then it was again almost as light as day. We were particularly cautioned by the sailors not to sleep with our faces exposed to her rays. One man of the 9th was affected by not paying attention to this, for as soon as it was dark he became quite blind.

One day the captain, after taking the latitude and longitude, told us that we should cross the line the next day. After the sun set, it being very dark, all at once we saw a large flame of fire on the sea not far from the ship, and a loud voice, that seemed to come from the fire, shouted out, 'What ship is that, pray?'

The captain, through his speaking trumpet, replied, *The Herefordshire.*

'Where are you bound for?'

'Calcutta' replied the captain.

'What have you on board?' again asked the voice.

'Troops' replied the captain, 'and who are you pray?'

'I am Neptune, the God of the Seas. Tomorrow at noon, I will pay you a visit.'

'Shall be glad to see you' replied the captain.

'Good night' said Neptune.

'Good night' said the captain.

In another moment the flame disappeared. The next morning, we were all in a great state of excitement, and the sailors were exceedingly busy in making preparations. A large sail was secured in the larboard waist, and half filled with water, and at the edge facing the quarter deck, a platform was placed. Everything being in readiness, we anxiously waited for the time when Neptune was to appear.

At last it was announced that a boat was at the side. We all flocked to it and there, to our amazement, was a boat full of the most grotesque figures we ever saw. The gangway was opened and the steps put down. A huge being, with a long beard and a trident in hand, this being Neptune, came first, then followed six of his acolytes. They walked across the quarter-deck to where the captain stood.

Neptune now demanded that all who had not been in his dominions before were to be handed over to him, that they might be shaved. Several unfortunate sailors were brought forward, one of the acolytes mounted the steps, two others got into the sail up to their waists in water, while the first sailor was brought up the steps by two others.

Now commenced the performance of shaving. The first acolyte had a pail of cow dung, tar, etc, mixed up and a huge brush and a piece of iron hoop. With this he smeared his face all over and then asked him a question. The moment he opened his mouth, dab went the brush and nearly filled his mouth with this beastliness. He then shaved him in a most cruel manner and they tilted him backwards into the sail of water, when he was seized by the two acolytes waiting for him and held under till he was nearly drowned—it was a cruel ordeal.

Several other poor unfortunate sailors were served in the same way— if they had attempted it with us, we should have fought for it. Those in the steerage, such as cuddy waiters, etc, escaped by each paying a certain number of bottles of rum. For several hours all kinds of fun was carried on. Some carried pails of water up the rigging and threw it down on the others, so that when the fun was all over, we had not a dry thread on us.

After passing the line, we were becalmed for several days. The sea was like a mirror, and we could see sharks swimming by the side of the ship. One day the captain saw a large shark astern that had been following us for several days; he ordered the shark hook to be baited with a piece of pork. It was no sooner thrown into the sea than the monster seized it. The rope attached to the chain which held the hook was passed through a block on the main yard-arm. About 50 soldiers now laid on to the rope, and he was soon drawn out of the sea, and suspended between the main yard and the quarter-deck.

The captain now called, 'Lower away, all hands stand clear.' The moment the monster reached the deck, he struck it a tremendous blow with his tail. One of the sailors pointed a capstan bar at him, when he made a snap at it and drove his teeth some distance into it. A sailor now went behind him and with one blow, cut off his tail. The tail part was cooked; it had much the taste and appearance of cod. The jaw bones were preserved for the captain; they were so large that I passed my body through them.

While in these latitudes, we frequently saw shoals of flying fish and several flew into the ship. When nearing the Cape [of Good Hope], we saw a whale, also a water spout. This being the season when the roughest weather was to be expected in these latitudes, the captain in consequence gave the Cape a wide birth by keeping well to the south; at one time we were 500 miles south of it. It was here we encountered a gale of wind, which lasted for three days. Fortunately it was right aft, so that with the foresail closely reefed and a stormy staysail to steady the ship, we sped over these mighty waves at the rate of 12 miles an hour. The scene was awfully grand: at one moment we appeared to be on the top of a wave as high as St Paul's; the next in a gulf with the hills on each side reaching to the clouds. All this time the stormy petrel was flying round us as unconcernedly as though it was a summers day. The weather too was very cold.

After this, we began to make the turn northward and soon experienced better weather. On nearing the line, we were becalmed for nearly a week, and again in the Bay of Bengal. During the voyage we saw but few vessels, and only spoke with one or two. We never saw land until we arrived at Sand Heads, Sāgar Island, which we sighted to our inexpressible joy, on 23rd October, after a voyage of five months. As soon as we dropped anchor, a number of boats came laden with cocoa nuts, bananas, oranges, lemons, melons and several kinds of fruit that we had never before seen. We at once commenced bartering with the natives.

The following day, we were transferred to small vessels, the *Herefordshire* drawing too much water to proceed further. We now sailed steadily up the river [Hooghly] towards Calcutta, this part between Sāgar Island and Calcutta being called Garden Reach. The scenery here is very beautiful, the banks of the river being studded with mansions and gardens.

On 24th October, with delight, we once more found ourselves on dry land; but how different everything appeared: the people black and generally clothed in white, the carts made of bamboo and pulled by bullocks. Our valises, for they contained everything we possessed, were put on these carts and we then marched off to Fort William.

On arriving at the outer gate, a Sepoy sentry presented arms, at the next gate was the guardroom and here the Sepoy guard turned out and saluted us. We now marched to a large barracks, forming three sides of a square, two sides of which were occupied by the 44th Regiment. We (the 26 men of the 11th and the 60 men of the 16th Lancers) were told off to a part of the other side. How different was this place to anything we had before seen, so large and lofty, and with no division of rooms – you could at one glance see the cots of some 200 or 300 men. Everything we saw struck us with astonishment. One thing I must mention was the pale faces of the men of the 44th Regiment: no doubt we looked strange to them with our sunburnt ruddy faces.

Tables spread with meat, curry, bread, butter and tea, with natives to wait on us, was all very amusing. Before night, we were all served out with a guttrey, which was to serve for a bed. The bedsteads were cane—bottomed.

At daybreak the following morning, we were aroused by the drums and fifes of the 44th beating the reveille. After answering our names, having no duties to perform I started off to take a survey of the fort and the bazaars. Everything I saw was strange and new. In the bazaar, I saw men buying cocoa nuts in their green state, for which they paid one pice; the seller then cut off the top with a small chopper so that you could drink the milk they contained (about half a pint). But before doing this, the canteen being close at hand, it was customary to get a drachm of arrack to put in; this made a most delicious drink.

We met with several men of the 11th, who had arrived in Calcutta six months before and were waiting for a vessel to convey them to England. They were invalids and amongst them was Private George Farmer, who had kept a diary for 24 years which was published 20 years afterwards by the title of *The*

Light Dragoon. After another 20 years had elapsed, the idea struck me that I should like to continue the record of the Old Regiment in which I had spent so many happy years.

One day, when strolling across the bazaar to look at the the Sepoys that were standing about outside their guardroom, they being on bazaar guard, one particularly, a very handsome fellow with a copper-coloured skin, took a great fancy to me. He appeared not to know how to make enough of me, and beckoned me to go into the guardroom with him, which I did, when two or three more came and stood around me and appeared to be viewing me with as much admiration and wonder as I was them. They then gave me a piece of sugarcane, and appeared much pleased when I began eating it.

The mosquitos soon found us out. Many were bitten on their hands and some on their faces as well. I, in adopting the following plan, prevented them getting at my hands; it was by sewing up my guttrey and making a bag of it and drawing it close round my neck before going to sleep. I found this an excellent plan, both in barracks and in camp. I adopted the same plan with my blanket during the Crimean campaign.

I one day met with a man of the 44th named Allen, who turned out a real friend to me during my stay in Calcutta, and I likewise made the acquaintance of a young fellow belonging to the Governor-General's Band, named Smith. One day I went with Smith to Lady Moira's School, an orphanage for girls, the daughters of soldiers, where they were kept and educated till they were marriageable. Soldiers in the Company's or King's Service, having obtained leave to get married, could select a wife from those that were deemed eligible. It was a splendid building, a few miles from Calcutta. At the main entrance stood a Sepoy sentry. Smith knowing some of the officials, we were admitted to a large room where there were from 12 to 15 girls, most of them marriageable.

One or two were Europeans; the remainder half-caste, threequarter-caste and so on, in fact there was every shade from white to nearly black. Some of them were rather pretty and, I have no doubt, put on their best looks for perhaps they thought we were looking for wives. We conversed with them for a short time and then left.

Shortly after this, there was a Ball at Government House. I went with Smith and got a seat amongst the band, so obtained a splendid sight of the ballroom. The Governor-General, Lord William Bentick, and Lady Bentick and all the élite of Calcutta were present.

One night we went to Kidderpore to see some friends of Smith's who lived in a pretty little cottage in a garden, in which were many banana and cocoa nut trees. Here we sat the greater part of the night drinking toddy (a juice that runs out of the cocoa nut tree). I was induced to smoke a hookah—the tobacco being mixed with sugar had a peculiar taste which made me very sick. This was the first and last time I ever smoked a mixture of this kind. At daybreak, we hired a Kidderpore coach, which gave us a fine jolting before we got back to Fort William.

One morning, much to my delight, I received a letter from the regiment from a comrade that came out the year before, informing me I was posted to 'E' Troop, together with the troops that the remainder of the detachment were posted to, which they were very pleased to know. Captain Bonds, the captain of my troop, now arrived from Meerut, having come to Calcutta to meet his daughter, who had been to England to be educated. He at once took command of the 11th detachment. During the six weeks we were in Calcutta, the 9th Regiment landed to relieve the 38th Regiment stationed at Chinsura.

The boats that were to convey us to Benares being now

ready, on 16th December 1835 we embarked and set sail. The scenery as we ascended the river was very beautiful, the banks being studded with bungalows and Hindoo Temples, but we now began to meet with what horrified me very much: dead bodies continually floating past, being carried down by the current. On enquiry I learned we would have no other water to drink, so that I was nearly famished for drink the first few days; but seeing the natives and our people drinking it without any compunction, I gradually fell into the way.

One day, in company with two or three more, I walked across an immense sandbank, about a mile from where our boats were, when we came to a stream of beautifully clear water quite unlike that in the river. I immediately went down on my hands and knees saying I would have my fill of it, which I did. We then walked along the bank of the stream (it ran parallel with the river) but we had not gone more than a few hundred yards when there lay a dead body, and a little further on another, both partly in the water. I felt very disgusted for the water I had so enjoyed, had but a short time before passed over them.

After a few days, we got beyond the influence of the tide. The natives then began to pull the boats against the stream, there being 8 to 12 to each boat according to the size for this purpose, besides one to steer who was the master. These boats have the appearance of floating houses, being thatched over and large enough to contain from 12 to 20 men. The men of the 11th were in two boats. We had with us detachments for every regiment up the country, except the 38th at Chinsura, they being on the eve of returning home, having given volunteers. When these joined us on our arrival at Chinsura, we numbered nearly 700 men, besides officers. Major Tronson (13th Light Infantry) was in command, and the regimental sergeant-major of the 13th Light Infantry acted as the sergeant-major, giving out the orders, etc. We had with us detachments for the following regiments: 3rd Buffs (Meerut); 13th Light Infantry (Karnāl); 31st Regiment (Ghāzīpur); 16th Lancers and 16th Foot (Kānpur); 49th (Bhāgalpur). The fleet now consisted of nearly 100 boats.

Each hour bought fresh scenes to our view—the banks of the river in many parts being strewn with skulls, skeletons, and bodies in every stage of decomposition. Sometimes we had to witness the horrid sight of a body stranded and surrounded by wild dogs tearing it to pieces, and a few yards off vultures standing looking on and waiting for their turn; then beings, just breathing their last, lying on the sand with their feet close to the water, and a thin white cotton cloth over them; their friends sitting a few yards off with bundles of wood close to them, ready as soon as the breath left the body to place it on the wood and set fire to it. These burning were very common: I have often seen the arms and legs protruding from the flames. One day I saw a Hindoo woman walk into the river up to her waist, with a baby across her arms (whether living or dead, I could not see) but after saying a prayer, she let it slip off her arms into the river.

In some parts of the river crocodiles were very numerous. On a sandbank one day, we saw six basking in the sun with their mouths open; if a boat approached, or they were fired at, they immediately plunged into the river. One day two or three of us were bathing, when I swam some little distance out; all at once I remembered about the crocodiles. Terror seized me, I turned my face to the bank imagining that one of these monsters was close behind me, and had the greatest difficulty in reaching the side. It was some little time before I recovered, for I felt that if I had had to go a little further, I should have been drowned. This was the last time I ever bathed in the Ganges.

Bayldon, the man who was tried at Maidstone for refusing to carry his kit, when in a state of excitement from having drunk too much arrack, jumped off the head of the boat into the river. The river at this part was broad and rapid. Instead of making for the bank, he turned his face to the stream and was being gradually carried down the river. I called out to the dandies to pull the boat to the side. I then sprang off and ran down the bank until I came opposite to him, and then called out as loudly as I could, telling him that he would be drowned if he did not make for the side. After a little time, he turned his face towards me, but I expected every moment to see him go down. At length he reached the side.

It is a singular fact that the bodies of women float on their backs and that men float on their faces. We often saw hawks and jackdaws on the bodies as they floated past us, pecking away.

The 24th December came and there appeared no probability of our having plum pudding the following day, when by chance I saw some trees bearing a sort of plum: it was green and about the size of a small Orleans. I gathered a lot and gave them to the cook, so that the following day I was not without plum pudding.

PART TWO

1836–38

Meerut and Kānpur—Famine in India—Victoria ascends the throne—Lord Cardigan takes command—Return to England

About the first week in January, we arrived at Rājmahāl. Here was a range of hills, thickly wooded, where we were told tigers abounded, and in the centre of the river was a pretty island, or rock, rising almost perpendicular to a great height. On it was a Hindu Temple, and there lived a fakir who subsisted on the offerings of passing boatmen. I here found the skeleton of a young crocodile about two feet in length.

On the hill nearest the river was a Hindu Temple which was approached by a winding path overhung with cocoa nut, palm and other trees; it was a lovely spot, the view of the river and the surrounding country was very fine. After a little parley with the fakirs (giving them some pice and consenting to take off our shoes) they allowed us to pass in. It was of circular form, about six yards in diameter; in the centre was a marble bull, and round in niches were idols of various forms.

About a week after this, we arrived at Monghyr. The town was about a mile from where our boats were lagowed. On going towards it, we had to pass over a bridge on which were assembled a number of men, women and children begging. One I remarked in particular; a man with a good face and body, walking on his hands and feet like a four-footed animal, he being compelled to do this in consequence of the joints of his knees being bent the reverse way to ours. Another had what is termed Elephantiasis, that is, the flesh of his legs growing so that only his toes were to be seen, the instep being entirely covered. Another had a ball of flesh protruding from the socket where the left eye should have been, about the size of a small racket ball, and completely covered with skin the same as his face. I sat some time on the parapet of the bridge looking with wonder and pity on these wretched people. In the town at a baker's shop, I met with some of the most beautiful white bread I ever ate.

A few days after leaving Monghyr, our dandies all ran away; we should have been left behind if we had not turned out and taken their places in pulling the boat, so as to keep up with the fleet. Before starting the following morning, a fresh relay was pressed from the nearest village.

On 9th February 1836, we arrived at Ghāzīpur. Here we left the recruits and volunteers for the 31st Regiment.

On 14th February, we lagowed opposite to Benares. From Calcutta to Benares by coach is 465 miles, but we had come nearly double that distance in consequence of the windings of the river. On the 16th, we crossed the river, disembarked and marched to camping ground not far from the Sepoy lines, about three miles from Benares. We found our tents pitched but no bedding, except what we had brought with us: viz. a piece of coarse sacking to put on the ground, our one guttrey (mine having been sewn up, as I before stated) and our valises for pillows. Thinking the ground would be rather hard, and seeing a jungle of very long grass not far off, I took a knife, cut a large armfull, and placed it on the ground under my sack. Being very tired, I soon fell asleep and did not awake till morning, when I found I was lying in a sop, everything on and around me being wet through. It appeared that a heavy straight-down rain had come on in the night and there being no trenches round the tents, it had run under. We employed ourselves during the day in drying our things.

The detachment of Sepoys that left Calcutta with us as our guard, was now relieved by a guard from the regiment stationed here; their tent was not far from mine. One day, seeing them pipe-claying their belts with bits of rag, I took them a sponge that I had brought from England, and showed them what a much better thing it was for the purpose. I gave it to them and they were much pleased with it.

The volunteers from the 38th were a drunken set; our encampment was constantly in an uproar. The two drachms of arrack that we each received daily was not enough for them, and they often bought from the recruits that did not care about it, giving fabulous prices, they having plenty of money. I saw one of them, that was suffering from the effects of what he had taken the night before, offer as much as two rupees for one drachm (a drachm is about half a quartern).

We were now cautioned to be very careful not to come into collision with the natives as they were much opposed to Europeans (this being the holy city of the Hindus and many deposed Rajahs living here). European soldiers had never been stationed in or near this city.

Feeling a great desire to see the interior of this great city that looked so beautiful from without, I, in company with two more, made up our minds to go on one of the five days we remained here. When about two miles from the camp and one from the city, we suddenly came across one of the 38th lying insensibly drunk by the roadside. To arouse him we were unable; to carry him with us was impossible, as we had many miles to go before getting back to camp. Fearing that he might be maltreated or killed by the natives, I looked around for a place to put him, intending to return the same way and take him back with us, when I saw a pretty little bungalow at a short distance and, to my surprise, a lady with a white face standing at the door.

I went over to her, and told her that I had found a man belonging to our camp by the roadside insensibly drunk, that we were going to Benares, and that on our return we would take him with us—and would she kindly allow one of her servants to have an eye to him till we returned? She replied 'No'—it was disgraceful for Englishmen to act as they did before natives; that they were missionaries and came to do all the good they could, and that we to do all the harm by the bad example we set. At the door of a schoolroom, where were a number of native children, stood a fair young English girl of about 18 years. Before leaving the drunken man, I found his name on his clothes, and placed him in as comfortable a position as possible.

Outside the city, we met several rich natives, mounted on elephants gaily caparisoned, and grand retinues attending them. We now entered the city and traversed many of the principal streets, but met with nothing European. The natives looked at us with astonishment for they seldom saw a white face in their streets.

At one of the shops in the great bazaar was a man selling apples and plums. I asked the price of the apples and he told [me] half a rupee each. I then showed him an anna and, pointing to the plums, gave him to understand that I wanted the value of it in plums. He would not take it from me but motioned to me to put it in the scale, which I did. He then put a few plums in the other scale and motioned to me to take them out after weighing them. Thinking I had not got the value of my money, instead of taking the plums, I took the anna and at once dropped it into my pocket, and was walking away. He instantly sprang up, seized a bamboo stick bound with iron, raised it over his head and told me to stop. I saw that if I moved, he would strike me. He made a great noise; in a moment I was surrounded, several being armed. One drew his sword and raised it over me in a menacing manner.

On looking for my comrades, I saw them in the distance, just leaving the bazaar. They did not see what was going on, consequently I was alone, surrounded by armed men, not knowing the moment I should be cut in two or have my brains dashed out. It now flashed across my mind, 'Oh, that I had my sword.'

Fortunately for me I had not (having only a small stick in my hand) for if I had, in all probability I should have been killed. But I was nothing daunted; showing a resolute front, I walked right through them, refusing to give up my anna, and overtook my comrades. We did not leave the city by the same gate we entered, so we did not pass the place where we left the drunken man. On arriving in camp, I at once went to look for him and found that he had arrived before us.

On 21st February, long before daylight, we were preparing for our first day's march by striking our tents and placing them on camel's backs (three camels carrying two tents), our gutreys and valises being packed up in the sacking and placed on ackreys: small native carts made of bamboo and drawn by bullocks.

After several days' march, we crossed the River Ganges on a bridge of boats just above Allahabad and, on 2nd of March, met the 31st Regiment marching to Ghāzīpur, where we had left their recruits and volunteers.

On 8 March, we arrived at Kānpur, having marched about 10 miles a day (Benares being 155 miles from Kānpur) and encamped about a mile from the cavalry lines. The detachment of the 16th Lancers and 16th Foot now left us.

The following day I went to the 16th Lancers' barracks with a letter from a sergeant of the 16th whose acquaintance I had made in Calcutta, he being on his way home invalided. The sergeant it was for treated me with great kindness, taking me to his room and giving me a clean fronted shirt and pair of twilled trousers, full from the waist cossack-fashion, starched and beautifully pleated down to the knees. I think I never looked so smart before. We then went to the sergeant's mess and had an excellent dinner. I spent the evening with him and then returned to camp.

The following morning, 10th March 1836, we marched from Kānpur. We now had but two detachments with us: viz. the 3rd Buffs for Meerut and the 13th Light Infantry for Karnāl. Of all the men I ever met with, the men of the 13th were the most wild and ferocious, they being all Irish. Their tents were now next to ours; we being English and very young, were positively afraid of them for one night, when they were all drunk, they threatened to murder all the English in camp. They used to fight amongst themselves like dogs, striking and biting each other when on the ground, and then kissing one another. We looked at them with perfect horror, for we had never seen such men before. Whatever the mild Bengalee must have thought of them, I cannot imagine. I remember well seeing one of them being marched a prisoner—he had an immense head with red hair, he was bareheaded and barefooted and of a most ferocious appearance.

A native with a flock of goats now followed us, so that we were well supplied with milk. My shoes being now nearly worn out, having had no supply of any kind of clothing since leaving England—in fact we had little except what was on our backs—I got a native in one of the villages to mend them. In doing so, he put the knot of his thread on the inside. The following day, having no socks, I found at the end of the days' march, that I had a blister on my foot. The next day, the sand getting into my shoes (for we often marched over deep sand) caused the blister to burst and I was unable the following day to put on my shoe, so was compelled to march with only one on. As we were passing through a village, the natives had a good laugh at my expense, seeing me with one shoe on and carrying the other.

One day we entered a vast burial district. After marching some distance between tombs of all sizes and shapes, we encamped on the border of it, about a mile from the River Ganges and close to a castor-oil plant field. After dinner we spent the remainder of the day in wandering amongst the tombs. At times they stretched as far as the eye could reach in every direction. It was here, we were told, that a great battle had been fought, centuries before, between two brothers named Husson and Orson.

Another day we encamped near the vast ruins of the city of Kannauj. It was here that Alexander the Great ended his conquests in India.

We were now but two days' march from Meerut, so the following morning I decided to march barefooted. Fearing that I should not be able to keep up with the detachment, I started off by myself as soon as the tents were struck. It was quite dark, but getting on the Great Trunk Road, I felt no fear of going the wrong way. After marching some miles (it still being quite dark) and having met no one, I heard in the distance a pack of jackals or wolves in full cry. They came nearer. I had nothing to defend myself with and escape appeared impossible: not a tree to get up, the road being on a level sandy plain. I stood still not knowing what to do, for the pack appeared to be getting nearer to me every minute. I now began to reproach myself for being so venturesome and wished myself back with my comrades, when all at once the pack (from the sound) appeared to change their course and their cry became gradually fainter. Soon after this, day began to break and I arrived on our new camp ground an hour afterwards.

I cannot express the delight we all felt when, in the afternoon, we saw several of the 11th come galloping into the encampment, mounted on ponies they had hired for the occasion. Some we knew, others were quite strangers to us. Now commenced such a scene of drinking and song singing, for our delight knew no bounds, to think that we had all arrived safely within a days' march of our new home—and the family that we were to belong to—as long as we were able to serve our King and Country. Our visitors left us an hour before sunset to return to Meerut.

We had now been nine months together; on the morrow we were to be separated, some going to one troop, some to another. Although only 26 of us, it must not be thought that we had always lived on the most amicable terms. There had been many little differences amongst us, there being two who were the principal cause of this.

All being much excited, we now began to quarrel amongst ourselves feeling that on the morrow we should be parted. I now came into collision with these two men that had made themselves particularly obnoxious to us all. After a few words with one, he struck me at the tent door. I at once sent him spinning over the tent ropes; we then had a regular set-to. After a few rounds, I bunged his eyes up so that he could hardly see; he then gave in. Seeing the other fellow standing near, I challenged him; we then had a set-to. After a few rounds, he gave in having received a good thrashing and a black eye. I was most fortunate, escaping without any marks on my face. Another fight or two was going on, and a few more black eyes and bruised faces were got.

The next morning, 4th April 1836, we paraded for our last days' march, it being nine months and ten days since we left Maidstone. (Meerut is 894 miles from Calcutta by road). A pretty set of ragamuffins we were when we formed up on the general parade at Meerut; with old Kilmarnock caps, jackets stained and threadbare, trousers various and many of us almost shoeless. The regiment turned out to look at us and gave us the name of the 'Fighting Draft'—so many displaying the effects of battle.

We were now told off to our troops and marched off by our sergeant-majors, and I was informed that my appointment of acting sergeant was at an end. Sergeant-Major Trotter now handed me over to an old soldier of the name of Jemmy Cook, who at once took me to the bazaar to buy a cot and many other things that I required. Everything I now saw filled me with delight: the barracks [were] built in open column about 50 yards apart, each building containing one troop—the 'E' Troop being the only one thatched, the other seven being pucker or cement. All had double verandahs, the inside being one open space except for the ends that were partitioned off for the sergeant-major and sergeants.

In standing at the end one could see every berth, the bedsteads standing two to each pillar; the roof being held up on arches from pillar to pillar, while each man's saddle hung with his sword belts and pistol over the head of his bed. At the foot of the bedsteads were boxes of various sizes, mostly mounted with brass, containing the ample kits of their owners—some men having dozens of pairs of white cotton trousers and shirts.

I next went over to the stables, and was struck with the beauty of the horses. 'E' Troop was called the 'Black Troop', having all black horses and, with the exception of two or three geldings in each troop, all were stallions. [It also had] the only three black men in the regiment: viz. Trumpeter Murray, Roderick the cymbal player and McKinley the big drummer. Roderick had a black wife but no children; McKinley was also married and had a large family. Murray and Roderick were West Indians while McKinley was an East Indian. Several men too had married half-caste and native women, so it really was the 'Black' Troop.

The horses wore shoes only on their forefeet, and they had ropes attached to their hind-legs just below their fetlock joints, these ropes being fastened to a peg driven into the ground about four yards behind them. They were called 'heel' ropes. They also had head ropes fastened to the collar and to pegs on each side, and were always fed from nosebags. These horses had been bred in the East India Company's studs at Hopper and Ghāzīpur, and were half-bred English and Arab.

The two right troops were bays, the third troop from the right chestnuts, the fourth duns, the fifth piebalds, skewbalds and horses of all colours, the sixth black, the next two troops greys. Their tails were not cut so they reached their fetlock joints, their coats were as sleek as moles, and their eyes large, bright and intelligent. Numbers of these horses were high and strong enough to mount big men over six feet.

I cannot express the pride and pleasure I felt to think that I belonged to such a splendid regiment, for on the first church parade I noticed that the right-hand man of the front rank, Corporal Stewart, stood six foot three, and there was not a man in the front rank under five foot ten. I, being a little over five foot nine, was in the rear rank. At this time the regiment was complete in men and horses—701 being the establishment.

A few days after joining, we paraded for Colonel Bruton's inspection. He was an old man and had seen much service in India, having been twice before Bhātpur with Lord Lake. He was wounded in the neck with a matchlock ball, which was a running wound up to his death. He spoke very kindly to us and advised us not to drink our grog withour water, saying we should all die if we did. The adjutant (McReady) accompanied him; he joined the regiment in France from the 23rd Light Dragoons and rose from the ranks. He was a grand specimen of a man, standing over six foot, and both he and the colonel were beloved by the whole regiment. A feeling of love and admiration for them both sprang up within me for the kind and fatherly manner in which they spoke to us.

We then went to the quartermaster's stores and received new shakos, then to the tailor's shop for new clothing.

The horse the sergeant-major told me off to I did not like: he was a great heavy gelding. However I kept him until I was dismissed and I then got permission to exchange with a man who had one of the prettiest little horses I ever saw. He was entirely jet black with four white feet, and a star on his forehead. I was delighted by the exchange but I had enough to do to ride him.

One morning, when riding across the plain in Watering Order, a loose horse galloped up and singled my horse out for a fight. Standing on his hind-legs, he put one foot on the top of my head and the other on my bridle hand, and was about to seize me, when I slipped off the other side and lay close to the ground. Their hind-legs now rattled against one another's ribs and hind-quarters over my head, and they roared like mad things. At last away they galloped to have another fight somewhere else, and I walked quietly back to barracks, thinking what a narrow escape I had had.

Just as the sun was rising, one morning when we were exercising our horses, the man riding next to me called my attention to something glistening just above the horizon, saying it was the snow on the Himalayan Mountains: they were about 200 miles off.

Soon after arriving in Meerut, the hot winds began to blow. During this season, which generally lasts from the beginning of May to the middle of August, we were not allowed to leave the barracks from 9am to 5pm. All the doors and windows on the side the wind blew from were made up with tatties (bamboo frames covered with a long grass root, called Cuss-Cuss which grows on the banks of the Ganges, having the appearance of large doormats). Natives on the outside were employed in throwing water on them, so that they were kept sopping wet all day; the hot wind, after passing through them, became quite cool. Most of the windows and doors on the opposite side being kept shut, we had barely sufficient light to see to read. During the day, the men employed themselves in reading, playing cards, etc.

About 6pm we went to stables, but not to clean our horses, there being a native to every troop horse in the regiment, called a sice, who was answerable for the horse he was told off to for which he received four rupees a month—two from the East India Company and two from the man the horse belonged to. My sice was a very nice fellow: his name was Nergin.

The great heat in June was very distressing. Several of my draught now went into hospital and, on 18th June, I was compelled to go in, having a fever. It gradually got worse. Calomel was much used at this time and the surgeon gave me a large quantity, but finding it did not affect my mouth he discontinued it. One of my draught now died in a bed opposite to me. I had eaten nothing for a fortnight and was reduced to a shadow; my tongue was quite black and I could take nothing but drink. What would I then have given for a little sparkling treacle beer, such as I had often drunk when a boy in Yorkshire. How I sighed for this during the long nights, looking at the punka waving solemnly over the beds of about forty sick and dying men. Another man was now carried out dead from the bed next to me, then one or two not far off.

One morning my comrade came to see me and advised that I should make out my will, but I did not consent. Dr Sandham was exceedingly kind to me, he would sit down on my bed and talk to me, so I made bold to ask him to let me have half a bottle of beer, having seen a man opposite that was getting better receive a glass from a bottle that was uncorked by his bedside.

What would I have given for the other half; how my eyes followed the attendant as he carried it away. The doctor said he was afraid it would do me harm, so I went on sighing for another 24 hours, and again saw the man get the beer. What the doctor thought on his next visit I could not tell, but I was certainly no better for I had now been nearly three weeks and had taken little else than tea and water. I did not again venture to ask for the beer but, to my inexpressible delight, he ordered it. Shortly after he left, the attendant came up to my bedside, uncorked a bottle and poured out a glass of sparkling ale, which I drank eagerly. It saved my life: from that moment I got better and in three weeks I was at my duty again.

One day while I was in hospital, I received a note from the man that wrote to me when in Calcutta. With it a paragraph that his friends in England had cut out of a newspaper. As nearly as I can remember, it ran as follows:

> What have the 11th Light Dragoons done that they should have Lord Brudenell to command them, an officer that was dismissed from the 13th Hussars for tyranny.

As soon as the weather permitted, I was sent to the Riding School to go through a course of drill, previous to the commencement of field days, and was again dismissed on 19th September 1836. The rainy season commences about the middle of August and continues till October, but this year (same as last) scarcely any rain fell.

In November the drill season commenced. We now had field days, sometimes under the colonel, at others under the adjutant when the non-commissioned officers commanded the troops, and sword drill on foot occasionally under the regimental sergeant-major in the afternoons. The last week in November, I received an order to go to the colonel's bungalow.

He spoke to me very kindly and asked me many questions—amongst others if I could draw. I replied 'A little.' The next day I was appointed lance-corporal.

The cold season is a very pleasant time in Meerut, as we could amuse ourselves out of doors in various ways: Long Balls was the favourite game. Woolhouse of the band was the don player: he could jerk a ball of 18 ounces, 90 yards. During breakfast, natives often brought in baskets of jackals, wild cats, hares and other animals, which we bought for a few annas each to hunt across the plain, as many of the men kept dogs. Other natives brought snakes which they carried in bags; for a few pice they would put one on the ground and then let loose a mongoose—these are little animals not unlike a ferret. Then they would fight, which always ended in the mongoose being the conqueror by killing the snake.

Our term of five years [at Meerut] having now expired, we received the order to exchange stations with the 16th Lancers. On 28th January 1837, we marched from Meerut and encamped about six miles off; shortly after the 16th Lancers marched past our encampment on their way to Meerut.

Near our encampment was a pool, which we had to ride into to water our horses. Two or three, getting loose, began to fight; this caused a hundred to get loose and several men were thrown off into the water. They then galloped through the encampment, causing great confusion. Some went back to Meerut, others wandered about the country and were not caught for some time afterwards. When a day or two's march from Kānpur, two of the native cavalry overtook us, bringing two of them.

On 31st January, we were reviewed by Commander-in-Chief, General Fane, near our encamping ground; Private Young of the 16th Lancers was his orderly. Forty years afterwards I met with Young; in conversation he told me he was orderly to the General on that occasion. I then remembered having noticed him when riding through our ranks.

On 1st February about an hour before daybreak, we struck camp and placed the tents on elephant's backs (two elephants carrying three tents) our baggage was carried on ackreys. The sices, while we were doing this, got the horses ready and the picket posts and head and heel ropes packed up, which were carried by camels. We then took our horses from the sices and stood around fires made from the grass the horses had not eaten till daybreak.

The mornings were cold. The horses felt it more than we did, for we had to keep them back from burning themselves; it was astonishing how quiet they became after a few days. There were two men in my troop who had guns. They generally, after each days' march, went out shooting and often met with good sport, bringing home numbers of peacocks and other birds, which were divided amongst the troop messes.

A cavalry regiment on the march in India has from 5000 to 7000 followers, besides elephants, camels and bullocks, to carry the tents, bedding, baggage and all merchandise belonging to the regimental bazaar. In a very short time after arriving at the new camp ground, a native town springs up as if by magic, where almost anything can be purchased from a sweetmeat to a coffin. At night the guard, mounted, formed a chain of videttes round the camp.

One day while on the march, several of us started off to a village we could see in the distance. Before getting to it, we had to pass through a tope (a small wood), when about half way through, all at once, we heard a violent rustling in the trees near us. On looking up, we saw between 20 and 30 large white monkeys with black faces. They grinned at us and some ran down the trees as though to obstruct our going any further. We halted and, for a moment or two, were undecided whether to go on or return. However we decided to go on, so proceeded. They then ran up the trees and followed us some distance, jumping from tree to tree. Had we molested them, I believe they would have attacked us. When we arrived at the village, we saw several tame monkeys sitting quietly on the houses and walls evidently petted by the natives, they believing that the souls of their deceased relatives had passed into them.

After an exceedingly pleasant march, the weather being fine the whole way, we arrived at Kānpur on 1st March 1837.

We soon settled down in our new quarters, but the station is not so nice and pleasant as Meerut; I did not like it so well.

On 16th March, a Brigade Order was issued that, as the morrow would be St Patrick's Day, there was to be no beating of drums, music or demonstartion of any kind. Some little time after this, a Hindu festival commenced. The native cavalry were allowed their horses, the native infantry their arms, and were supplied with blank ammunition by the East India Company. Night after night, for several nights, they were suffered to parade the station, passing through our lines with lighted torches, beating tom-toms, blowing horns, shouting, discharging their pieces—in fact making noise enough to keep the station awake for hours. A short distance from our lines on the plain, they erected immense idols of wickerwork, filled with combustibles and fireworks, which were set fire to and burnt on the last night of the festival in the presence of thousands of natives shouting and gesticulating. The expense of these idols was largely contributed to by the European officers of the native regiments.

By about the middle of April, the heat became very oppressive and the hot winds began to blow, so that the tatties were put up. On 23rd June they were taken away, and brought back again on the 28th; on 20th July they were again taken away and on 12th August brought back; on the 18th were taken away for the last time. It was the most remarkable season ever known.

The rains now commenced and with them great sickness, principally the cholera. At one time we had about 200 men in hospital and in a few weeks lost 35 men, 7 women and 30 children. The rains, as in the two preceding years, were very scant; famine amongst the natives was the consequence. They died around us by hundreds and numbers could at all times be seen floating down the Ganges. It was piteous to see these poor wretches, some begging, others picking up bones or any offal they could find round the barracks. Although tens of thousands died from sheer starvation, little was known of it in England.

On 21st October, we paraded in Review Order with white trousers and marched to the general parade ground, where all the European and native troops were assembled, to hear the general read the Proclamation of Queen Victoria's ascension to the throne. We gave three cheers and the ceremony ended. The troops present were the 11th Light Dragoons, the 5th and 7th Native Cavalry, three troops of Horse Artillery, two batteries of Foot Artillery, the 16th Foot and four regiments of native infantry. Lieutenant-Colonel Lord Brudenell, of whom I have before spoken, was on parade this day for the first time, (he having joined at Kānpur on 10th September) but Lieutenant Colonel Bruton commanded.

On 23rd October, Lieutenant Colonel Bruton resigned the command of the regiment and Lieutenant-Colonel Lord Brudenell took command.

On 25th October, we had our first field day of the season under our new colonel. It was a dreadfully hard one. After so many months of inaction, the men were all completely prostrated. Besides regimental field-days, we occasionally brigaded with the two native cavalry regiments and the horse artillery.

On 18th November, we received news that the 3rd Light Dragoons had landed in Calcutta to relieve us. Great indeed was the joy of all who wished to return to their native land. Volunteering opened for the 3rd Light Dragoons and the 16th Lancers on 22nd November for three days. On the evening of the first day, all being in a state of great excitement, I came to blows with a man that had insulted me. Being seen by a sergeant-major, I was confined and the following morning was deprived of my lance-corporals' rank.

On the third day of volunteering, a circumstance occurred for which I could never quite forgive Lord Brudenell. An old man, John Dowling, who had completed his service and was going home to be discharged, was confined a few days before for being drunk on piquet (at other times for the same offence, he would have been awarded about eight days congee house). Lord Brudenell ordered him to be tried by court-martial. A general parade was ordered and we marched to the Riding School. When the court-martial was read, to our amazement he was awarded corporal punishment. No one present supposed for a moment that Lord Brudenell could be hard-hearted enough to carry it out, particularly when the old man turned round to him and, in an imploring tone, said, 'My Lord, I hope you won't flog me. I am an old man and just going home to my friends, and I should be sorry for such a disgrace to come on me now.' 'Tie him up said Lord Brudenell.

The farriers then commenced their brutal work. My heart

heaved and I had great difficulty in restraining myself from bursting into a flood of tears. After the parade, loud were the denunciations against him, all—both officers and men—feeling the change that had come over us.

An extra days' volunteering opened the next morning. Numbers that had made up their minds to return to England, volunteered in consequence of this exhibition—158 volunteered to remain in India (110 in the 3rd Light Dragoons and 48 in the 16th Lancers).

Field days were still continued, volunteers having to attend: many of them at times very unfit as there was much drinking going on. One morning Private Peter Cain, a volunteer, was observed by his captain, when parading the troop, to be drunk:

'Cain,' he said, 'you are drunk.'
'No, captain' replied Cain 'it's my horse.'
Of course Cain was soon in the guard room.

A few days before our time for leaving, all the saddlery having been packed in crates ready for the voyage, we received an order in the evening that there was to be a field day the following morning. The consequence was we were up half the night unpacking and preparing for it.

At length the long looked-for morning arrived, 4th December 1837, when the left wing of the regiment paraded under the command of Major Jenkins and, headed by the Band, marched to the ghat and there embarked on board boats waiting to receive us. As soon as all was ready, we set sail.

During the day a man named Simpson of my troop died. In the evening, we lagowed on the opposite side of the river, it being then the King of Oude's territory. I was one of the fatigue party ordered to dig the grave. We clambered up a high bank and commenced digging under a large tree a short distance from the river; a little further on we could descry a village. The ground was very hard, and it got quite dark before the grave was near deep enough, so that we had to send for a lantern, which one held while another dug. We had not been long at work when the natives in the village, hearing us, came in a body to see what we were doing; they were told we were digging a grave to bury our dead.

They said, 'Throw it into the river, same as we do.'

We replied, 'It is not our custom.'

They then appeared determined that we should not proceed, so that we were obliged to desist.

The Sepoy guard that was accompanying us, was then sent for and formed a chain of sentries round us. The body, sewn in a guttrey, was placed on the ground near the grave; we then continued our digging. When the grave was considered deep enough, the body was committed to the ground and the regimental sergeant-major read the funeral service. It was a sight never to be forgotten.

Dropping down the river with the stream, with sails set, is very pleasant in comparison to ascending it; we went further in one day than we did in three when going up.

On 9th December, we arrived at Allahabad and lagowed just round the point where the River Yamuna empties itself into the Ganges. This is the point on which the fort is built and where the Hindus from all parts of India come to worship and procure holy water. Many hundreds were encamped close to where we were lagowed, some belonged to the higher classes as their surroundings denoted. The water of the Yamuna is perfectly clear, so that we could see to the bottom of the river, whereas the water of the Ganges is always thick with sand. I went over the fort: it appeared very strong and completely commanded the two rivers and the surrounding country.

On 14th December, we arrived at Benares, and on the 24th at Ghāzīpur. The 44th Regiment was now stationed here, so I went to the barracks and spent a short time with Allen (the man that had behaved so kindly to me when I was in Calcutta). I likewise went to see Lord Cornwallis' monument and the East India Company studs.

On 29th December, we passed Monghyr. A few days afterwards, when lagowed at Rajmahal, Private Mason took a leapt from his boat for a swim, when a crocodile seized him and we never saw him again.

On the morning of 10th January, we came in sight of a fleet of boats being dragged up the river, which we found to contain the sick, women and baggage of the 3rd Light Dragoons. As we sailed close past, we had little conversations with them.

On 14th January we arrived at Berhampore and, on the following day, at Calcutta. We now learned that Lord Brudenell's father, the Earl of Cardigan, had died on 11th August 1837, consequently Lord Brudenell had succeeded to the title. Here we remained on board the boats for three days and, on 18th January, embarked on board small brigs, the ship that was to convey us to England being then quite ready. These brigs were like huge barges of a most unwieldy build, intended to take merchandise to and from Calcutta to large ships lying at Sand Heads. We did not reach the ship until the 20th.

The misery we endured on board the boats for three days and

two nights was dreadful. No rations were issued: in fact there was no place to cook them if there had. No place to lie down (the deck by day being too hot, and the dew at night was so heavy that we should have been wet through), so the only place to get was the hold amongst the ballast, which consisted of huge stones, so large and irregular that it was impossible to find a place anywhere to lie down. What with hunger and the misery of being unable to lie down to sleep, [this] surpassed anything I ever met with in all my career.

Glad indeed we were as we sprang on to the deck of the noble ship *Thames* that was to convey us to Old England.

I at once got something to eat and was soon fast asleep. The next morning we set sail but, so remiss had the authorities been, that no hammocks or bedding of any kind had been provided. Consequently both men, women and children had to sleep on the decks until we arrived at Madras on 26th January. Hammocks were then issued to us from the stores at Fort St George.

We were much amused and surprised at the way in which the natives came off to us in their catamarans. These are two or three planks fastened together, on which they sit and manage to surmount and ride over the largest waves. The surf here is very heavy.

On 31st January 1838, we weighed anchor and set sail for the Cape of Good Hope. On arriving within a day or two's sail from there, a strong headwind set in, almost amounting to a gale, accompanied with rain, which continued for nearly a week, at the end of which we were much further off.

The wind now abated for a short time, when we hoped by tacking to make headway, but the wind again sprang up and we were prevented from entering the Bay for nearly another week. At last to our great joy, we sailed into the harbour and dropped anchor. The day before, Troop Sergeant-Major Warwick died and was commited to the deep. The day after, 27th March, I attained my 21st birthday.

During the eight days we remained here, there was always something of interest going on, the town and Table Mountain full in view. The clouds sometimes enveloping the mountain round the summit, gave it the appearance of a huge table with a white cloth.

One day we were surrounded by a shoal of fish named rock cod and in a short time some forty or fifty of us were fishing, every device being resorted to, as they bit at everything we threw overboard. As soon as they were pulled up, they were prepared for the galley. After a few hours, everyone had had his fill, but the fishing did not cease—if anything it was carried on with renewed vigour—for nearly all hands joined in the sport. It was fine fun to see them pulled up. They were now thrown carelessly on the deck and this continued till the waists of the ship were covered. At last the captain thought we had had enough of it, so he ordered the decks to be cleared, when we had to commence and throw back into the sea those we did not require.

Major Jenkins allowed small parties to go on shore each day. One day I went in company with six or eight more and we ordered dinner at an hotel. While it was preparing, we went through the town and to the barracks (the 27th Inniskilling Regiment were quartered here). Of course to the canteen we must go. The wine, which we drank from tumblers, was one shilling a bottle. Soon after leaving, I began to feel the effects of it. Seeing a Hottentot driving a mule cart with six mules (two abreast), I sprang on the back of the second mule, which commenced kicking furiously. The next moment I was thrown in between the six and should in all probability have been killed, if the Hottentot had not by some means stopped them, when I managed to extracate myself from the traces. After dinner we again strolled about the town and, just before sunset, returned to the ship.

During the time we were anchored here, the natives brought off to us all kinds of fruit and bread. The bread was very acceptable, for the biscuit on board was frightfully bad, the insides being little more than a mass of dust having been eaten by the weevils (these are small insects that generate in old biscuits). The rations altogether were very bad; very different from what we received on our outward voyage.

On the morning of 4th April 1838, we weighed anchor and, after a very pleasant run, having the trade winds with us the whole way, and sometimes having the stunsails set, we dropped anchor at St Helena on 15th April. I regretted much that I could not get on shore to see Napoleon's Tomb, but no one was allowed. The following morning we set sail and, on the 20th, passed the island of Ascension. On the 24th we crossed the Line.

We all now began to look anxiously forward to the time when we should come in sight of Old England. To our inexpressible delight, on the afernoon of 2nd June, we descried a pilot boat which made towards us. The captain then engaged a pilot and he came on board. In the evening we saw the Tilley Lights.

On the following day, Captain Roebuck went on shore taking with him the letters. The remainder of the voyage we were generally in sight of the coast. We lost but one man more during the voyage: Private J Rudd of 'G' Troop.

On 8th June we dropped anchor at Gravesend and at once commenced to disembark. We then marched eight miles to Chatham; all our baggage was conveyed to the Town Hall, put inside the railings, and a guard placed over it. We were billeted in the town. The first place I looked out for was a cook shop, where I had a jolly good dinner.

The following morning we marched 11 miles to Sittingbourne. Many of the men fell out during the march in consequence of their feet getting blistered: the weather was dreadfully hot. Many of them were old and much worn, having gone out with the regiment in 1819, and some had been longer in India, having volunteered to the 11th from the 8th, 21st, 22nd and 24th Light Dragoons.

The following day, 10th June, being Sunday, we halted. How delightful it was to spend the day in a pleasant country village after the uncomfort for five months on board ship, and to wander through the lovely lanes that abound in this delightful county.

Major Jenkins, being of a naturally kind disposition, and fearing that our entry into Canterbury would be anything but credible. Some of the men being sick and footsore, and the march being a long one (16 miles), he arranged for conveyances: viz. omnibusses, cabs, etc;

After parading (the conveyances being close at hand), he ordered us to mount, when all rushed to try to get on the outside. I have seen the Old 11th under many circumstances but this, I think, was the most ludicrous of all. The major was mounted. When all was ready, off we started, not at a trot but at a steady walk. The train was rather a long one, having all our baggage, women and children with us.

When within a few miles of Canterbury the major, riding some distance in front, met with a post-chaise containing Lord and Lady William Bentick, his Lordship being the head colonel of the regiment and having just returned from India. The major came galloping back to us, calling out 'Dismount men, and form up.' In a few minutes we were formed up on the roadside. His Lordship had halted during this time. When we had drawn swords and all were ready, His Lordship's carriage proceeded at a walk. As he passed, He and Her Ladyship frequently bowed. After passing us, they increased their pace and were soon out of sight. The major then gave the order 'Mount men,' when we again got on to the carriages.

On arriving at the entrance to the town, we dismounted and the carriages were dismissed—with the exception of one or two that were retained to take on several men that had managed to get too much to drink and were unable to march. On arriving at the barracks we were told off to rooms. The beds had been filled by our recruits that had arrived from Maidstone a day or two before.

On 25th June 1838, the headquarters division, under the command of Major Rotton, disembarked at Herne Bay and arrived at Canterbury about 11pm. The total number that returned from India with both divisions was 347 non-commissioned officers and men, of which number 120 were discharged; but the recruits from the depot made up the regiment to the home establishment: viz. 333 non-commissioned officers and privates, divided into six troops.

The regiment having so much money on their arrival at Canterbury, and having no horses, Lord Cardigan gave the men a fortnight's leave. No parades being ordered during this time and no guards being mounted except what were absolutely necessary, every man was allowed to do nearly as he liked. This gave them an opportunity of getting rid of their money without getting into trouble. Unfortunately there were no regimental savings banks; had there been, many no doubt would have availed themselves of their benefit.

Lord Cardigan at this time was away in London. At the end of the period he returned; he then drew the reins with too tight a hand, giving most severe punishments for trivial offences (there being no code to guide commanding officers). The consequence was the men became reckless, some, after being ordered punishment which they considered too severe, walked direct from the office over the barrack wall, preferring to be tried by court-martial and sent to jail. Many a man in consequence, that would have made a moderately good soldier, never did any good afterwards.

One man was drummed out—it was the most laughable performance. After his court-martial was read—the sentence being, 'To be discharged with ignomy from the Service', the regimental sergeant-major cut the facings and buttons off his jacket and the stripes off his overalls. The regiment then formed a street, the front rank facing to the rear, down which the prisoner was marched—this was between a file of the guard and of the band in front playing *The Rogue's March*. He was then turned out of the barrack gate. About this time, we had a number of men in jail, and a greater number at kit drill.

Lieutenant and Adjutant Ready now left the regiment and Regimental Sergeant-Major Knowles succeeded him. Sergeant-Major Anson, who joined with the recruits, was appointed regimental sergeant-major; he drilled me at Maidstone when I joined. Young horses now began to arrive to remount us, so that we became busy enough—every man having to break in his own horse. Several recruits too joined, and the regimental sergeant-major told me off to drill them. I had not been long at this, when I was again appointed lance-corporal. I was likewise told off to a very nice little horse, which I broke in.

I now belonged to 'A' Troop, Captain Lawrie being the captain and Ennis the troop sergeant-major. He afterwards became adjutant and received captaincy during the Crimean campaign; he was always a great friend to me, doing me a good turn whenever he had an opportunity. I often went to see him many years after we had both left the service, and followed him to his grave in December 1882. He died in his 75th year.

PART THREE

1839–53

'Prince Albert's Own Hussars'—The Queen's Duty—Appointed sergeant—In aid of civil power in Ireland—England and return to Ireland

During the latter part of the year 1838, our principal employment was breaking in the young horses—the regiment now being completed.

In the spring of 1839, we received the new Victoria percussion carbines (the old flint and steel ones being returned to the Tower) and new accoutrements. The 11th was the first regiment that received percussion arms. Field days now commenced and on 11th June, our first inspection took place by Major-General Sleigh, this being the anniversary of the arrival of the 1st Division of the regiment in Canterbury. The following distinguished personages reviewed the regiment during the summer and autumn: His Royal Highness the Duke of Cambridge; Lieutenant-General Sir Hussey Vivian; Lieutenant-General Lord Charles Somerset Manners KCB; General Lord Hill; Field Marshal the Duke of Wellington, all expressing their approbation of the progress which had been made towards the efficiency of the regiment.

Our greatest trouble all this time was the white sheepskins that we had brought home from India, they having been cleaned there by the natives with something that had turned them a very bad colour which all the cleaning we could give them would not alter. Unfortunately for us, Lord Cardigan would admit of no excuse; white they must be, and white they could not be got. Some were much worse than others; the unfortunate owners of these were perpetually at extra drill and extra parades –

sometimes the whole regiment had to parade in the afternoon, each man with his sheepskin, all the officers attending. Just before one of these parades, a number of the men were sitting on the grass near the barracks, beating the chalk out of their sheepskins and singing *Britons never shall be slaves.* Lord Cardigan passing and hearing them, sent the adjutant with an order that they were not to make so much noise.

One poor fellow who had tried every device to get his sheepskin white, and was sick at heart at all the punishment he was receiving in consequence of being unable, was told by one of his comrades in fun to try soot and grease. Being a rather simple sort of fellow, and without giving the thing a thought, he did try it. The consequence was he completely spoilt it. At the next parade, as a matter of course, he was confined and marched to the office with his sheepskin to show Lord Cardigan, who ordered that he was to pay for a new one. This circumstance caused great merriment throughout the regiment. Shortly after this, a waggon arrived from London laden with bales of new sheepskins. Imagine our delight when we found out they were black instead of white.

Early on the morning of 7th February 1840, 100 men paraded in review order under the command of Major Rotton and marched to Dover, to meet and escort His Royal Highness Prince Albert of Saxe-Cobourg (he having come to England to marry the Queen). It was a most wretched march, the weather being very cold and a drizzling rain falling nearly the whole way. We were wet through, not being allowed to cloak. On arriving at Dover about 11am, we dismounted on the beach. Here we waited over two hours, till the Prince was ready to start, during which time we fed our horses but nothing was provided for us, nor were we allowed to leave our horses to get anything. We then escorted the Prince through Dover and as far as the windmill or Barham Downs; another escort of the 11th was here waiting that escorted the Royal Party to the Fountain Hotel, Canterbury. Lord Cardigan and the officers of the regiment in the evening dined with the Prince and his brother Duke Ernest. The rain now came down faster, and we cloaked and proceeded on our march back. It was quite dark before we arrived at Canterbury; we were then completely saturated. What with hunger, cold and being wet through, this without exception was the most wretched day I ever spent during the 26 years I was in the regiment. Major Rotton, in preventing us from having any refreshment, was only carrying out Lord Cardigan's orders.

The following morning, another escort from the left wing of the regiment proceeded with the Royal Party to Sittingbourne; escorts from the Life Guards then took them on to London. At this time I had been promoted to full corporal in 'C' Troops.

About the middle of March, the following general order was received and read to the troops, accompanied by a regimental order that we were not to shave the upper lip. At this time only the Life Guards and Hussars wore moustaches.

Horse Guards

12 March 1840

My Lord,
I have the honour to acquaint you, by the direction of the General, commanding in chief, that Her Majesty has been graciously pleased to direct that the Eleventh Regiment of Light Dragoons shall be armed, clothed, and equipped as Hussars, and styled the 'Eleventh', or 'Prince Albert's Own Hussars'.
I have &etc
J Macdonald, Adjutant General

Lieutenant Colonel the Earl of Cardigan
Commanding Eleventh or
Prince Albert's Own Hussars

At the end of April 1840, His Royal Highness Prince Albert was appointed the head colonel of the 11th Hussars. It was in May 1840 that Captain R A Reynolds was placed under arrest for having ordered wine at the mess table, that it was usual to place on the table in black bottles. Lord Cardigan, disapproving of this, ordered him under arrest. Shortly after Captain Reynolds left the regiment, but did not leave the service, for in 1858, he was assistant adjutant general.

At the latter end of June 1840, the regiment marched from Canterbury and relieved the 12th Lancers at Brighton and Chichester. During the summer, we received our new Hussar clothing; when all were completed, Lord Cardigan paraded us through the streets of Brighton. It was about this time that Lord Cardigan fought a duel with Captain Harvey Tuckett, late 11th Hussars, for having written an anonymous letter to *the Morning Chronicle,* animadverting in severe terms on his Lordship's conduct in placing under arrest Captain R A Reynolds for challenging His Lordship to fight a duel. He at this time was Captain of 'C' Troop, the troop I then belonged to. I have often, on parade, witnessed Lord Cardigan's overbearing manner to Captain Reynolds, which he did not submit to quietly, often replying in a manner that I was surprised that his Lordship did not then and there place him under arrest. Captain R A Reynolds was tried by a general court-martial, of which Sir H Pakenham was president, and was cashiered. The troop was not at all sorry at losing him. Major Jenkins died about this time and was buried with military honours. He was with the regiment in the Peninsula, at Waterloo and Bhuāpur, and 19 years in India, having gone out and returned with it.

In April 1841, the regiment marched from Brighton to Hounslow and Hampton Court, to take the Queen's Duty, sending an officer's detchment to Kensington to furnish escorts and a letter party at the Horse Guards. The night before marching from Brighton, Private W Rogers was absent all night. For punishment he was ordered to march on foot and lead his horse; this he refused to do. On arriving at Hounslow, he was tried by court-martial and awarded 150 lashes. This he received without emotion in the riding school, after divine service on Easter Sunday.

During the year 1841, the regiment was frequently employed in furnishing escorts (the Queen always travelling by road at this time) from London to Windsor; and on one occasion to Brighton; on another to Newham in Oxfordshire and to Woolwich; also to Panshanger in Bedfordshire. On the last of these, I, being corporal of one of the escorts (there being relays stationed along the road) had the honour of riding at the near carriage door, Prince Albert being on my right and the Queen on his right, the sergeant having been sent by the Queen to put up in a cottage near at hand a private of the escort that had been taken ill. Instead of looking to my front, I turned my head to the right to look at the Queen, feeling that I had escorted her many times, but had never had an opportunity of having a good look at her; when suddenly she turned her head and fixed me, so that I was unable for a moment or two to turn my eyes to the front. On 9th November 1841, being Lord Mayor's day, a party of 100 men under the command of Acting Sergeant-Major Dungate marched from Hounslow to London to take part in the procession. As we passed near Buckingham Palace, the people told us that a Prince had just been born. The corporation provided us with a most sumptuous dinner at an hotel near the Blackfriars Bridge (our horses being put up and fed in stables near at hand) and we likewise received 5d each.

At the latter end of January 1842, we furnished escorts for the King of Prussia on his way to Windsor, to be present at the christening of the Prince of Wales; and on 28th January, marched to Windsor and were reviewed with the Royal Horse Guards, the Queen, the King of Prussia, Prince Albert, the Duke of Wellington and other distinguished personages being present. On 4th February the 11th escorted the King of Prussia to Woolwich to review the troops stationed there.

On 20th April 1842, the regiment was reviewed by the Queen on Wimbledon Common, on which occasion His Royal Highness Prince Albert marched past at the head of the regiment and saluted Her Majesty. Field Marshal the Duke of Wellington was present at this review.

About a fortnight previously, I marched from Hounslow to Tilbury Fort, in command of a letter party consisting of three men, for the purpose of carrying despatches to Warley Barracks to regiments of infantry assembling there previous to embarkation for India. When I marched the party into the fort, and formed up in front of the office, the governor, after inspecting us, ordered his horse out and took us to a small public house just outside the fort; two of the men he billeted there. The governor then said that I and the other man were to be billeted at Orset, a village about halfway between Tilbury and Warley, and that he would go part of the way with us, to show us the way. He quite took command of his little party, giving the words 'Trot,' 'Walk' as if he had a troop or regiment under his command. He told me he was in the cavalry in the Peninsular and had seen much service.

I used to go occasionally to Tilbury to visit the two men. The governor was always very pleased to see me and, when we left at the end of April to join the headquarters of the regiment at Watford (then on the march to York), he gave me a letter for Lord Cardigan expressing his approval of the manner in which the duty of my party had been performed, which told very much in my favour afterwards. The following day, after joining the headquarters at Watford, I was sent on to draw billets. One troop marched to Barnsley, two to Sheffield, the remaining three troops and headquarters to York.

Regimental Sergeant-Major Anson had now succeeded to the adjutancy. During the time I was in York, I was an instructor in the yard, drilling a squad of new recruits.

At the beginning of January 1843, I was appointed lance-sergeant and marched with Captain W C Forrest's troop to Sheffield to relieve one of the troops quartered there. The day before they marched I was sent on to draw billets. Next day, before the troop arrived, a keen frost set in so that they had to lead their horses into Selby, the roads being covered with ice. Before marching, my horse and that of my man had to be roughed so that we were much delayed. A frightful snow storm came on soon after we started, so that we were in danger of being blown off the road; the horses staggered under us. It was long after dark when we arrived in Doncaster.

The next days' march was equally bad, the rain falling in torrents accompanied by thunder and lightning. When a few miles from Sheffield, in passing down a lane we came to a wicket gate and path leading to a church. I involuntarily halted saying 'I think I have been here before,' so dismounted and gave my horse to my man to hold.

On walking about 20 yards down the path on my left, I came to a spot where I had stood when a boy to see my grandmother interred—and there was the tombstone with her name. I stood for a few minutes, thinking over her great love and kindess to me, for she had brought me up from an infant, taking me from my mother when I was a baby. The following day, 12th January 1843, I took over the part of the barracks allotted to the troop.

A little circumstance occurred about this time which I think worth relating. A man by the name of Blandford, who rode a little bay horse, used, when we turned out for exercise, to start off at a gallop round the barrack yard—much to the amusement of his comrades. When spoken to about it, he said his horse ran away with him, so the captain and the sergeant-major came to the conclusion that his horse did not have enough to carry. So they ordered that Blandford should turn out every morning in Marching Order for exercise with the troops, who were in Watering Order, till his horse became quiet like the others. We generally rode through some part of the town, when Blandford, with busby, pelisse slung, sword and carbine, became a great source of attraction, the Sheffield boys shouting out, 'A, that'st Mester,' thinking that he was the commander. It was not many mornings before Blandford's horse became as quiet as the others.

On 17th April 1843, I was appointed sergeant in Captain Douglas' troop. At the end of April 1843, we commenced the march to Liverpool for embarkation to Ireland. The night before marching, Private Clarkson fell into the river which runs past the barracks, and was unfortunately drowned. We left his body to be buried by the regiment that relieved us.

We had a pleasant march to Liverpool and embarked the following day for Dublin. On arriving there, the Acting Regimental Sergeant-Major Gilleland with the recruits and young horses were sent on to Newbridge, and I was appointed to assist in drilling the recruits and keeping the accounts of the detachment. Regimental Sergeant-Major Graham was left at York sick, where he died a few months afterwards.

At the end of June 1843, the detachment at Newbridge joined the Headquarters at the Royal Barracks, Dublin. During the summer, frequent field days and cavalry brigades took place

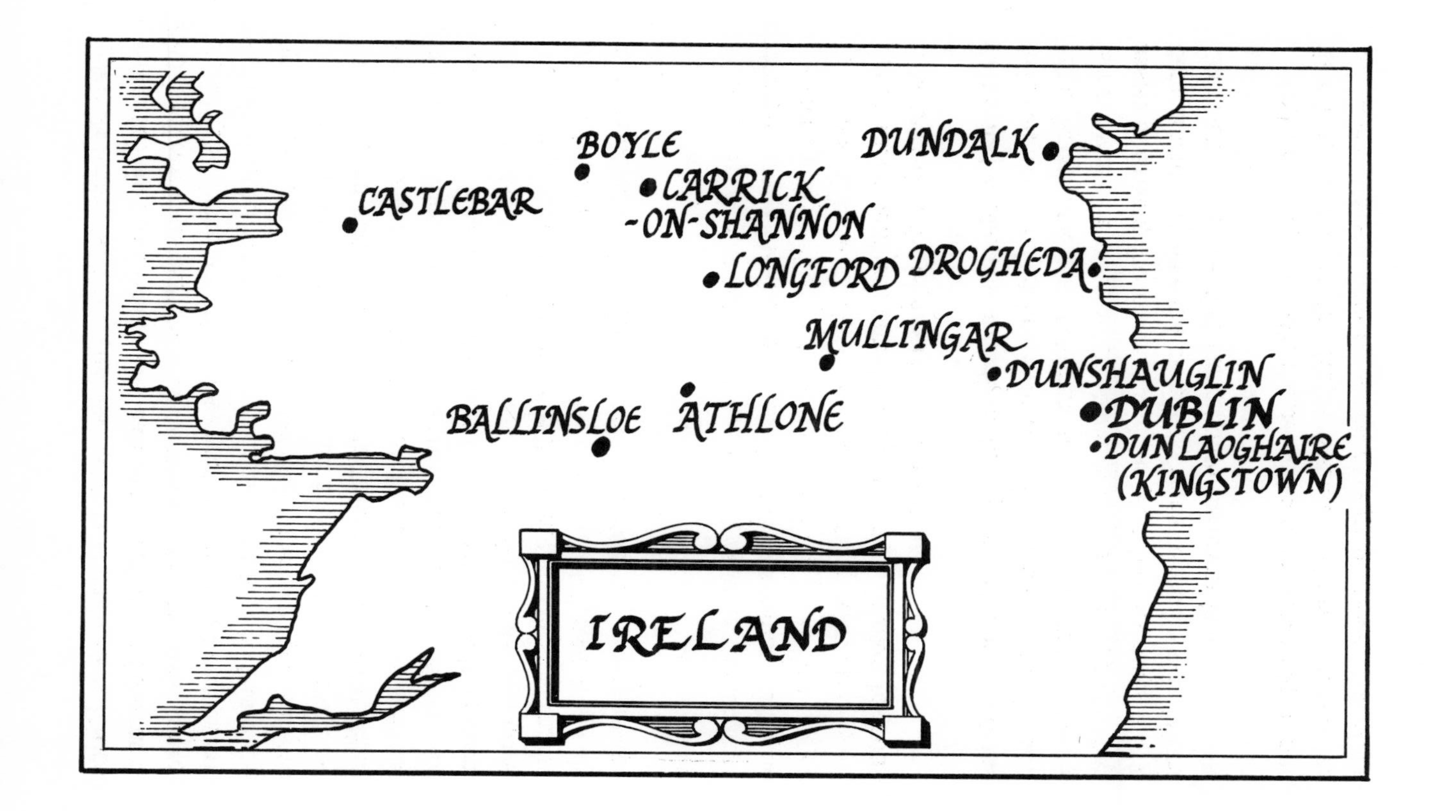
BOYLE
DUNDALK
CASTLEBAR
CARRICK
-ON-SHANNON
LONGFORD
DROGHEDA
MULLINGAR
DUNSHAUGLIN
DUBLIN
DUN LAOGHAIRE
(KINGSTOWN)
BALLINSLOE
ATHLONE
IRELAND

under the command of Lord Cardigan in the Phoenix Park. About this time, the 11th, a troop of horse artillery and the 60th Rifles marched to Clontarf to suppress a repeal meeting being held there, which a proclamation of the Lord Lieutenant had prohibited. Each man carried a day's rations and a feed of corn for his horse.

On arriving at Clontarf, where the meeting was to be held, there was not a person to be seen. After a time we dismounted on the sands and fed our horses, remaining there till evening. On our march back, by the roadside sat an old woman. Just as Lord Cardigan was passing her, she sprang up and shouted, 'Arrah bad luck to ye's. We'll have the repeal in spite of your red a.... Three cheers for Daniel O'Connor!' Lord Cardigan and all within hearing had a good laugh at the old woman.

It was about this time too that the 11th escorted Daniel O'Connor to Kilmainham Gaol. We were frequently confined to barracks during his trial and held in readiness to turn out at a moment's notice.

In April 1844, the regiment changed barracks from the Royal to the Portobello with the 3rd Dragoon Guards, and in August marched to Dundalk. The recruits and heavy baggage, under the command of Lieutenant Sandes went by train to Drogheda, the line being just opened. On arriving at Drogheda, the baggage had to be removed from the train and then loaded on to the ordinary country carts. Afterwards each cart had to be weighed in the town on the weigh-bridge and it was night before the start was made for Dundalk, which was reached between 8am and 9am the next morning. After daylight, the recruits of the 8th Hussars with their baggage were passed going in the opposite direction. On arriving at Dundalk, we were all completely prostrated for the want of rest.

While quartered at Dundalk, two remarkable incidents occurred. Lance-Corporal Davidson, when on duty at the canteen at noon, allowed a defaulter to pass into the canteen unobserved. Corporal Davidson was placed under arrest. Major Jones ordered him to be reduced, and given seven days dry room and kit drill. He was then taken to the dry room with his kit. About an hour after, when the troops were at dinner, he loaded his carbine and shot himself through the heart. He was a promising young soldier and much respected by his comrades.

Private Thomas, a good-for-nothing soldier, when drunk went to the officer's quarters and took a coat from a peg in the anteroom belonging to the Reverend Allpress, the chaplain, who was dining with the officers. He put the coat on and laid down by the back—or watergate—of the barracks and went to sleep. He was tried by court-martial for disgraceful behaviour, and his sentence was to receive 100 lashes and to be drummed out of the regiment. The chaplain, who was a most kindly man, bought him a suit of clothes and paid his expenses to London.

The only place available for field days was on the sands when the tide was out. On one occasion, the tide hemmed us in so that the water was up to the horse's girths; the consequence was the crimson overalls were much discoloured by the salt water. The same evening, Lord Cardigan ordered that the whole regiment was to be put under stoppages for new overalls. This caused great discontent amongst the men, many that had two good pairs objected to it. Those men that did not object, received a new pair at the expense of his Lordship.

During the time we were quartered at Dundalk, the sergeant-major of 'F' Troop slipped down a flight of stone steps, and was discharged in consequence of the injury he received. I was appointed troop sergeant-major in his stead.

In April 1845, the regiment marched to Newbridge. On arriving at Dunshaklin several of the men of 'F' Troop were billeted on an undertaker. In one of the rooms were a number of ready-made coffins. These some of the men filled with straw and slept in, there not being enough beds in the house to accommodate them all. The regiment, after remaining in Newbridge a short time, removed to Dublin for the drill season and was quartered in the Island Bridge Barracks, then returned to Newbridge. During the time the regiment was quartered here a squadron marched to Mullingar in aid of the civil power to be present at the execution of Bryant Scery, who had been condemned to death for the attempted murder of Sir Francis Hopkins, as it was supposed that a rescue would be attempted, but the strong military force brought into the town overawed the people. He was hanged outside the jail. We remained in our billets, ready to turn out at a moment's notice.

The following day we commenced the march back to Newbridge. In April 1846, the regiment marched from Newbridge to Dublin, remaining there one night. The following day we embarked for England. The 'F' and 'E' Troops marched with the headquarters to Coventry where they were quartered for two years. Captain J H Forrest now sold out and Captain Sandes succeeded him in command of 'F' Troop.

One day Dr O'Callagan met with Prince Louis Napoleon in the town and brought him into the barracks, first taking him round our troop stables, then to the officer's mess-room. The messman's wife, a French lady, gave him a ring little thinking he would one day become Emperor. In his prosperity he remembered her, and appointed her mother to have charge of a rural post office.

In consequence of the great scarcity and high price of

potatoes, this being the year of the great famine in Ireland arising from the failure of the potato crop, the issue of them to the troops had to be discountinued and extra bread provided in lieu. Major Jones, fearing that the scurvey might break out for lack of vegetables, ordered parties from each troop under a corporal to go daily into the country lanes and gather nettles. The barracks being in the centre of the town, the men could not avoid being seen by the inhabitants. This annoyed them greatly, more particularly when the girls called them 'donkey robbers.' One day two of them, instead of gathering nettles, filled their sacks with dock leaves. When brought before the major, they pretended they did not know the difference.

Cornet and Adjutant Sutton, who had succeeded Cornet and Adjutant Anson in Dublin, now returned to the Royal Horse Guards, the regiment he originally belonged to, as adjutant, and Troop Sergeant-Major Ennis was appointed in his stead. Regimental Sergeant-Major Dungate, who, it will be remembered, I spoke of at the commencement, married the daughter of a master baker, who had a fortune of about £2,000.

Lord Cardigan was seldom with us during the time we were quartered in Coventry, Major Jones being generally in command.

His Lorship, for the sake of neatness had had the valises altered and made so small that they would not contain the men's kits, so that one pair of overalls had to be carried under the pilch on the stretcher of the saddle. In marching order, this made a most uncomfortable seat, besides destroying the men's best overalls. General Brotherton, who commanded the district, having heard of this, came to Coventry and ordered the troops to turn out in Marching Order. After inspecting us, he caused a number of men to show their kits and satisfied himself that the valises had been made smaller than the regulation. This he reported to the commander-in-chief, when an order came that the valises were to be made larger at the expense of Lord Cardigan. This must have given the general a little satisfaction in the way of retaliation on his Lordship for the way he had treated his son in Canterbury, by refusing to pass charger after charger that the general had sent to mount his son. So pointed was the annoyance that Cornet Brotherton was subject to that he soon left the regiment. I remember on one occasion, being drill corporal at the time, being ordered by the regimental sergeant-major to take Cornets Brotherton and Cunningham to setting-up drill, Lord Cardigan having seen them, as he considered, walking in a slovenly manner across the barrack yard.

Although Lord Cardigan was considered one of the strictest and most severe officers in the army, still he always saw for himself and did not at once take the evidence of others, but enquired into matters—particularly if he suspected that any injustice was being practised on the non-commissioned officers or men by those in authority over them. This, in a great measure, reconciled the men to the strict régime to which they were subject. His Lordship had a wonderful gift for remembering men's names.

After the regiment returned from the Crimea Lord Cardigan, then being Head Colonel of the regiment and Inspecting General of Cavalry, on reference to the regimental books, found that several troop sergeant-majors had been reduced to sergeants by Colonel Douglas. He told him he could not understand it, adding 'I commanded this regiment 16 years and never reduced a troop sergeant-major.'

On 13th June 1848, the headquarters marched from Coventry to Hounslow, arriving there on the 20th. Shortly after, Her Majesty and Prince Albert reviewed the regiment on Hounslow Heath. The ground being very soft and slippery, several of the horses fell, which much annoyed Lord Cardigan, so that he threatened to send us all to everlasting riding school. A few minutes after this threat, his and Trooper Connor's horse fell together. His Lordship's foot, being in the stirrup iron under the horse, was severely injured so that we did not see him again for several months. As he lay on the ground, all smothered in mud, one of the men in the ranks exclaimed in a loud tone, 'Behold the Lord is down,' which caused a tittering amongst the men. I have no doubt the officers joined in it, for they were under the law as well as ourselves.

During the time of the review, Prince Louis Napoleon drove on to the ground in a carriage drawn by four horses with two postillions. He was not recognised either by her Majesty or any of the nobility. At this time he was a resident in London, before the end of the year he was elected President of the French Republic.

On 27th June 1849 the regiment was reviewed a second time on Wimbledon Common by Her Majesty and Prince Albert. The Duke of Wellington and many distinguished personages were present, when the following manoeuvres were performed:

March past by squadrons
Rank past by threes, with carbines
Trot past by squadrons
Trot past by troops
Change front to the rear by the wheelabout of divisions, and gallop past, left in front
Line to the rear on the rear troop, skirmishers from 1st and 2nd squadrons, right divisions

1. Retire in a column of troops from the left
   Line to the left about on leading troop
   Skirmishers in and advance

2. Retire in a column of troops from the right
   Line to the rear on the 1st squadron and advance
3. Retire in a column of troops from the right
   Line to the rear on the 2nd squadron and advance
4. By echelon of troops, change position right back
5. Take ground to the right by troops
   Change direction to the left
6. Inverted line to the left on 1st squadron and attack to the front in direct echelon of squadron from the left
7. Column of troops from the right of squadrons to the left
   Change direction, wheel into line and advance
8. Advance in column of troops from the right
   Wheel into line and advance
9. Retire in direct echelon of squadrons from the right echelon change direction to the right and form line on 3rd squadron
10. Close column of squadrons on the 2nd right in front
11. The column takes ground to the right and changes direction to the left, by right shoulders forward
    Halt, front, forward
12. Deploy on 1st squadron and advance
13. Retire by alternate troops, covered by skirmishers from left divisions of 1st and 2nd squadrons
    Right thrown back quarter circle
    Skirmishers in, advance
14. Open column of squadrons in rear of the 1st wheel into line and advance
15. By threes, change position right back
16. By threes, change position to the left and advance
17. Advance in direct echelon of squadrons from the left at two-thirds distance
18. Oblique line to the right and attack
19. By threes, change position half left back
20. Retire in a column of troops from the right close column of squadrons to the rear on the 3rd squadron

21. Attack to the front by squadrons in succession and retire by threes from the flanks of squadrons
    2nd and 3rd squadron re-form on original ground
    1st squadron re-form after retiring a short distance and the left troop extend to skirmish
22. The column takes ground to the left, halts, fronts and deploys into line on 2nd squadron
    Skirmishers called in; and the 2nd and 3rd squadrons attack to the front
    Right troop of the 1st squadron pursues across the front after the attack
23. Retire by alternate squadrons covered by skirmishers from 3rd squadron
    Re-form line and attack to the front
24. Retire by threes from the outward flanks of the line
    Re-form line and attack to the front
25. Retire by threes from the right of squadrons
    Halt, front, wheel into line, and advance in Parade Order

NB Most of the advances to the front were made so close to the line of spectators, that the regiment was reigned back to gain wheeling distance previous to breaking into column before retiring.

At the 6th manoeuvre, Lord Cardigan inverted the line and forgot he had done so. The adjutant perceiving this, galloped out and told His Lordship, but he must have got confused for, instead of giving a word of command that would have replaced, he galloped up to Her Majesty and asked permission to re-form the regiment before proceeding. This was the only time I ever knew his Lordship to make such a mistake. The Life Guards kept the ground on this occasion.

At the latter end of the summer of 1849, 'F' Troop marched to Hampton Court and was quartered in the Palace Barracks, the other troop occupying the new barracks. On 14th May

1850, the squadron under the command of Captain Douglas marched from Hampton Court en route for Ipswich, arriving there on the 18th. Near Chelmsford, we met the squadron of the 16th Lancers that we were relieving. They formed up and saluted us as we passed; the last time we met was a days' march from Meerut. The two squadrons then dismounted and had about half an hour's chat together. I met two or three that went out to India with me in 1835; they wore three medals each, but looked quite old men—the hard campaigning that they had in India had told on their constitutions. Nearly every man in the squadron wore one, two or three medals.

At the latter end of the summer, 'F' Troop, now under the command of Lieutenant Sykes (Captain Sandes being on the lord lieutenant's staff at Dublin), marched from Ipswich to Norwich to join the headquarters. During the time we were quartered there, 'F' and 'A' Troops, under the command of Captain Douglas, proceeded by rail to Great Yarmouth to aid the civil power in quelling a riot caused by the sailors, who were opposed to the new Shipping Act. The squadron formed up with drawn sword on one side of the great square, which was filled with people. The Riot Act was read; Captain Douglas then gave the word: 'March.' As we advanced across the square, the people dispersed as if by magic, running up the narrow streets and on to the beach. I was then sent with six men to prevent the people returning to the square by the street near the beach. The heads of the vessels being, on one side, all in darkness and gas lamps on the other in front of the houses; this brought us in full view of the sailors on the heads of the vessels, who pelted us with stones. There was no getting at them. I was struck twice, once on the forehead and once under the eye, which caused the blood to run down on my belts. Several of the men and horses were also struck, but no one was seriously hurt either amongst us or the people. About midnight they had all dispersed; we were then billeted. The following day (Sunday), the soldiers and sailors fraternised and there was no more rioting. The next day we marched back to Norwich.

On 23rd April 1851, the headquarters and three troops marched from Norwich, arriving at Nottingham on 1st May. During the time we were quartered there, we lost, by death, Sergeant J Norris, Corporal Bassett Smith (my brother), and three privates. The non-commissioned officers, as a mark of their sincere respect, erected tombstones over the sergeant and corporal.

In June, Lieutenant F Sykes succeeded Captain Sandes to the command of the troop. About the middle of April 1852, the headquarters marched from Nottingham to Liverpool for embarkation for Dublin. On arriving at Dublin, they at once proceeded to Newbridge. During the months of May and June, we had frequent field days under Lord Cardigan on the Curragh.

On 1st July, 'F' Troop under the command of Major Jones marched to Athlone, arriving there about the 6th. About the 20th, they proceeded to Carrick on Shannon, remaining there a few days, then returning to Athlone. At the latter end of the month, they joined the headquarters at Newbridge. The regiment at this time had detachments at Castlebar, Ballinasloe, Boyle and Longford—the General Election taking place at this time. At the latter end of the summer, the regiment marched to Dublin and was quartered at Island bridge Barracks and the Royal Barracks.

In December 1852, Lieutenant E A Cook succeeded Captain Sykes to the command of 'F' Troop., During the summer of 1853, [we] had frequent brigade field days under Lord Cardigan in Phoenix Park. About midsummer, we exchanged quarters with the 16th Lancers, they coming to the Island Bridge, and we going to Portobello Barracks.

On 2nd September 1853, His Royal Highness Prince Albert reviewed, in Phoenix Park, the cavalry and artillery forming the Dublin Garrison. The following regiments were present: the 1st and 2nd Dragoon Guards; the 11th Hussars and 16th Lancers and the 'I' Troop Royal Horse Artillery. Lord Cardigan commanded.

The brigade formed in parade order for a Royal salute:

1st Dragoon Guards (4 squadrons) on the right
2nd Dragoon Guards (3 squadrons) on the left
11th Hussars (3 squadrons) in the centre
16th Lancers (3 squadrons) in the centre
RHA (6 guns) on the right of the line.

The manoeuvres were as follows:

1. Brigade forms close column in rear of first squadron of regiments
2. Brigade forms contiguous columns on the Hussars
3. The contiguous columns will take ground to the left by threes
   Halt, front
4. Brigade will change front to the right and form columns *en masse* on 1st squadron of 1st Dragoon Guards
5. Brigade will deploy on 1st squadron of 1st Dragoon Guards
   Guns to the front and fire till the movement is complete
6. Brigade will advance in echelon of regiments from the centre
   Guns to the outward flanks of the leading Regiments
7. The 1st and 2nd Dragoon Guards will form line on the Hussars and Lancers
   Guns unlimber and fire until the movement is complete
8. The brigade will change front, left back, covered by skirmishers from the Hussars: 1st Dragoon Guards by

echelon, remaining regiments by the open column
Skirmishers are called in, and the guns fire two or three rounds when their front is clear

9. The brigade will advance in echelon of regiments from the right
   Form line on the 1st Dragoon Guards
   3rd squadron of Hussars and 1st squadron of Lancers pursue from centre to flanks
10. The brigade will attack to the front
    Guns unlimber after the attack and fire two or three rounds
11. The brigade will change front, left back, 2nd Dragoon Guards by echelon, remaining regiments by open column
    Guns unlimber and fire two or three rounds
12. The brigade will advance in echelon of regiments from the right
    Echelon halts and guns action left
13. The regiments will change from to the left
14. The brigade will form line on the 1st Dragoon Guards
15. The Hussars and Lancers will advance with the guns
    The 1st and 2nd Dragoon Guards will form second line by the open column
16. Guns unlimber, fire two or three rounds, and the first line attacks to the front
    The first line retires by threes from the right of squadrons, pass to the rear and form second line
    The Dragoon Guards attack to the front
17. The Dragoon Guards retire in a column of troops from the outward flanks of the line and the brigade forms quarter distance columns of regiments (or four lines) on the Hussars
18. The brigade will attack to the front by regiments in succession and retire in a column of troops from the outward flanks
    Guns fire both before and after the attack

19. Regiments will form close column and right in front, on second squadron of regiments—1st Dragoon Guards on 3rd Squadron
20. The brigade will attack to the front by squadrons in succession and retire by threes from outward flanks
    Guns fire before and after the attack
21. The brigade will deploy into two lines on 2nd squadron of the 1st Dragoon Guards and 1st squadron of Lancers
    March past by squadrons
    Trot past by troops
    Gallop past by troops, left in front
    Advance in parade order

PART FOUR

1853–54

War declared with Russia—A long sea voyage—Arrival at Varna—Enemy encounters at the Almá—Arrival at Balaclava

Dublin, Christmas 1853. The 11th (Prince Albert's Own) Hussars were quartered in the Portobello Barracks. War with Russia at this time was the principal topic of conversation, at the Mess, at stables—in fact everywhere when we met and had an opportunity of discussing the subject. One evening an illustrated newspaper was brought to the mess-room; we all eagerly crowded round as it contained illustrations of the different Russian regiments: artillery, dragoons, lancers, cossacks and infantry. Many remarks were made, but little did we think that before 12 months were up, we should have been face to face and actually engaged with this same Russian Army, and that some of us would have met with a soldier's death on the battlefield.

After many months of fruitless negotiations with the Emperor Nicholas, war was proclaimed on 27th March 1854. Previously we had made many preparations in anticipation. On 9th March 1854 we received a notification from the general commanding that we were for foreign service. The following day the order arrived from the Horse Guards, with a detail of all the arrangements, viz: we were to take out four troops of 74 men and 62 horses each, and 4 women per troop. If deficient of men or horses, we were to be made up from the 16th Lancers, they being the nearest light cavalry regiment, being quartered at Island Bridge Barracks, Dublin. By breaking up the band and putting them in the ranks, we had men sufficient, but we required about 30 horses to complete. Lord Cardigan now joined, having been away on leave.

By 22nd March 1854 the service troops were complete and everything in readiness for embarkation. From this time till we received the order to embark, we had frequent field days in Phoenix Park under Lord Cardigan and skirmishing drill under the adjutant who, to give the men a better idea of skirmishing, formed them in two lines opposed to each other. There were many very young soldiers, so that this drill was of great service to them as it gave them an idea of what they would be required to do if they were in the actual presence of an enemy. One morning an order was issued that all our sword were to be collected; they were then placed in a waggon and sent down to Dublin to be ground and sharpened—men from the Tower of London having arrived to see this properly carried out. When they were re-issued, an order was given that they were not again to be drawn till required, when in presence of the enemy. A certain number of whetstones per troop were likewise issued, to be taken with us. This little preparation made one think seriously of what was before us, as it looked more like warfare than anything we had before witnessed.

All being now in readiness, we anxiously looked forward to the day when we should leave Dublin for embarkation. We now learned that five transports had been hired to convey the regiment to the east. The officer's mess plate with the heavy baggage of the regiment was deposited in the Dublin Bank. The depot marched to Newbridge, there to remain till the regiment returned.

At length the order came that the transport *Asia* (721 tons), that was to convey 'F' Troop had arrived at Kingstown. On the morning of the 9th May, we paraded under the command of Captain Cook as follows: Cornet Houghton; Pay-Master Healey; seven officer's horses—two of which belonged to Lieutenant Dunn, who had remained behind on leave; 43 non-commissioned officers and privates; and 39 troop horses.

These were all the *Asia* could accommodate. The remainder of the troops, viz: 31 non-commissioned officers and privates and 22 troop horses, came out on board other ships. We had a pleasant march to Kingstown, arriving there about 11am. The morning was beautifully fine, but we had no sooner formed up on the wharf opposite the ship, than the sky suddenly became overcast and the rain poured down upon us with unsparing severity, speedily drenching both men and horses. As soon as it abated, we dismounted and commenced unsaddling. The men also took off their busbies and pelisses, and put on their forage caps; these with the saddlery and arms were put by each man into his corn sack and sent down below. Ship collars were placed on the horse's heads; then commenced the process of shipping them, which was attended with much trouble and danger as some of the horses resisted violently. After four hour's hard work, they were all placed safely in the hold without a single accident. By 4 o'clock, everything was on board and the men were comfortably seated at their dinners. The arrangements for our comfort were admirable; we were all on the lower deck. The captain kindly had a corner partitioned off for me and I messed with the purser, so that I was more comfortably put up than I could have anticipated.

Wednesday 10th May 1854 At about 6am, the *Asia* was towed out of the harbour. The wind being favourable, all sail was crowded, so that the coast of Erin gradually disappeared from our sight. The sea now became rougher, and many of the men suffered very much from seasickness. The wind for several days was variable.

Sunday 14th May 1854 We were in the Bay of Biscay—paraded in full dress for Divine Service. Captain Cook read prayers; the ship rolled heavily so that we had a difficulty in standing. The weather after this became beautifully fine and pleasant, wind favourable. Passed the island of Madeira on the

16th, many vessels in sight. The next day we were off Cape St Vincent. Both we and our horses were now getting accustomed to our new quarters. I had brought some sticks and baskets for the men to practise attack and defence, and for amusement, when they were tired of this, dancing and singing songs were resorted to, so that the evenings were spent pleasantly, everyone on board seeming happy—Captain Cook leaving all the arrangements to me. The men's conduct was so good that I do not recall having to report one of them.

The trumpeter sounded 'Stables' three times a day, and every man attended to his horse as far as possible the same as in barracks. Several barrels of vinegar were shipped for the purpose of refreshing the horses, by sponging their heads well over with it, particularly their nostrils. Slings were provided too for the horses to rest on. These I soon began to suspect must be made on a wrong principle for, if a horse slipped, they rather tended to throw him down than support him, and there was more difficulty to get a horse up, and more danger of him being killed with one on, than if he had fallen without one. So convinced was I at last, after watching the thing narrowly, that I discontinued their use. The consequence was that every horse was disembarked at Varna in splendid condition; this I believe did not happen with any other sailing vessel that went out, nearly all losing more or less—one as many as seven before leaving the Channel. The other four vessels that took out the 11th lost 11.

One day I was in the hold looking at the working of the slings and puzzling my brain to find some better way when, on a sudden, an idea struck me: *four* ropes instead of *two*. I immediately jumped up saying I had it. I at once commenced making a model which, after a few days, I completed to my satisfaction. I then wrote a description of the working of the two slings, pointing out the disadvantages of the one and the advantages of the other. I also made a drawing representing a horse in each of the slings, at an angle of about 10 degrees. In the instructions we received before sailing, we were requested to report on the working of the slings at the end of the voyage for the information of the authorities at home, so that I felt I had found out something that I hoped would benefit me some day or other, but unfortunately, it has brought me nothing but disappointment, expense and trouble.

18th May 1854 Passed the Bay of Trafalgar; the following day the town of Teneriffe (in the distance could be seen the African coast). About 6pm, passed the Rock of Gibralter; no boats put off, consequently we were not able to send letters. The fair wind that we got as we cleared the Irish Channel carried us through the Straits of Gibralter. With a light wind and calm sea, we moved steadily on within sight of the Coast of Barbary.

20th May 1854 Off Fez. Since entering the Mediterranean, we have seldom been without the company of one or more transports laden with troops, all steering for the same destination.

24th May 1854 Paraded in Full Dress to fire a *Feu de Joie* in honour of her Majesty's Birthday. Firing omitted in consequence of the horses; hoisted the Ensign and gave three cheers.

28th May 1854 Off Algiers.

29th May 1854 In the evening passed the Bay of Tunis. Spoke to transport containing part of the 13th Light Dragoons. About 9pm we were near another transport (No. 62) containing part of the 3rd Field Battery, Royal Artillery, which left the Downs on 13th May. Our trumpeter hailed them with a salute on the trumpet, which their trumpeter returned. It being a lovely night, we sailed together abreast within a very short distance, so that we could speak with them. They threw up a rocket and burnt port fire so that we could see every man on board distinctly and they us. They then gave three cheers for 'Prince Albert's Own' and we returned the compliment by giving three cheers for the Royal Artillery; they then sang *Rule Britannia*, afterwards we sang *Cheer Boys Cheer.* They informed us they had lost one horse that day. So we went on together, trumpets sounding and singing songs alternately, as happy as men could be; not giving a thought of what was before us and not knowing that every third officer and man would never return.

Thursday 1st June 1854 Sighted the island of Malta, but did not arrive at the entrance to the harbour till the evening of the 2nd, where we lay all night. The following morning we were towed in, when we at once commenced taking in water. The town had a very enchanting appearance—the houses rising one above another in terraces, interspersed with orange trees.

A number of bum-boats came alongside with all sorts of wares, provisions and fruit. The rowers were of different nationalities: Greeks, Maltese, Sicilians—and the greatest rogues and cheats I ever met with, charging us enormously for everything we purchased. We were informed by the authorities that our destination was Varna, and that we were not to remain in harbour more than 10 hours. The order was most peremptory, for before we had completed taking in water, a tug came alongside and took us in tow. When about three miles out, it left us. The wind being fair, we set all sail and went rapidly on our way, making 11 knots an hour. By 9pm, the Malta lighthouse was scarcely visible.

Sunday 4th June 1854 Beautiful morning, no land in sight. Church parade at 11am, prayers read by Captain Cook. The ship making about six knots an hour. The weather continued beautifully fine and wind favourable, the nights too being moonlit, so that everything went pleasantly with us, being always in sight of many other transports.

Wednesday 7th June 1854 About 6pm sighted the mountains of the Morea; the following morning entered the Archipelago. The *Asia* steering on the morning star. The scenery became more enchanting as we proceeded, range beyond range being tipped with crimson and purple hue. The white sand on the highest mountain tops had much the appearance of snow. We soon became nearly surrounded by land—the Morea on our left, the island of Cerigo on our right. About midday, came in sight of the points of the mountains of Candia on our right front at a distance of about 30 miles. At this time 15 ships were in sight, nearly all sailing in the same direction. The sunset was most magnificent and the surrounding scenery charming in the extreme; the moon being nearly at the full, we could distinctly see all around us.

Saturday 10th June 1854 At 4am came in collision with Transport No. 40, artillery on board, she breaking our spanker boom and we their studsail boom. This was occasioned by her crossing astern and, the wind suddenly dropping, we drifted astern (faults on both sides), which occasioned the accident. Damage to our ship £3.

Passed many islands during the day, some remarkably high. About 5pm off a large fertile island which appeared to be cultivated in every part, a town distinctly visible. The occasional pleasant fragrance of fruit blossom made our sailing very agreeable. The night was beautifully fine. About 10pm quite becalmed.

Sunday 11th June 1854 Beautiful morning, light breeze, 49 sail in sight. Church parade at 11am, prayers read by Captain

Cook. Passed several small islands, at times we appeared to be surrounded by land, not being able to see any outlet. The sun set at 8pm. The blood-red tints on the edges of the clouds and summits of the mountains had a splendid effect. The moon rising eastward behind an immensely high mountain of Scio had a beautiful appearance with its bright silvery light tinging the mountains, shipping and sea.

Monday 12th June 1854 Beautiful morning. About 9am passed the Gulf of Smyrna; about 12 noon off the island of Mitileni. About ?.30 opposite to a town at the point of Cape Baba, the surrounding country appearing to be well cultivated, trees on all the hills in sight, which reached far away into the country. About midnight between Limnos and Tenedos.

Tuesday 13th June 1854 Sun rose at 4.30. Fine, clear, but exceedingly hot morning. About 4pm off the ruins of Troy, the town and citadel of Tenedos in sight. After passing the island, came in sight of the mouth of the Dardanelles. On our right was Fort Asia, on our left Fort Europe. These forts command the mouth of the Dardanelles. When opposite to and about a mile from Fort Asia, we suddenly ran aground—the captain never having been this way before, had kept quarter of a mile too much to the right of the channel. Every endeavour was made during the night to get her off, but all to no avail. Two guns of distress were fired and blue lights burned, but no-one came off to us till the following morning about 11am, when a boat from Fort Europe containing three Turkish officers and several soldiers arrived. After giving instructions to the captain, they returned to shore to inform the British Consul so that a steamer might be sent to draw us off.

During the morning, about 10 transports passed us, containing French and English troops, much to our mortification, for every endeavour had failed to get us afloat. Many steamers too

THE AEGEAN SEA
BALCIK
NOS KALIAKRA
DEVNA
VARNA
GREECE
CONSTANTINOPLE
(ISTANBUL)
USKUDAR
(SCUTARI)
MAMARA
ADASI
GELIBOLU
TROY
LIMNOS
OTTOMAN
EMPIRE
IZMIR
(SMYRNA)
Khios
Athens
CYCLADES
DODECANES
Rhodes
IRAKLION
CRETE

passed us, but all gave us a wide berth—the water round us being only three fathoms deep. About midday, the commander of Fort Asia, with several Turkish officers, a pilot, trumpeter and several artillery soldiers came on board. The soldiers giving us every assistance under the direction of the pilot, but every effort failed. About 4pm they left us. At 8pm our Consul came on board and remained all night.

Thursday 15th June 1854 At 4am three Turkish boats came to our assistance with officers, interpreter, pilot and a number of soldiers. Every device that could be thought of by the captain and pilot was carried out, but all to no avail.

Captain Cook then consulted with me as to the advisability of passing the horses over the side and letting them swim ashore; this could have been done in the event of our not being able to get off. In the evening a steam tug arrived.

Friday 16th June 1854 In the morning, the anchor and chain cable were put into two boats lashed together and dropped into deep water some distance from the ship. By the exertions of all on board and the steam tug, we were got afloat by 8.30am; we then dropped anchor in 16 fathoms water, having been aground 61 hours. Fortunately the weather was beautifully calm the whole time. The tug then left us. At 1pm, we weighed anchor and set sail with a fair wind. The Turks now left us, except the interpreter and our Consul, who went with us to Gallipolli.

Spoke to two French Brigs having cavalry on board, who played a salute which we returned. About 5.30 pm, passed the town of Abydos. At sunset were opposite a large fort, which fired a gun to indicate that we were not to proceed further, so dropped anchor within 300 yards of the shore in 26 fathoms. There were eight French and three English transports anchored not far from us. At this point the current was very strong—the width of passage about five miles. During the night at intervals of about 10 minutes, we could distinctly hear the wild cries of the dervishes on the minarets, of which there were several not far distant.

Saturday 17th June 1854 Weighed anchor about 11.30am. Wind favourable, making 11 knots. Passed several forts armed with heavy guns. The scenery on both sides was very beautiful. Passed Gallipolli at 4pm. A division of the French Army had disembarked here and was encamped in the surrounding country. About 9pm, were taken in tow by a man-of-war steamer.

Sunday 18th June 1854 About 4am the following morning passed the island of Marmara. About ?am, to our great delight, came in sight of the minarets of Santa Sophia and shortly after Constantinople came in full view. The city has a magnificent appearance as you enter the Bosphorus; the beauty of the situation can hardly be exceeded, the aspect from the sea being particularly grand. About 12.30, cast anchor between Centari and Constantinople.

The following morning I was sent by Captain Cook to Constantinople to post our letters. After doing so, I met with a Mr Brown, engineer in the Sultan's Mint; he, being able to speak the language, assisted me in making purchases—one purchase was a huge basket of eggs, for which I paid 14s 6d. These were given by the captain to the men as a treat, they receiving nine each. I spent several hours with my new friend, who showed me through the bazaar and several other places of interest.

Tuesday 20th June 1854 Sent all our heavy baggage to Scutari to be placed in stores there, being only allowed to take with us what we could carry in our valises. Since we have entered the Dardanelles, it has been one constant scene of excitment: English, French, Turkish transports sailing together cheering one another.

Thursday 22nd June 1854 Weighed anchor at 2.30 and was taken in tow by a war steamer. The scenery as we passed up the Bosphorus was enchanting in the extreme: palaces, mansions, forts, houses of various colours built close to the water's edge with balconies built close over the beautifully clear water for the owners to sit upon and smoke their pipes in the cool of the evening. Ships of war, colours flying; transports laden with troops, bands playing; small boats, called caiques, flitting about with their gaily dressed boatmen—altogether it was a scene never to be forgotten. As we sailed out of the Bosphorus into the Black Sea, the two immense forts that guard the mouth saluted us by hoisting the Turkish flag.

Friday 23rd June 1854 About 10am, came in sight of Varna but, by some unaccountable mistake, the captain of the steamer took us 10 miles beyond the entrance of the bay, nearly to the lighthouse at Kaliakra. He then returned and made direct into the harbour, which had a most animated appearance—the French and English fleets lying at anchor, transports innumerable, disembarking troops and war material. About 2.30pm dropped anchor after a most delightful voyage of six weeks and two days and, what was more satisfactory to all concerned, was that every man and horse was in perfect health—many far better than when we started.

Saturday 24th June 1854 About 8am, commenced disembarking, which took us three hours. One horse managed to disengage himself from the slings, so fell into the sea and swam ashore. Tents, picket posts, ropes and camp kettles we brought with us, so that in half an hour after the disembarkation was completed, the horses were all picketed and the tents up. Our encampment was on the left of the harbour, about three miles from Varna and within a hundred yards of the salt water, which was very fortunate for us as we could enjoy the sea-bathing to our heart's content, which I believe everyone did. At least I know I did, for I made a rule that, as soon as I awoke, nearly every morning to run down to the sea and plunge into it. When we landed the 8th Hussars and 17th Lancers, with one squadron of ours, were encamped about eight miles off under the command of Lord Cardigan—they forming the advance guard. The 13th Light Dragoons and some artillery were encamped near us. Part of the 1st Royal Dragoons disembarked on the afternoon of the same day that we did. On landing, we learned that our lieutenant-colonel, Lord Cardigan, had been appointed major-general and that Major Douglas had succeeded him. Lord Cardigan had commanded the regiment since 1837. Lord Lucan with his Staff was encamped on the hillside a short distance from our encampment, he being the divisional general commanding the cavalry.

Sunday 25th June 1854 All the cavalry in camp paraded for Divine Service at 6am. Lord Lucan and staff present.

My duties frequently took me to Varna, all our rations and forage being drawn from there. Our daily rations were: meat 1lb, bread 1½lb, coffee 1oz, sugar 1½oz, for which was stopped 4½d *per diem*. The officer's rations were the same and drawn with ours, except that they got no coffee or sugar: all they paid was 1½d daily. The women got half a man's allowance free. Four women per troop having been allowed to accompany their husbands, which was a mistake as women on campaign, unless they could be employed in the hospitals, become a useless encumbrance.

The town of Varna is like most Turkish towns, ill-paved and

most of the houses in a dilapidated state. It is inhabited chiefly by Turks, Greeks and Bulgarians. On the left of the road to Varna was a large swamp, alive with frogs, which was a great source of thankfulness to the French, as it provided them with suppers after their own hearts. I was often amused to see them catching, skinning and cooking them. The French at this time had about 20,000 men encamped in the neighbourhood.

Sunday 2nd July 1854 Colonel Douglas in command of the headquarters disembarked today; there are two more transports yet to come. A few days after, I went to his tent and showed him the model of the horse sling I have before mentioned, also the sketch and instructions, and explained to him the working of the invention. After carefully examining it he appeared much pleased and said, 'I have no doubt, Sergeant-Major, that this will turn out a good thing for you some day.' I then asked him how I had better forward it to the authorities at home. He replied, 'You had better send it through Lord Lucan. He, being in command of the cavalry, will be in constant contact with them.'

The following day, I took it to Lord Lucan's tent and handed it to him understanding, as a matter of course, that it would be sent home, by him, in my name as my signature was attached to the letter of suggestions. What was done with it, and who took credit for my invention, I have never been able to learn to this day (27 years since). But this I know: the slings were altered as I suggested for the following year, those that were issued to the troops coming out had four ropes instead of two. Consequently scarcely any casualties occurred, whereas in 1854 about 200 horses were lost to the service before arriving in the Crimea. During the time I was in the Crimea, I was constantly expecting to hear from Lord Lucan, or the authorities, relative to my invention and for many years afterwards, but made no application, thinking that when it was finally settled that my invention should be adopted, I should be communicated with.

In the beginning of 1877, a paragraph appeared in the daily papers that the Admiralty had ordered 2000 horse slings or hammocks as they then called them. On 6th March 1877, I had an interview with the head clerk at the Admiralty, who showed me a miniature model horse in a hammock which I at once recognised as being in all the main features precisely the same as the one I gave to Lord Lucan. I aso learned that a Special Committee in 1869, of which Colonel the Honourable H H Clifford was President, had recommended the final adoption of the present horse hammock. The book that contained the report was marked 'Private and Confidential,' consequently I was not allowed to see the inside of it. Why the report of a committee simply investigating the best mode of slinging horses on board ship should be kept a secret is a mystery to me.

On 10th March in the same year, I wrote to Lord Lucan sending him a copy of the letter I handed to him at Varna. After waiting a month and receiving no reply, on 10th April I called, but did not succeed in seeing him. On the 24th, I again called and obtained an interview. After many questions, and finding I was perfectly clear on the subject, he said he did not remember the circumstances. I told him his aides-de-camps would, as they were present at the time, and if he enquired, he would find what I stated was correct, and would he kindly intercede with the authorities for a recognition of my invention. He refused, saying he could not be troubled, and that I had better apply to the quarter-master general. I did so, stating all particulars, and received a reply from Major-General Cambell, surveyor general's department, stating that nothing was known in the department about my invention, and referring me to the Admiralty, as they now had the supplying of the horse hammocks, it having been handed over to them after the Special Committee, which sat in 1869, had approved of the present pattern. I then applied to the Admiralty and received a similar reply, that nothing was known of my invention there, and referring me back to the Horse Guards.

Feeling satisfied that I was being shuttlecocked from one department to another, I gave the affair up in disgust and disappointment feeling I had been robbed of my invention by someone—neither the Horse Guards nor the Admiralty denying the fact that the invention was mine. The fact of the alteration of the mode of slinging horses on board ship must have been made by the suggestions and representations of someone, the question is who is that someone? When did he first suggest it and what was his reward? These are the questions that should have been answered me, when I claimed to be the original inventor. If the authorities had only given me credit for the invention, it would have been some satisfaction.

Friday 7th July 1854 The 11th now having all arrived, we marched under the command of Colonel Douglas to join the advanced regiments, which were encamped at Devna 19 miles distant, made a short march and encamped. During the night, a violent storm of wind and rain accompanied with thunder and lightning burst over us. The horses becoming frightened, and the picket posts losing all hold of the ground, the order was given 'Every man to his horse.' There we stood, holding our horses in torrents of rain till we were completely saturated. Most of the tents too were blown down, so that we were in a nice plight when day broke. Fortunately the day was beautifully fine, so that we were able to get our clothes and blankets dried, and to clean up before marching.

As we neared Devna, the scenery became very beautiful. The valley is about seven miles in length and two in breadth, and has a small river running through it. On the high ground on our left our infantry and artillery were encamped under the command of Lord Raglan. Higher up, on the opposite side of the valley, were the cavalry. Near the bridge we passed over to our encampment was a small village. The scenery and surrounding country here has a most romantic appearance, and is well supplied with springs. We pitched our tents on the left of the line facing the north, the 8th Hussars being on the right; the 13th Light Dragoons next; then the 17th Lancers next to us and on our left a regiment of Turkish cavalry. The 'I' Troop RHA was encamped near us, all under the command of the Earl of Cardigan. The regiments of Heavy Cavalry, viz: the 4th and 5th Dragoon Guards; the 1st Royal Dragoons and 6th Inniskilling Dragoons and a regiment of Turkish cavalry; and the 'C' Troop RHD were under the command of General Scarlet, Lord Lucan commanding the division. We had several divisional field days, in which the Turkish cavalry took part. About the beginning of August, the Light Brigade and the 'I' Troop RHA under the command of the Earl of Cardigan, made two marches of about 12 miles each and encamped on high ground near the village of Yenibazaar in sight of Shumla. This placed the Light Brigade about 24 miles in advance of the Army and in rear of the centre of the Turkish Army at Silistria. Up to this time, the regiment had been remarkably healthy but on the 7th we lost two men, and several more before the end of the month, principally from cholera.

It was now that Lord Cardigan mounted his major-general's cocked hat, but it either did not fit him, or he preferred his busby, for we did not see him many times in it. Lord Cardigan's promotion brought about other changes in the regiment: Captain Peel succeeding Colonel Douglas as Major, Lieutenant and Adjutant Ennis becoming Captain—this left the adjutancy vacant. Unfortunately for us (the 11th), Colonel Douglas allowed Colonel Lawrenson of the 17th Lancers to persuade him that his quartermaster would make us an excellent adjutant— although at the time our two senior sergeant-majors were both eligible and both became adjutants of other regiments within the next two years. I have heard on good authority that Colonel Douglas afterwards deeply regretted this act. If he did not, I know the whole regiment did, for a worse rider, a worse drill, a greater humbug never before held the rank of adjutant in the British Army. The 17th might well be glad to get rid of him: they certainly got the laugh of us.

Our horses at this time were in first-rate condition, the commissariat being able to get a plentiful supply of forage. We too were able to purchase many things from the natives, such as milk, onions and eggs.

Friday 11th August 1854 This morning the Turkish general commanding at Shumla paid Lord Cardigan a visit.

Friday 25th August 1854 We the 11th paraded with the 'I' Troop RHA and marched to Yesetippe, en route for Varna to embark for the Crimea, leaving the 8th, 13th and 17th to follow under the command of Lord Cardigan. Before marching off, His Lordship addressed us, saying that he had selected us to lead the van, being the most effective regiment in the brigade, and that we should, in all probability, be the first to meet the enemy. We had been very fortunate compared to the other regiments having lost, during the month, only one sergeant-major and two privates. My troop so far had lost but one man and two horses. The English Army from cholera alone had lost up to this time over 600 men.

Tuesday 29th August 1854 The Light Brigade, having all now arrived at Varna, encamped not far from the sea waiting for the order for embarkation. The Rifles and several other regiments marched past our camp this morning and embarked. In the evening, the brigade to which the 88th belonged, marched past and encamped about quarter of a mile from us.

Their major was taken seriously ill just as they arrived and fell off his horse.

Wednesday 30th August 1854 Lord Lucan inspected our brigade in watering order. During the time we were on parade, the 88th buried their major under a large tree between the camps.

Friday 1st September 1854 Lord Cardigan with the 8th and 13th embarked today.

Saturday 2nd September 1854 6am and Sir De Lacy Evan's brigade, who have been in camp about a mile from us, have just struck tents and are now marching off for embarkation to the tune of *Cheer, Boys, Cheer.* The country looks quite deserted to what it was a few days since, the greater part of the army having embarked.

Monday 3rd September 1854 Lieutenant Saltmarsh died of cholera and was buried near the encampment. We now heard that the French had lost from fever and cholera nearly 7,000 and that they had about 12,000 sick in hospital.

Tuesday 4th September In the morning we embarked on board the *Kent* transport leaving behind, under command of Captain Ennis, all the men and horses that were considered not fit for active service. We then sailed and joined the fleet that was assembling at Balčik Bay. We then formed six lines, each line consisting of sailing transports towed by a steamer; we were then covered and flanked by the line of battleships of the three nations.

Thursday 7th September 1854 About 10am the whole fleet moved off—a sight never to be forgotten—the day was beautifully fine. At night, each ship showed at the masthead the same number of lights that corresponded with the line it belonged, so that the sea was illuminated as far as the eye could reach. No hammocks or berths were provided (every available part of the ship being taken up for the horses) so that the men had to shift for themselves. The cholera still followed us. During the voyage we, the cavalry, lost over 20; the infantry more than treble that number; and between 300 and 400 had to be left on board sick.

Thursday 14th September In the morning we all eagerly crowded the head of the vessel to witness the landing of the French and English infantry. For nearly a mile, flat-bottomed boats filled with armed men—our Light Division being first—were being towed by the sailors rowing in other boats. We saw them leap cheerily on to the beach. Grave thoughts now passed through my mind: how many of these fine fellows will never again leave that shore!

Friday 16th September All the infantry had landed, and we were ordered to hold ourselves in readiness to disembark the following day. Early next morning, three day's rations and three day's forage was issued to each man; the former consisted of 3lbs of salt-pork cooked, 3lbs of biscuit, and a small quantity of tea and sugar. The pork became so rancid the second day that we could not eat it. A ration of rum, about half a quartern *per diem,* was likewise handed over to the quartermaster for issue on our landing but, by some mishap or mismanagement, this was lost.

Orders were now given that our valises containing our kits, and our pelisses, were to be left on board and that we were to take one clean shirt only, which was to be rolled in the blanket and strapped on the back of the saddle instead of the valise. Each man's saddle, bridle bit, cloak, blanket and carbine being packed in his corn sack, and he fully equipped, all being now in readiness at about 8am we descried the sailors rowing towards us towing flat-bottomed boats. They were soon alongside. It was now Lieutenant Dunn offered me his regimental sword, he having provided himself with a second before leaving England. I gladly accepted it (it being far superior to my own) and have never since worn any other.

Now commenced the slinging and drawing the horses out of the hold by the sailors. Each man, as his horse came up, descended into the boat. They had nothing on save their collars and snaffles. As they were lowered into the boat, they were placed close together side by side, heads outwards, their masters standing to their heads. Ropes were passed around the boats through iron uprights about three feet high; by this means they were prevented from jumping or falling into the sea. Each boat contained about 16 horses. When ready we were towed to the beach. When near it, the sailors turned their boat from in front of us and the impetus with which we were going carried the forepart of the boat well on to the beach. The ropes around the boat were then removed, and the horses readily jumped one after another on to the shore, the depth being about three feet. Each man now saddled. In about 10 minutes, we were all mounted.

Shortly afterwards we marched inland, about three miles, then took up a position in front of the infantry, threw out piquets, then picketed our horses and bivouacked. My man Sampson brought me some boards from an adjacent village; these, spread over with hay, made a tolerably comfortable bed. With the aid of a waterproof sheet, with which I had provided myself before leaving Dublin, and with a few sticks I formed over it a covering. As darkness fell, we lighted fires and made ourselves as comfortable as circumstances would permit, considering it was our first night on another man's territory—and that man no less a personage than the Emperor of Russia, his army of 65,000 men within a few miles distance, and his

Cossacks hovering round us. The word 'Cossack' had rather a formidable sound to us at this time, but we learned to thoroughly despise them. Our horses all stood saddled. Each man lay down within a few yards of his own horse, rolled up in his blanket and cloak fully dressed, having his sword by his side ready to buckle on and his bridle also in readiness, so as to be up and mounted in a few minutes.

About midnight, we were awakened by musketry fire, the bullets whizzing over us. Thinking the Cossacks were attacking us, the brigade was soon mounted and in line, ready. Lord Lucan and Lord Cardigan were in front. On enquiry, it turned out to be a false alarm. It appeared one of the infantry sentries, from some cause or other, fired, it was then taken up by the whole line. One unfortunate circumstance occurred through this alarm. Lieutenant Annersley, seeing Lieutenant Dunn's servant who was running to bridle up his master's horse, and taking him for a Russian from the fact of his wearing a long grey coat, he being a private servant—the only one with the regiment, fired and shot him through the thigh. Colonel Douglas severely reprimanded Lieutenant Annersley for this act of indiscretion.

Monday 18th September 1854 The following day we sent out detachments to scour the country for supplies of forage and transport. Towards evening, we saw them returning with a long train of waggons drawn by bullocks and driven by Tartars, and a number of camels. The waggons were laden with forage and poultry, and most of the men had fowls and ducks hanging to their saddles. So plentiful were they, that I had two ducks and two fowls given me by the men of my troop that had been on the expedition. Having no opportunity of cooking them that night, I took them with me the following day packed up in my haynets.

Tuesday 19th September 1854 About 9am, the Allied armies commenced the march towards Sebastopol. The French and Turks consisted of 37,000 men with 68 guns, the English 27,000 including 1,000 cavalry and 60 guns. The French and Turks marched next to the sea, then came the British infantry in columns of divisions, the artillery between the divisions. We the 11th, the 13th and the 'I' Troop RHA formed the advanced guard, the 13th skirmishers in front, the 8th and 17th protected the left flank, the 4th the rear.

After marching across beautiful undulating country for some 10 miles, we came to the River Bulganak. It was but a small stream, not more than knee deep. We rode through it and ascended the hill in front; the 11th and 13th being now some distance in advance of the main body of the Army, the Cossack skirmishers retiring before us. On gaining the crest of the hill, we came in sight of the main body of Cossacks, spread out in skirmishing order in a beautiful valley about a mile across and two miles in length. The scenery was magnificent. The 13th skirmishers were still in front. As we descended the hill, the two regiments being in line, we lost sight of our Army. When about half way across the valley, we halted: the Cossack skirmishers were twice as many as ours.

It was now that the first shot of the campaign was fired. A Cossack directly in front of the 11th raised his carbine and fired. It was instantly taken up by the whole line. Our trumpets now sounded the 'Fire,' so that we beheld for the first time skirmishing in reality, for we could now hear the bullets. This continued for some little time, when the crest of the hill in front suddenly became lit up with the glitter of swords and lances. Lord Cardigan now gave the order, 'Draw Swords—skirmishers In—Trot.' The ground in front of us was uphill. As we moved off we began to throw off our haynets. Most reluctantly I threw off mine. By doing so both my horse and myself lost a part of our suppers. We had not proceeded far, when an aide-de-camp galloped up with an order from Lord Raglan that we were to retire. His Lordship had seen from the hill behind us that the enemy were in force just below the brow of the hill in front of us. The Cossacks now called in their skirmishers and were galloping rapidly across our left, ready to take us in flank should we charge their regular cavalry, or they us. It was a clever move. The Horse Artillery gave them a shot or two which made them keep a respectful distance.

The 1st and 3rd squadrons now went about and retired about 100 yards. During this time, the 2nd and 4th remained halted facing this body of cavalry. No other troops were visible to us at this time. The 1st and 3rd squadrons now halted and fronted; we then went about to retire through their intervals. We had not proceeded far, when I heard the rattle of wheels behind us. On looking round, I saw a Russian battery coming at a gallop down the hill behind us. They then halted and unlimbered; we could distinctly hear the trails come to the ground. In another moment a loud report, and a cannon ball passed through us, followed quickly by a round from every gun in the battery. A body of infantry had followed them and formed square. Our 'I' and 'C' Troops RHA had come up and were behind us at this time, unlimbered for action. The 11th now inclined to their left and the 13th to their right. The moment we had cleared the front, they opened fire and soon compelled not only the artillery and infantry to retire, but the cavalry also. The 8th and 17th had now come up to our support. In this affair Private Henry of the 11th had his foot shot off—from the effects of which he died on the 6th of the following month. A sergeant of the 13th lost his right hand, also two men were wounded and five horses killed.

We now retired to near the crest of the hill and dismounted. Our quartermaster then came up and handed over to me a sack of biscuits and a stone bottle of rum to issue to the troop. The captain came first, receiving his double handful of biscuit, then his half gill of rum, which he drank out of a little tin measure that

I carried in my haversack; then the lieutenant and so on till all had received. Unfortunately for me and the sergeant that assisted me, the measure being short, there was none left for us, which was rather hard, this being the first issue since leaving board ship.

At dusk we retired to the Bulganak and watered our horses, then fed, bridled up, and linked them with the collar chains, placing men on the flanks to keep them in line. This they had great difficulty in doing, the horses becoming very uneasy from the restraint. I got up several times in the night to superintend getting them in line again. This was the only night during the campaign that the horses were bridled up and linked, instead of picketed. The army bivouacked in order of battle.

Wednesday 20th September 1854 In the morning I felt as if I really wanted a breakfast, having had little save biscuit and very dirty water since leaving board ship. After seeing the horses watered and everything in readiness to march, I sent my man down to the river for a tin of water. Seeing a party of the Guards round a fire, I went over to them and asked the sergeant if he would allow me to put my tin on their fire to make some tea (we, at the time, not having a single fire in our bivouac, the men's whole time since daylight having been taken up with their horses) he readily consented. I had a little conversation with him during the time the water was boiling: he was a fine handsome young fellow. I then put my tea and sugar into the tin and stirred it up—but had to wait till it settled as the water was so muddy, there being, after I had drunk the tea, about a tablespoon full of mud at the bottom of the tin.

Just before marching, the 'E' Troop had to perform the melancholy duty of burying their captain (Captain Cresswell) who had died during the night of cholera. Lieutenant Saltmarsh, who died at Varna, belonged to the same troop. The troop was most unfortunate for a few days afterwards they lost their sergeant-major.

Between 8am and 9am we commenced the march for the Alma—the 11th and 13th forming the advanced guard, the skirmishing line being found by the 11th closely followed by a line of skirmishers from the Rifle Brigade. The Light Brigade protected the left flank and rear of the army. About 11am, we were close to, and in line with the French and on their right, next the sea, came the Turks. The front of the three armies covered an extent of about three miles. Our infantry were in columns of divisions, the artillery between the divisions. After marching some distance, the three armies halted on a gentle slope, beyond which we could not see—but we felt we were not far from the Russian Army, for the order was given to load and the colours were uncased. On the brow of the hill could be seen Lord Raglan and Marshal St Armand scanning the country beyond. The trumpets now sounded the advance.

As we crowned the summit of the hill, we came suddenly in view of one of the most magnificent sights that ever man beheld. As I stood up in my stirrups and gazed around, I thought to have the privilege of seeing such a sight was worth a man's life. We were now full in view of the Russian Army that crowned the opposite heights of Alma, their lance points, swords and bayonets glistening in the sun—it was a lovely day. Between us ran the River Alma. On our side were two or three small villages and homesteads close to the river. Between us and them was a gently sloping plain, about a mile across.

From our elevated position we could see over the forest of bayonets on our right and far away over the Black Sea, which was covered with the combined fleets, all steaming and sailing in the same direction that we were going. The colours of our infantry regiments were unfurled. Glorious sight! At one glance could be seen the armies of four of the mightiest nations of Europe in battle array, and the fleets of three of them (the Russian fleet being at this time safe in the harbour of Sebastopol with one of our warships on guard at the entrance).

The trumpets again sounded the advance, and we gently descended the hill. Our skirmishers now came in—the Rifle Brigade remaining extended, covering the front. The Russians now set fire to the village of Bourliouk. At this time, we (the 11th) were close to the left column of infantry (the Light Division) and in line with them. It was now, for the first time, that I caught sight of three women following close in the rear of the infantry regiment next to us. They were the wives of some of the men and had persisted in landing, although an order had been given that all the women were to remain on board ship.

The infantry again halted, and we took ground to the left front, this bringing us directly in front of the enemy cavalry. We were now all anxiously waiting for the next move, when a flash of light from the hillside, followed by a loud report and a cannonball, striking the ground in front of us, bouncing over our heads and rolling far away behind, told us the battle had commenced. They gave us another shot or two, then turned their fire on the artillery and infantry. It was about the fourth cannonball that took a driver's head clean off; the troop he belonged to, 'C', was on our right front at a little distance. The enemy's skirmishers in the enclosures of the farmhouses now commenced firing, our skirmishers replying to them. Their bullets reached us for I heard the sound and saw the dust fly up near my horse's feet. The Light Division had now deployed and I saw a shell burst just in front of their line making a great gap, several men being struck down. The order was now given for them to lie down. The Rifles at this time had got to the enclosures and were driving the enemy's skirmishers before them.

After a time, the whole line sprang up and advanced, soon reaching the walls of the farmyards, over which they went. We (the cavalry) now dismounted for a short time. After a while, we saw that the Light Division had gained a footing on the hillside and were fighting their way up towards the Russian Great Redoubt. Lieutenant Dunn kindly lent me his field glass, through which I could see distinctly that our Light Division, which consisted of the 19th, 23rd, 33rd and 95th regiments, were close to the Great Redoubt and then had taken possession of it. After a few minutes, to my dismay, they turned about and began to retreat—the supports not having been pushed on sufficiently soon to aid them in holding the ground they had so nobly won. We, at this time, were watching their cavalry; they changed their position two or three times, as if intending to take our infantry in flank. Had they done so, we would have immediately advanced and taken them in flank.

To our relief, we now saw the Brigade of Guards, and the Highland Brigade advancing up the hillside against columns of the enemy. It was at this time that an aide de camp galloped up to the 11th and called out for the sergeant-majors, giving to each of us a gun spike, saying, 'These are all we have' and adding, 'You may have an opportunity of using them presently.' Soon after this, another aide de camp galloped up with an order for the cavalry to advance. Lord Cardigan giving the order, 'Threes right. Gallop.' The 'I' Troop RHA accompanied us.

When passing through a narrow road that led to the river, one of the guns turned over into the ditch. This compelled us to halt for some minutes as they had a difficulty in getting it out. During this time, a shell from the heights dropped into the garden a few yards from where I was and buried itself in the earth. I expected every moment to be knocked over when it should burst. Fortunately for me and all those near it had a bad fuse, consequently it did not explode.

The ford we passed through was very shallow, the water quite clear running over pebbles. How both we and the horses would have liked a drink, but there was no time for this. Up the hill we went at a gallop, passing many of the Highlanders lying wounded. When near the top, we met with the Russian dead and wounded lying about. We (the 11th), being in front with the artillery, reached the crest of the hill almost at the same time as the infantry. The order was now, 'Front form the Line' so that we formed close to, and in line with, the 79th Highlanders. The artillery advanced about 50 yards in front of us, unlimbered and instantly opened fire on the columns of infantry that were retreating up the opposite hill—the shrapnel shells making a hissing sound as they cut through the air, carrying with them death and destruction.

A battery of Russian artillery now suddenly made its appearance on the crest of the opposite hill, unlimbered and opened fire on us and our Horse Artillery, the cannonballs striking the ground, bouncing over our heads and rolling down the hill as far as the Alma. Our artillery now turned their fire on them, and we retired over the crest of the hill, just out of sight. In a few minutes, our troop brought so well directed a fire to bear on them that they limbered up and retired. We then advanced and halted again in line with the 79th Highlanders. At this time, the crest of the heights of the Alma were crowned with the bright scarlet uniforms of the British infantry.

Lord Raglan with his staff now rode along in front of us. then went up a cheer as I doubt the like was ever heard on earth before. In their excitement, some of the Highlanders threw their bonnets in the air. We stood up in our stirrups and shouted—the excitement was very great. I believe we all felt greater joy than we had ever experienced in our lives before. We had won a great battle and we were now on the very ground on which we had seen the Russian Army so strongly posted but a few hours before. An order was now given for the cavalry to pursue. Lord Cardigan shouted 'Right Threes. Gallop.' The road we took, being the only one available, was down the hill to our right front. This brought us directly in front of our own infantry. They cheered us on as we passed up the opposite hill. Where the infantry columns were when they were overtaken by the fire of our artillery, the ground was literally covered with dead and wounded.

On arriving at the brow of the opposite hill, before us was a vast plain. In the distance could be seen the Russian Army in full retreat, with many stragglers. We now sent out pursuers to make prisoners of all that could be overtaken. A number were brought back—most of them wounded. One (a Pole, not wounded) appeared rather glad that he was taken. The ball part of the granade [sic] of his helmet had been shot through, which I appropriated and have now in my possession. Sergeant Bond, during the pursuit, received a bayonet wound in the face from a prisoner he had taken who pretended to surrender, then treacherously made a point at him. Bond would have cut him down, but an officer galloped up and told him to spare the scoundrel. At this moment it was perceived that a swarm of Cossacks were rapidly approaching, so that the pursuers had to retreat and this Russian escaped. (It is singular that Bond was the only man of the cavalry that was wounded, and not a single horse—although we had, during the day, at three different times been exposed to a cannonade—and once been under rifle fire).

We now dismounted. Just before dusk, the 4th Division bivouacked on the ground we then held and we retired to the Alma to water our horses. Afterwards we bivouacked near the road, where the Causeway Battery was placed and about quarter of a mile from the bridge. After picketing the horses, I heard there was a haystack about a hundred yards off, so assembled about a dozen men with their nets to go and get hay for the troop. Near the stack was a Russian soldier lying on his back with his knapsack under his head. His eyes were shut and he was breathing. I could not at first see where he was wounded. At last I saw a little blood and water coming from under the peak of his cap. On lifting it up, there was disclosed a bullet wound directly in the centre of his forehead. I then replaced his cap and lifted his head up to see if the bullet had gone through. It had, for directly opposite the hole was another, out of which his brain was oozing: he was insensible. The following day, when the men returned from getting hay, I enquired if the Russian was still alive. They said he was, but he died during the day.

There being some huts near our bivouac, we utilized them for firewood. I had the good fortune to get some planks; these, covered with hay, made me an excellent bed. Just before dark, double rations were issued of biscuit, fresh meat and rum which we stood much in need of. As we sat round our bivouac fire waiting for the pots to boil and talking over the incidents of the day, never I should say were men happier. One said, 'I wonder if we shall get a medal for this battle.' I said 'But what will the people of England say when they hear of it.' This was the thought uppermost in my mind, and so the conversation went on until the meat was cooked. What a glorious supper—how we enjoyed it—then we drank success to the campaign. After a time, the men rolled themselves up in their cloaks and blankets, each man lying down near his own horse, so as to be ready to mount at a moment's notice. The horses remained saddled.

About midnight I awoke. All was quiet, the bivouac fires had burned out, and the whole Army appeared wrapped in sleep. I got up to see that my troop horses were all right and that the sentry was on the alert. Seeing a light flickering in a small bivouac tent, and two or three persons passing to and from it, I enquired of the sentry what was going on. He told me that Lieutenant Annersley had been seized with the cholera. He died on board ship a few days afterwards. Several men too fell ill, for within the next few days we lost six. The next morning, one, a corporal that died during the night, was conveyed, rolled up in his blanket, a little distance from the bivouac and buried. Seeing one man interred who had died of pestilence was more depressing than seeing all the hundreds that surrounded us that had fallen in fair fight. One was the work of man, the other a visitation of the Almighty.

Thursday 21st September 1854 Was beautifully fine. After watering our horses at the Alma near the bridge, on our return I asked the colonel for permission to go back to the river to have a bathe. This he readily granted. It was a great boon, which I enjoyed very much. Near where I bathed, was a sergeant of the infantry lying dead; he had been killed just as he was in the act of ascending the embankment. Near him was a letter which I picked up (someone must have ransacked his pockets, then thrown it down) it was from his wife in Gibralter. I afterwards met with a sergeant of his regiment and handed it over to him, requesting him to forward it to his wife.

In the afternoon, I strolled over the field of battle. What a scene! Our wounded had been brought in and most of the dead collected, but the Russians lay where they fell in every conceivable attitude. Numbers I noticed had been shot through the head. Near our bivouac was a row that had been taken in flank by one of our cannon balls—several had the tops of their heads carried away. Opposite the Great Redoubt, an officer of the 23rd lay dead on his back in front of one of the embrasures. On the highest point of the hill were several wounded Russians sitting huddled together. As I stood looking at them, an infantry soldier came up. He, perceiving that one of them had a good pair of boots on and his being worn out, took hold of one of them and tried to drag it off. The Russian resisted, drawing his leg up, the infantryman then threatened to strike him, so he quietly submitted. I should have prevented this, but I felt that the Russian could manage better without them than the other man as he had to march.

A great pit, about fifteen feet square with a pillar about three feet left in the centre, had been dug in the hillside near the Great Redoubt to bury our dead. A staff officer stood on the pillar in the centre and, as they were carried down and placed side by side, he was told what regiment they belonged to, which he noted in a book. Most of the dead were without any covering except their uniforms, their faces exposed; others that had been dreadfully torn had been gathered together and put in blankets, so that they no longer resembled anything human. As I gazed with pity and sorrow on this ghastly work, a sergeant of the Guards was borne past me. I at once recognised him as the same that I spoke to at the Bulganak. I could bear the sight no longer so returned back to our bivouac, feeling sick at heart. Not far from the pit was a long line of dead Russians placed side by side, ready to be interred in another pit by themselves.

Friday 22nd September 1854 The left squadron of the 11th was ordered to turn out to accompany an aide-de-camp on a reconnaisance. After passing over the bridge, we turned to the right taking the main road leading up the valley of the Alma. On our right, between us and the river, were vineyards and gardens. The Tartars were gathering their grapes; as we rode along, they handed up bunches to all who asked for them. They appeared to be a quiet, inoffensive people. After marching about two miles, we came to the village of Tarkhanlar, through which we passed. Many of the women stood at their doors, many with babies in their arms. The headman of the village was interrogated as to the whereabouts of the Russian Army. He could give us no information. After marching some distance further, we crossed the Alma and ascended the highest hill but, as no signs of the enemy were visible, we returned by the same road.

After passing through the village some little distance, Sergeant-Major Pettit who was riding next to me in rear of the squadron, complained of illness. I offered him some rum from my bottle, but he could not take it. He then told me he could not ride any further—poor fellow, he had been seized with cholera. I immediately galloped up to the head of the column and told the captain. We then sent back to the village. The headman sent his carriage in which he was conveyed back. He died on the 25th.

Saturday 23rd September 1854 To our inexpressible joy, the morning had arrived that we were to leave this field of blood—the stench that arose was enough to sicken the strongest man. I felt that I could not bear it much longer. On reaching the great plateau beyond the heights of the Alma, the delightful sea breeze soon made me feel as well as ever. We occasionally met with traces of the enemy, such as helmets, knapsacks, clothing and newly-dug graves.

After marching some six or seven miles, we (the 11th) and the 'I' Troop RHA, instead of keeping with the main body of the Army, were detached to the village of Durancoy about three miles to our left front, which lay in a deep ravine. We had to descend a narrow circuitous road cut out of the hillside, in some places only room for two men abreast. We were obliged to be very cautious—the artillery particularly so—as in many places there were deep precipices on our right. At the bottom of the road was a pretty villa, surrounded by an orchard and vineyard; the inhabitants had fled. It was a most romantic place. We were now on the main road about half way between Bachcisraj and Sebastopol which are 20 miles apart.

Our advanced guard took a Cossack prisoner in the village. It appears he was down one of the roads which had no outlet. Seeing the leading files pass the top of the road, he must have imagined they were alone for, instead of turning to his right and trying to pass them, he turned to his left. Consequently he galloped right into the officer's party. Lieutenant Inglis immediately seized his lance and took it out of his hand, then ordered him to dismount and sent him back in charge of one of our men. He was an ill-favoured young fellow. His lance was a rude pole with a spike about nine inches long, his horse was very small in comparison to ours. Colonel Douglas took it for a bat pony for himself.

Just before dark, an order arrived that we were to retire by the same road and bivouac on the plateau beyond. Now commenced a most tedious and dangerous march back, as darkness had set in before we had proceeded far. It was midnight before we got settled down and our horses picketed. An order was then given, 'No fires to be lit. No noise to be made.' No rations had been issued since the day before, so that those that had no biscuit left were hungry enough. There was no help for it, we were a long way from the main body of the Army. Fortunately the ground was covered with a kind of heather, so that we had nice soft beds—a luxury we did not often meet with.

During the following morning, the commissariat brought us rations: biscuit and fresh meat. The camp kettles had been boiling for some time and we, with hungry eyes, had been waiting and watching them, when an aide-de-camp came with an order that we were immediately to take ground to the right to join the main body of the Army. The horses were soon bridled and everything in readiness, but what was to be done with the boiling pots? We could not leave them behind, nor yet take them with us as they were, for they had to be packed one in another and carried on a spare horse, so there was nothing for it but to empty them on the ground. As we marched off it was grevious to leave our yesterday's dinner behind us.

The weather was beautifully fine, but very hot; we suffered much from thirst. In the afternoon, we were halted not far from the bridge leading over the Belbic. An infantryman passing with his canteen full of water, I proposed an exchange to him saying, 'If you will give me a drink from your canteen, I will give you a drink of rum from my bottle.' He readily agreed to this. At last the order came for us to march. The infantry at this time were passing over the bridge and we were ordered to ford the river; it was not deep, except near the bridge. One of my horses, as soon as he saw the water, bolted with his rider and plunged into the deep part, both disappearing for a moment. After a little however, he regained his feet. Neither were any the worse for a good ducking. Opposite the part we were fording, sat Lord Lucan, storming and threatening that he would flog any man that attempted to water his horse, so that the men that passed over directly opposite him had great difficulty in forcing their horses through the water, as they plunged their heads into it eager to drink, not having been watered since we left the Alma. What could have been Lord Lucan's reason for this I never could make out, for a greater piece of cruelty I never witnessed. The men's canteens were empty and they too, like their horses, were suffering severely from thirst. It was a cruel deprivation as the water was beautifully clear running over pebbles. Lord Cardigan sat some little distance from him, lower down the stream, evidently indignant for he rendered no assistance in enforcing the order.

On our right, as we ascended the opposite hill, were vineyards teeming with the largest and most luxuriant grapes I ever saw. Many of the men jumped off their horses and with their swords cut off immense bunches, which they handed up to their comrades, so that nearly every man as we rode along was eating grapes.

The 11th, under the command of Lord Cardigan, was now sent on a reconnaisance down the main road leading to Sebastopol. It was between two hills. The dust of the road was like powder, and a foot deep in many places, so that we could see but a short distance. When nearly at the bottom, Captain Walker who was an aide-de-camp to Lord Lucan and who was riding on the brow of the hill above us, called out that there was a masked battery on the opposite hill which commanded the road. Lord Cardigan immediately gave the order, 'Threes about. Gallop.' So back we went much quicker than we went down, expecting every moment to be assailed with shot and shell. Fortunately for us there was no battery there. Had there been, they could have caused us frightful havoc.

It was dusk when we returned to our bivouac; we then watered our horses at the Belbic. The Scots Greys had landed during the time we were away and were bivouacked near the river. Rations were issued and once more we got the kettles to boil, but this time their contents were not destined to be thrown on the ground. This was the first real meal we had had since leaving the Alma.

My man Sampson, being an excellent forager, got a good supply of wood from the fences close at hand so that I had a splendid fire long after all the other bivouac fires were out and most of the men were asleep. The orderly room clerk and a sergeant of my troop were lying on the ground enjoying it with me, when out of the darkness (it was a very dark night) came two figures. After looking at us for a few moments, they seated themselves on the ground close to the fire and entered into conversation. One was no less a personage than the Earl of Cardigan, the other Colonel Douglas. Unfortunately I had nothing to offer them, or I certainly should have done so for I looked on them as guests, although they had come without invitation.

Monday 26th September The following morning Colonel Douglas ordered me to turn out my troop, to take a dozen led horses, and proceed along the road running east and parallel with the Belbic till I arrived at a farmhouse where, he had heard, there was plenty of forage. After marching along a pleasant road for about two miles, we came to a neat farmhouse of good dimensions on the left side of the road with a large farmyard and good-sized granary. I then placed sentries to watch the surrounding country, so that we might not be surprised by the enemy. We then filed into the farmyard. I immediately dismounted and ascended the granary steps. At the top was a balcony with large folding doors in front, which I opened. The room—a moderate sized one—was empty, a small room on the right was also empty. On opening the door to the left, I was agreeably surprised to find about a waggonload of barley. I called out to the men who came rushing up with their sacks; in a short time, they were all filled and securely fastened on the saddles of the spare horses.

We then proceeded to the stackyard; there were three stacks of hay. I selected the one I considered best, a man was then lifted up who pulled off the thatch, then turned it down in flakes. Whilst this was going on I observed some of the men crawling through the hedge, there being an orchard adjoining the trees covered with beautiful ripe apples. I instantly ordered them back, telling them as soon as all the haynets were filled and all ready for starting back, that they should then have a turn at the apples. When all was ready, I gave the word. It was laughable to see them bundling through the hedge. In a short time all our haversacks were full.

It was now that a solitary Tartar made his appearance with one of our men who had been into the house. He stood looking listlessly at us. The man that came with him, brought out a large likeness framed, which the Tartar gave me to understand was the master of the house. When all was ready, we marched back with our booty. I felt somewhat proud of it, for there was enough corn to supply the regiment for the day. The name of the farm was Kutor Farm so that when we were there, we were just four miles from the village of Aterkoi, where was Prince Menshikoff with the Russian headquarters and a strong escort of Cossacks. How little we thought we were so close to our enemies and how easy it would have been for them to have captured us when we were foraging, had they know we were there.

It was late before we commenced the march. After going a few miles along the main road, we made a sharp turn to the left. This brought us into a wood, the road in some places being very narrow, so that we could only advance by files. The Rifle Brigade in single file was close to us on our right. They were pleased to get a share of our apples, which our men handed to them as they rode along. We had not proceeded far when from the brushwood on our right came Captain Walker and, following him, a Russian infantry soldier that he had taken prisoner, having found him wandering in the wood. At this time we could not see any other part of the Army. We were not far from the McKenzie Heights.

After some time I happened to look to my right rear, when to my surprise through an opening in the trees I had a full view of Sebastopol. I called out involuntarily, 'Sebastopol.' All within hearing halted and for a few moments sat gazing at the beautiful town with it's church spire and white buildings reflected in the sun. This was our first view of the prize we hoped soon to seize. Soon after we heard firing in our front. We then began to push on as quickly as the nature of the ground would permit, soon coming to an open space, where were a number of waggons and other vehicles and carriages laden with flour and bread and baggage. The Greys, the 8th Hussars and part of the Rifle Brigade had arrived there before us and had put the baggage guard to flight. Consequently most of the baggage fell into our hands. In the first waggon we came to, was an officer cutting up loaves with his sword and giving to the men as they passed a slice each. I got a piece. It was new so I though I had got a treat and eagerly took a big bite, for we had not had any bread since leaving home—only biscuit had been issued. Imagine my disappointment when, on chewing it, I found it to be sour, bitter and nauseous in the extreme. I was glad to spit it out and dash the piece I had in my hand to the ground.

We now formed line in the open space where the two roads met, being close to McKenzie's Farm. It appeared this baggage had left Sebastopol early in the morning, and had passed along the valley parallel to us, but a little time before it had then turned sharp to the left up the road leading to the heights. This brought it directly in our front, so that escape was impossible. The Greys, 8th Hussars and some of the Rifle Brigade, being some distance to the left of us and opposite the top of the hill, this enabled them to secure this prize, as prize indeed it was; the officer's carriages were laden with valuable baggage belonging to the 11th and 12th Russian Hussars. I managed to secure an officer's undress jacket and shabrack embroidered with gold lace, a dress shirt, towel, a large bag of Turkish tobacco and some scores of cigarettes. After securing these articles to my saddle, I walked round to the front of the troop with a double handful of the cigarettes, giving one each first to the officers, then to the non-commissioned officers and men of my troop. In a short time we were all smoking, the other part of the regiment looking on with envious eyes for, at this time, I do not think there was a bit of tobacco in the regiment. In my troop, I know there was but one pipe and that had not been used for some time.

While we were standing smoking, a party of the Greys marched past us with three Russian Hussars prisoners. As an artillery man was passing that had just secured a shrine about two feet high and two broad, we asked him to let us look at it. He placed it on the ground and opened two folding doors. In the centre was Christ crucified, the Virgin Mary and the Apostles standing round with their hands closed as in the act of prayer. By some mechanical device, the figures raised their heads and eyes towards the cross; they were all of solid silver and gold. Who eventually became the owner of it, I never heard. Among the bagagge too was found much silver plate. Trumpeter W Smith of the 11th, who was this day field trumpeter to Lord Lucan, secured a silver punch ladle, beautifully engraved. I have often heard him tell the following story:

> 'As we were riding down the hill from McKenzie's Farm, I took the ladle out of my holster to look at it. One of Lord Lucan's aide-de-camps, passing at this moment, asked me to let him see it. I handed it to him. He said, 'I will show it to Lord Lucan' and galloped up to him. On seeing him afterwards, I asked him for it. He said Lord Lucan had kept it and that he had no doubt he would give me something for it.
>
> About two month afterwards, having heard that Lord Lucan had been ordered home and that he was about leaving the encampment for embarkation, I made bold to go to him and asked him if he would kindly make me some remuneration for the punch ladle. He flew in a great temper, ordering me away, saying he would have me flogged for plundering. However he thought better of that, for he left five shillings to be handed to me—much to my annoyance as I would rather have had the ladle.'

This was rather sharp practice of the noble Earl for he must have known that the officers first pillaged the baggage, then gave permission to the non-commissioned officers and men to take anything they chose. When this permission was given, I ran over to an officer's carriage that was a little way in the wood, opposite to where we were dismounted, and jumped up on to the spokes of one of the off wheels. As I leaned forward to pull the things out, my busby nearly touched the cocked hat of an aide-de-camp that was standing on the opposite wheel and on the next wheel was an infantry officer—both as busy as myself pludering—no, that is not the word: taking what we had permission to take.

After remaining here some time, we descended the road that the baggage came up, into the valley of the Tchernaya, and bivouacked on the banks of the river between the village of Tchorgoun and the Traktir Bridge. Shortly after we had settled down, two bullocks were driven into the bivouac, hamstrung, then killed. Every man helping himself, cutting steaks and pieces off where he liked. In a short time there was little left but bones and hide.

Just before dusk, I marched my troop some little distance up the stream to water our horses. As we were doing so, two Tartars came galloping widely towards us, their hair flowing (having lost their caps), calling out and indicating they were being pursued by Cossacks. I instantly ordered the troop to form up on the bank ready to receive them. The Tartars passed on to the bivouac and gave the alarm. In a short time Colonel Douglas with the other three troops joined us. No enemy appearing, Colonel Douglas ordered me to ride out in the direction the enemy was supposed to be coming and ascertain if there was any cause for the alarm. It was now nearly dark. I at once drew my sword and galloped off. After riding about quarter of a mile, I came in sight of two Cossacks, who appeared to be watching us. They being on higher ground, I could see them distinctly. After satisfying myself that no forward movement was being made by the enemy, I returned and reported to Colonel Douglas what I had seen. A line of videttes was now thrown out in this direction and no further alarms occurred during the night.

Tuesday 26th September 1854 The following morning we commenced the march around 8am towards Balaclava about four miles distant. After passing over the Traktir Bridge and up a pleasant road between two hills, we came to the North Balaclava valley (the same the Light Brigade charged down on the 25th of the following month). The road we passed over was just in front of where the Russian guns were placed. How little did many a fine fellow of our brigade think that, that day, the following month, he would be lying dead, unburied on that very ground. Many a man this day rode over his own grave.

On arriving at the rise in the ground at the opposite side of the valley, named the Causeway Heights, we came suddenly in view of the beautiful valley, village and harbour of Balaclava and the villages of Kadikoi and Kamara. We now descended the valley, passing through the village of Kadikoi, which was about a mile from Balaclava, our Rifle Brigade leading the way in skirmishing order. We (the Light Brigade) now halted, the infantry advancing up the heights on both sides of the harbour. There being no enemy in sight, we thought we had made an easy conquest of the place but, to our surprise, a shell from a small fort just beyond the village and near the mouth of the harbour, came whizzing through the air towards us followed by several more. Presently we heard firing from the sea; our shipping had opened fire on the fort. This caused the commander to hoist the white flag and cease firing. We now saw our riflemen enter the fort and, shortly after, one of our warships steamed majestically into the harbour, so that without loss of life, the village, fort and harbour fell into our hands—many of the inhabitants being still in the place.

When Lord Raglan with his staff rode into the village, they offered them bread and salt as a token of goodwill and friendship. During the afternoon, several more of our warships steamed into the harbour. The prisoners taken in the fort, consisting of several officers and two companies of infantry, were put on board ship and sent down to Constantinople. The villagers remained in the village for a few days. They were then sent away beyond our lines as we required the houses for our stores. We (the 11th) bivouacked on the north side of the village of Kadikoi, where we found an abundance of forage, there being several farms in the neighbourhood.

In the village was a water trough, well supplied with water. As I was returning with my troop from watering their horses, I saw a drummer boy of the Guards sitting on a pony looking over a wall. On going to see what he was so intently looking at, I found it was a number of fowls in the backyard of a pretty villa. I said, 'Would you like one of those?' he replied 'Yes.' I too thought I should, so told him to jump over and get one each for us, and I would hold his pony. He was soon over the wall and in full pursuit, but it was no easy matter. The fowls flew about and made a great noise, when the back door of the house opened and a fine portly lady draped in black satin made her appearance and looked at me with an enquiring air, as much as to say: What do you mean by intruding on my premises? I at once raised my hand, extending two fingers, then pointing at the fowls, as much as to say: We require two fowls. She turned round and called out. When a manservant appeared, she then ordered him to assist the drummer boy in catching two fowls. When they were caught and killed, the drummer handed them to me, then jumped over the wall and mounted his pony, when I gave him one. I then thanked the lady for providing us with a supper and we galloped off. The weather was beautifully fine, and not cold, so we felt no inconvenience from being without tents.

Wednesday 27th September 1854 Yesterday we had marched south, today we commenced the march due west, the 11th forming the advance guard. It was a grand sight to see our skirmishers spread across the hills of the Chersonesskij, leading the Army direct for Sebastopol, which was about five miles off. Lord Raglan and Sir John Burgoyne were with us, so that we accompanied them in their first reconnaisance of the town of Sebastopol. The only enemy we met with were a few Cossacks that retired as we advanced, giving us an occasional shot. Corporal Williams, who was with the skirmishing line, had a button shot off his jacket.

As we approached Sebastopol, we passed several farm-houses, vineyards and orchards. At last we came in full view of the town. What a glorious sight to look down on the beautiful town and harbour, and the Russian fleet riding at anchor. As we sat gazing at them with admiration, a cannon ball came whizzing along towards us, as much as to say 'Halt.' After a time we retired, and bivouacked close to the farmhouse that afterwards became the English headquarters. Adjoining it was a large vineyard and wine press with numbers of empty hogsheads ready to receive the wine. The grapes were quite ripe and immensely large.

Nearby was a field in which was a nice little fat bullock. We were not long in utilizing him. He was driven into the bivouac, then hamstrung. We had two or three men who had been butchers, so that he was soon killed and skinned. Every man that now liked, helped himself; fires were soon lighted, then commenced the cooking in right earnest. The colonel came to me saying, 'I should like the heart, sergeant-major.' 'You shall have it, Sir', I replied, at the same time ordering one of the men to take it to the colonel.

At dusk we began to settle down for the night. One of the men rolled a hogshead into the bivouac. After securing it, he crawled inside intending to sleep in it. This was not permitted him for some of his comrades, when they thought he was asleep, commenced rolling it (much to the amusement of us all) so that he was glad to crawl out.

Thursday 28th September 1854 The 4th and the 11th were the only two cavalry regiments in front, being attached to the second and third divisions of infantry, the remainder of the cavalry being in the valley of Balaclava.

Sunday 1st October 1854 We bivouacked in rear of the windmill, sending out piquets to the front and right. A few days afterwards our tents were brought up from on board ship, having now been six weeks without shelter except for our cloaks and blankets. Fortunately we only had one or two slight showers of rain during the time, but the dew sometimes fell heavily. I have often when waking found my face and hair very wet.

Sunday 15th October 1854 Marched to the valley of Balaclava and joined the Cavalry Division, our duty being to protect the rear of the army and send out piquets in that direction. Frequent alarms now occurred, our spies bringing intelligence that the Russian were preparing to attack our rear. On the night of the 23rd, we stood to our horses all night about halfway between Canrobert's Hill and our encampment.

The following officers and non-commissioned officers embarked for active service in 1854:

Lieutenant-Colonel the Earl of Cardigan, commanding 11th PAO Hussars
Major Douglas

'C' Troop
Captain Peel
Lieutenant Inglis
Cornet Annersley (died on board ship 28th September 1854)
Troop Sergeant-Major Silver

'D' Troop
Captain Dallas
Lieutenant Trevelyan
Cornet Vansittart
Troop Sergeant-Major Parker (died in Bulgaria 23rd August 1854)

'E' Troop
Captain Cresswell (died at the Bulganak 19th September 1854)
Lieutenant Saltmarsh (died in Bulgaria 3rd September 1854)
Cornet Roger Palmer
Troop Sergeant-Major Pettit (died at the Tchernaya 25th September 1854)

'F' Troop
Captain Cook
Lieutenant Dunn
Cornet Houghton (Mortally wounded at Balaclava, died 22nd November 1854)
Troop Sergeant-Major Loy Smith

Pay Master Healey
Adjutant Ennis
Quartermaster Kounts
Surgeon St Croix Cross
Assistant Surgeon Wilkin
Veterinary Surgeon Gloag
Regimental Sergeant-Major Bull

Lady Elizabeth Butler's famous painting, "After the Charge".
Loy Smith is depicted mounted on the far right.
Reproduced by kind permission of Queen's Park Art Gallery, Manchester.

Mr George Loy Smith
by C.E. Marshal 1887
"The Queen God Bless Her"
Reproduced by kind permission of The Illustrated London News.

Loy Smith's jacket (as shown in Lady Butler's painting) worn at the battles of Inkerman, Balaclava and the Alma.
Reproduced by kind permission of City Museum, Sheffield.

Artist's impression of the Charge of the Light Cavalry at Balaclava.
Reproduced by kind permission of The Illustrated London News.

Carrying the frostbitten to Balaclava. *Reproduced by kind permission of The Illustrated London News.*

The Seige of Sebastopol.
Preparing a train for the trenches. *Reproduced by kind permission of The Illustrated London News.*

One of "Prince Albert's Own" on sentry in the Crimea.
Cap and gloves—English.
Coat and boots—Russian.
Cavalry camp near Kadikoi, 5th February 1855.
Drawn by George Loy Smith.

Reproduced by kind permission of City Museum, Sheffield.

One of "Prince Albert's Own" watching a Cossack vidette near Balaclava.
Cavalry camp near Kadikoi, 5th February 1855.
Drawn by George Loy Smith.

Reproduced by kind permission of City Museum, Sheffield.

Flowers gathered by Loy Smith from the "Valley of Death" a year after the Charge.

Reproduced by kind permission of City Museum, Sheffield.

Loy Smith's boots worn over two winters in the Crimea. They were a present from the Sultan of Turkey.

Reproduced by kind permission of City Museum, Sheffield.

The road to Sebastopol.
Commissariat waggons, conveyance of fascines etc. *Reproduced by kind permission of The Illustrated London News*

The officer's encampment at Balaclava, 11th Hussars.
Painted by George Loy Smith. *Reproduced by kind permission of City Museum, Sheffield.*

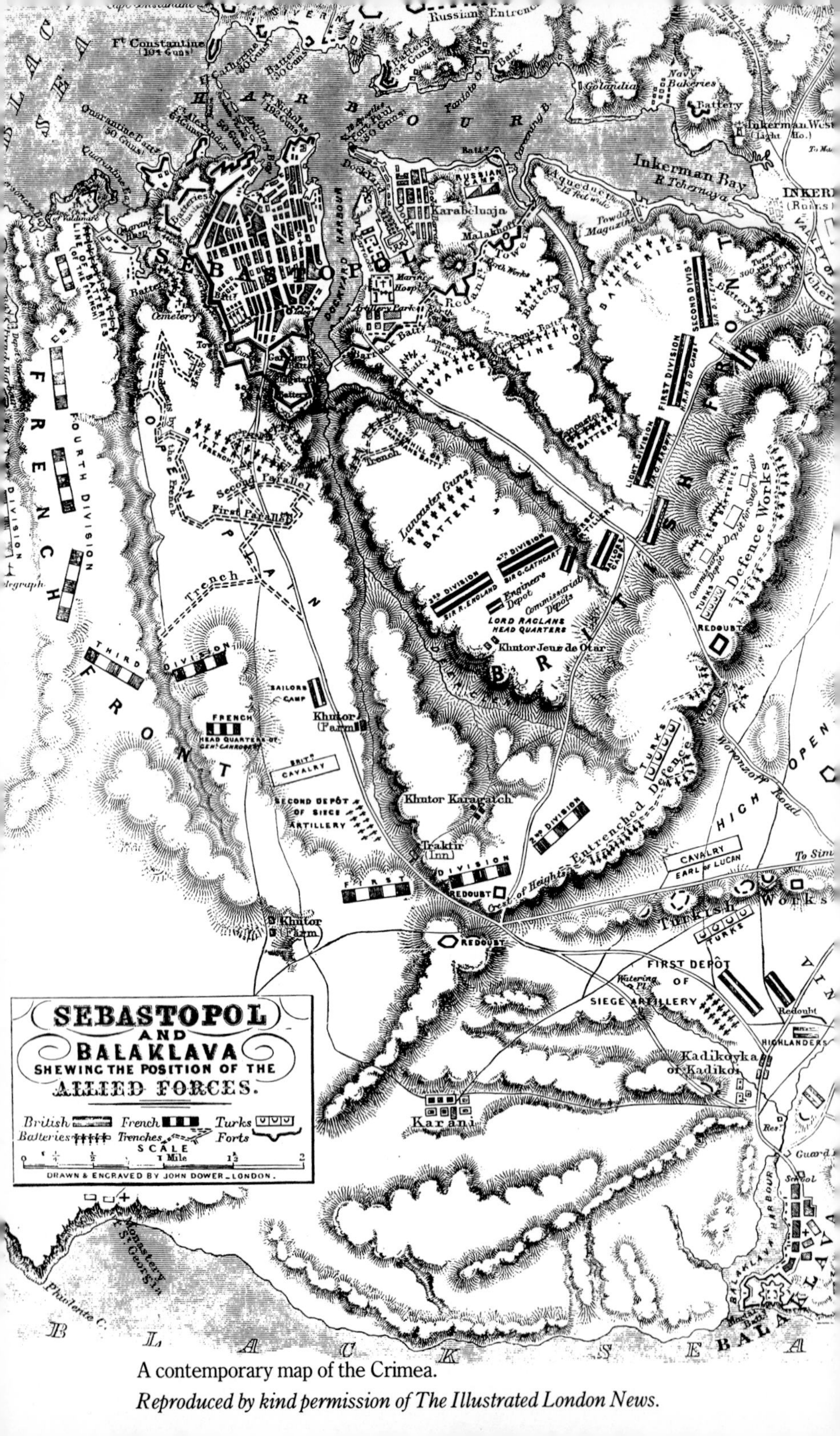

A contemporary map of the Crimea.

Reproduced by kind permission of The Illustrated London News.

PART FIVE

Wednesday 25th October 1854

The Charge of the Light Brigade

Wednesday 25th October 1854 On this morning, as had been the custom since landing in the Crimea, the Light Brigade was mounted and in line a short distance in front of their encampment an hour before daybreak, their right pointing to Balaclava, their left to No.5 Redoubt. Canrobert's Hill, which lay to the east, being directly in their front at a distance of about a mile and a half. As the first glimmer of light shewed itself on the horizon, a flash of fire directly under it followed by a loud report, told us that the Russians were about to attack. As the cannonade increased, and was replied to by the Turks on Canrobert's Hill, we (the Light Brigade) were ordered to advance. Colonel Douglas, giving the words, 'Eleventh, Attention,' addressed us saying, 'Now men, in all probability we shall met the enemy today. When you do, don't cut but give them the point, and they will never face you again.' We then advanced across the plain to within about a quarter of a mile off Canrobert's Hill.

By this time it was sufficiently light to see our videttes along the brow of the Causeway Heights, on which were Nos. 2, 3, 4 and 5 Redoubts. They were circling right and left rapidly, which indicated they could see the enemy cavalry, artillery and infantry advancing. As we neared the hill, we heard the shouts of the Russian infantry storming the Redoubt No. 1 on Canrobert's Hill on the side furthest from us. The next moment we saw the Turkish flag hauled and the Russian flag run up. The Turks were now driven out on our side; they appeared to fight bravely against overwhelming odds for, as the last of them came over the parapet, I noticed that the Russians were close at their heels and, as they retreated down the hillside, many of them turned around and fired. As they gained the plain, a number of Cossacks swept round the foot of the hill, killing and wounding many of them. Some of them, unarmed, raised their hands imploringly, but it was only to have them severed from their bodies. This we had to witness close in front of our squadrons, feeling the while that had a dozen or two of us been sent out numbers of these poor fellows might have been saved.

The Light Brigade, as also the Heavy Cavalry, were now ordered to retire. The left squadron of the 11th took up a position on the right rear of the 'I' Troop RHA that was stationed between No.s 2 and 3 of the Redoubts on the Causeway heights, firing into the valley beyond (the same which the Light Brigade charged down subsequently) up which the main body of the enemy was advancing.

Their artillery now opened fire on the Redoubts No.s 2 and 3 and on our troop of artillery. This soon compelled the Turks to evacuate No. 2 and, shortly after, No. 3 also, and eventually they were driven out of No. 4. These Redoubts were armed with our ship guns, nine in number, seven at least of which fell into the hands of the enemy. (These guns are now in St Petersburg labelled 'Taken from the English at Balaclava'). The fire brought to bear on our troop of artillery was very heavy. The troop consisted of four six-pounder guns and two twelve-pounder howitzers. I saw one shell burst which wounded Captain Maude, the commanding officer, severely and killing his horse. One gun was disabled, one man and twelve horses killed, and a number of men wounded. Each gun fired about thirty rounds of shot and shell. The ammunition being nearly expended and the position becoming almost untenable, an order was given for them to retire. As we retired, I observed that one of the guns was being drawn by one horse, the other five having been killed. We (the 11th) being out of sight of the enemy and on the right rear of the troop, sustained no loss.

Shortly after we took up a position on the left rear of our encampment with our backs to Balaclava, facing the opening at the top of the valley through which it was thought the Russian cavalry would come, so as to prevent them getting in our rear. We were out of sight of the enemy, but expected every moment to see them. Occasionally we heard a bullet from the Russian infantry that had occupied the Redoubts.

Lord Cardigan now gave the order, 'Draw swords.' Our Heavy Cavalry was in our rear behind our encampment—that is, their left was rather towards our rear, but we were some distance apart. The Cossacks that had pursued the retreating Turks now came boldly on, galloping into our encampment and wounding the spare horses that had been left tied up in the lines, for we had retired without being covered by skirmishers, nor yet had any troops been left to protect the encampment. Lord Raglan, perceiving this, sent an order by Major Fellows that this should be done. Major Fellows, having another order from Lord Raglan to convey to the commander at Balaclava and meeting Mr Gloag (the Veterinary Surgeon of the 11th Hussars), directed him for the sake of dispatch to convey this order to Lord Lucan: that a detachment was to be left for the protection of the camp. On Mr Gloag giving the order to Lord Lucan, he made him repeat it no less than three times. The tents at this time were all lying on the ground, the ropes having been let loose soon after the battle commenced by the guard left in the encampment, the object being to prevent the enemy so readily seeing the situation of it.

There was now a pause in the battle, during which a portion of Heavy Cavalry had moved towards the middle of the inner

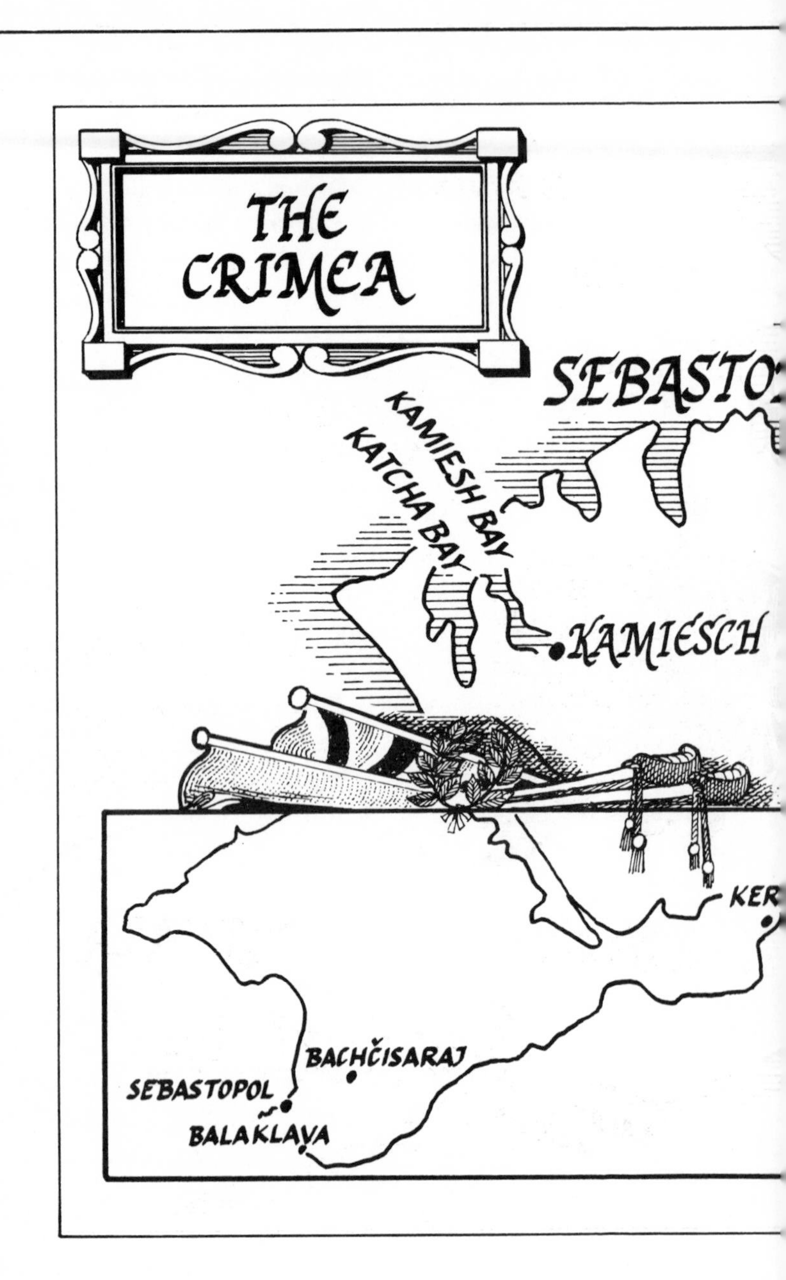
THE CRIMEA
SEBASTO
KAMIESH BAY
KATCHA BAY
KAMIESCH
KER
BACHČISARAJ
SEBASTOPOL
BALAKLAVA

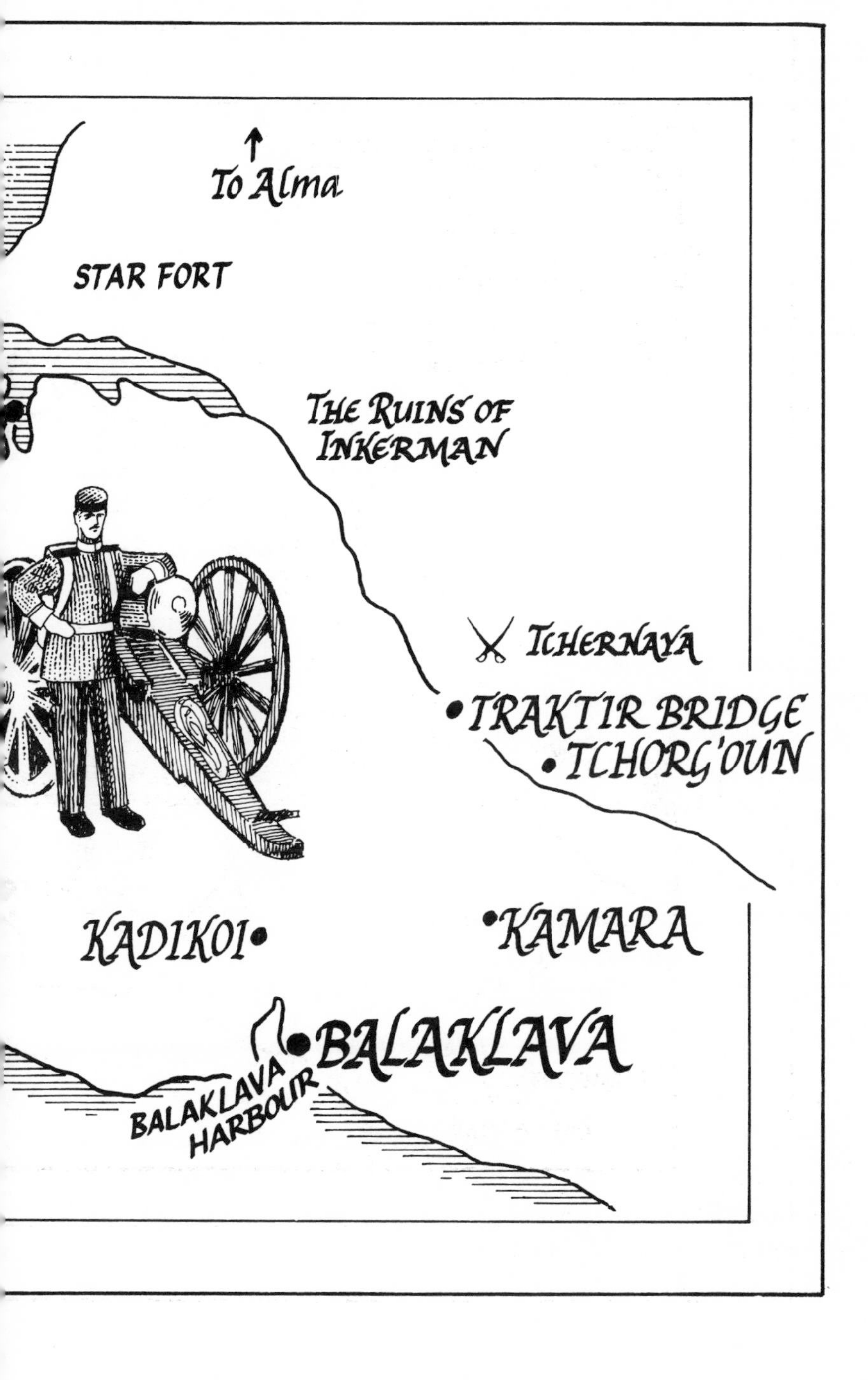

To Alma
STAR FORT
THE RUINS OF INKERMAN
TCHERNAYA
TRAKTIR BRIDGE
TCHORG'OUN
KADIKOI
KAMARA
BALAKLAVA
BALAKLAVA HARBOUR

plain in the direction of Balaclava, when suddenly the French artillery stationed on the plateau opened fire over our heads down the North Valley on a strong body of Russian cavalry advancing up it. The 'I' Troop RHA, which was about two hundred yards in front, delivered fire and retired on us. Had this body of Russian cavalry, consisting of the 11th and 12th Hussars with several squadrons of Cossacks, come on a little further, they would have been brought face to face with us immediately on crowning the hill but, just as we were expecting them, we saw the head of the column crown the Heights near No. 4 Redoubt. They then steadily descended the hill and halted not far from the front of our encampment.

Our Heavy Cavalry now advanced and charged into them; we then expected to be ordered to sweep down on their right flank. Had we done so at the proper moment, I feel that few of them would have escaped, being either killed or made prisoners. But, much to our chagrin, we were held as spectators of this unequal combat for more than ten minutes. We could distinctly hear the din and shouts of our people, being only a few hundred yards off. Our excitement became very great and I am of the opinion that nothing but the strict discipline under which we were held prevented us breaking loose to assist our comrades of the Heavies. But, to our joy and relief, we saw this mass of Russian cavalry retreat over the Causeway Heights the same way they came. Had we received the order, in all probability the charge down the North Valley would not have taken place.

We shortly took up a position facing directly down the North Valley. We could distinctly see the Russian position. The 11th was on the left of the first line, the 13th Light Dragoons on the right and the 17th Lancers in the centre; the 4th Light Dragoons and 8th Hussars formed the second line. We had not been in this position long when Lord Cardigan received the order from Lord Lucan to attack the battery of guns which was placed across the valley immediately in our front about a mile off. There was likewise a battery on the Fedioukine Hills on our left and the enemy had possession of the Redoubts No.s 2 and 3 on our right, where another battery and battalions and riflemen were posted. This Army in position numbered about 24,000 and we (the Light Brigade) not quite 700. Strange as it may seem, although 12 Horse Artillery guns were at this moment close at hand, the divisional general made no use of them before he ordered the attack. It had been the custom on brigade field days for artillery fire to precede a cavalry attack. Had this simple rule been followed out on the Causeway Heights for a few minutes before we moved off, it would have been of the greatest advantage to us, for it was the enemy's guns and infantry posted there that caused us the greatest losses—both going down the valley and returning. This was a most unfortunate omission for us.

It would also appear incredible that, although we had been on active service four months, that no gun spikes had been issued (to the Light Brigade at least) except one to each of the four troop sergeant-majors of the 11th at the Battle of the Alma, although we had been in the presence of an Army with a powerful artillery. (At the Battle of Aleewal in 1846, a sergeant and 12 men on the flanks of each squadron of the 16th Lancers carried mallets and gun spikes. Sergeant Lee spiked one of the enemy's largest guns on that occasion.)

The trumpets now sounded the advance. The 13th and 17th moved off and the 11th were ordered to support them as soon as they had advanced about one hundred yards. We moved off, soon breaking into a gallop, but did not actually cover the 17th the whole way down, consequently we swept down the valley much nearer to the Fedioukine Hills than any other regiment. As we moved off, the Russians opened fire from all their batteries. The round shot passed through us and the shells burst over and amongst us, causing great havoc. The first man of my troop that was struck was Private Young, a cannon ball taking off his right arm. I, being close on his right rear, fancied I felt the wind from it as it passed me. I afterwards found I was bespattered with his flesh. To such a nicety were the enemy's guns elevated for our destruction that, before we had advanced many hundred yards, Private Turner's left arm was also struck off close to the shoulder and Private Ward was struck full in the chest. A shell too burst over us, a piece of which struck Cornet Houghton in the forehead and mortally wounded him.

When Private Young lost his arm, he coolly fell back and asked me what he was to do. I replied, 'Turn your horse about and get to the rear as fast as you can.' I had scarcely done speaking to him when Private Turner fell back, calling out to me for help. I told him too to go to the rear. I then galloped after the regiment. Happening at this moment to look to the rear, I saw the Chasseurs d'Afrique charging up the Fedioukine Hills at the battery that was taking us in flank.

We now came under a terrific fire, for the infantry in and about the Redoubts kept up a continual fusilage as we came opposite them, but the men hung well together, keeping their line and closing in as their comrades fell back wounded or killed. Many riderless horses were now galloping along with us, forcing their way into the ranks and keeping their places as well as though their masters had been on their backs. Many of these horses belonged to the first line, for we now frequently met with their lifeless bodies. I was particularly struck with one of the 17th Lancers lying on his face with his arms stretched out and a short distance from his right hand was his lance with the pole broken.

As we neared the battery, a square of infantry that had been placed a little in advance of the guns, gave us a volley in flank.

The very air hissed as the shower of bullets passed through us; many men were now killed or wounded. I, at this moment, felt that something had touched my left wrist. On looking down I saw that a bullet, which must have passed close in front of my body, had blackened and cut the lace on my cuff. Private Glanister had his lower jaw shattered by a bullet entering on the right side, and a bullet passed through the back of Private Humphries' neck, just missing the spinal cord. At this time we were at a sweeping gallop. In another moment we passed the guns, our right flank brushing them, when about a hundred yards in rear Colonel Douglas halted us. During the advance, Lieutenant Trevelyan and Cornet Houghton had fallen out being wounded, the latter mortally. Regimental Sergeant-Major Bull, Trumpeters Smith and Keates had their horses killed or wounded, so that the only leader in front of the right squadron was Troop Sergeant-Major Teevan. Troop Sergeant-Major Joseph and I were the only two left as serrefiles.

It now became my particular duty (the adjutant having remained behind when we received the order to attack, and the regimental sergeant-major's horse having been wounded) to note every word of command the colonel should give, as I now considered the adjutant's duty devolved on me. After halting, the word was, 'Come in on the centre' so that the squadron interval was filled up. During the advance, which had not taken many minutes, we had lost (as near as I could calculate) about 50 men, so that we had about 80 left. I am sure we had quite this number from what I witnessed afterwards.

As we advanced, the 11th, 4th and 8th were in echelon. The fact of our right flank brushing the guns brought the 4th directly in front, so that they drove right into them where those of the 13th and 17th that had not yet retreated, were still fighting.

We (the 11th) were now but a short distance directly in front of the same Russian Hussars and Cossacks that our Heavy Cavalry had charged in the South Valley. Lord Paget at this moment galloped up on our right flank. Colonel Douglas, seeing him, called, 'What are we to do now Lord Paget?' He replied, 'Where is Lord Cardigan?' and galloped away—his regiment, the 4th Light Dragoons, being at this time at the guns sabring the gunners. Colonel Douglas, seeing there was no time to lose, having no order to retire and expecting any moment we should be charged by this body of cavalry in our front, called out, 'Give them anuther charge, men. Hurrah!' At this moment I particularly noticed the gallant bearing of Lieutenant Dunn. He was a fine young fellow, standing six feet three, mounted on a powerful horse and wielding a terrific sword, many inches longer than the regulation. His heroic conduct throughout the affair inspired all around him with courage. He saved the life of Sergeant Bentley when surrounded by Russians by cutting them down left and right. So conspicuous was his gallantry that Colonel Douglas justly recommended him for the Victoria Cross, which he received at the hands of Her Majesty. Strange to say he was the only officer who rode in the Charge on whom this honour was conferred and, much stranger still, Kinglake never mentions him, but mentions the name of a junior officer no less than four times.

Waving our swords over our heads on we galloped, expecting the next moment to be amongst these Russians but, to our surprise, when no more than 20 yards off, they wheeled about and galloped away in front of us. We were shouting and feeling rather amused, for they were 20 to 1—there not being at this time more than 80 of us (the 11th) left. We now lost all hold of the other part of the brigade, for we saw nothing more of them till we returned to the ground we charged from. The 4th [Light Dragoons], after sabring the gunners, retired with the remnants of the other regiments.

After galloping a short distance, on looking round, I saw one of the guns some distance to our right being taken away. It was a large brass gun with carriage painted green, drawn by six horses; there were only three men—drivers—with it. Feeling that it had escaped from the battery, and knowing that the 4th Light Dragoons had possession, I at once formed the resolution to retake it. So, seeing three men riding independently in the rear of the regiment, they having just been crushed out, I called to them to follow me, saying, 'Let us take this gun.' I at once galloped off, supposing they were following me. When within a short distance of it, I saw a Hussar officer and three Cossacks, who had detached themselves from the main body for the protection of the gun, and who were coming rapidly between me and my regiment. I was now considerably to the right rear of it (about two or three hundred yards) and within fifty yards of the gun. On looking round, I found I was alone; that the three men had not followed me as I had expected. Feeling it would be madness to attempt the capture singlehanded, I instantly halted, turned about and galloped off in the direction of my regiment. The first Cossack and the officer might have engaged me on my track, but they hesitated, calling out to the other two who were a little distance in their rear. This hesitation allowed me to rejoin my comrades. If there had been any troops—either of ours or the Russians—any distance in rear of the guns at this time, I should have seen them, for I went beyond the left flank of the battery. This act was witnessed by several of our men—more than 20 years afterwards, one of them mentioned it in a letter.

I noticed at this time one of the 17th Lancers in our right squadron. His was the only flag that waved either with us or the cavalry we were pursuing, the Cossacks having no lance flags, the remainder being entirely Hussars. I afterwards learnt there was one of the 13th Light Dragoons there as well. His name was Nicholson. Beyond these, and one or two stragglers that joined us on our way back, we were not in any way mixed up at any time with any other part of the brigade. Nor yet did we receive at any time, during the Charge or returning, any word of command from any other officer than Colonel Douglas.

We were now nearing the extreme end of the valley, about a mile and a half from our position, still pursuing this body of cavalry. In their confusion, I saw one of their leading Cossacks fall from the bridge into the aquaduct, there being no parapet. Near the bridge was a moderately steep hill, which formed the end of the valley, up which they rode a short distance; their rear being at the foot, close to us. They now halted, but remained for a few moments with their backs to us, looking over their shoulders. Seeing there were so few of us and without supports, they turned about and we sat face to face, our horse's heads close to theirs. As we looked up at them, they had all the appearance of a vast assemblage in the gallery of a theatre. The stillness and suspence during these moments was terrible. At last it was broken by their officers calling out to their men to follow them and break through us, which they themselves attempted to do by driving their horses at our front rank. But their men failed to display the same courage as their leaders, and our men showed a firm front, keeping close together and bringing their swords down to the right front guard, and so kept them at bay. Many of them now took out their pistols and fired into us, and the Cossacks began to double round our flanks and get in our rear. Many of the flank men now became engaged and were killed. Our position became every moment more critical, for we were in danger of being surrounded, overwhelmed and killed to a man. But, had a few more of our own squadrons come up at this time, I am of opinion that this body of cavalry would have surrendered to us, for we, numbering now not more than 80 sabres, held this Russian Hussar Brigade in a corner at bay for some minutes.

I looked anxiously around, hoping to see our supports coming to our assistance, when instead I saw a body of lancers in the act of forming across our rear. They must have formed the reserve, for they were out of sight when we passed down. They appeared to come out of the road leading to the Traktir Bridge, which is between two hills. I at once knew they were Russian by their lance flags, they being green and white. I thought to myself: none of us have many more minutes to live. Colonel Douglas at this moment caught sight of these lancers and, supposing them to be our 17th, shouted out, 'Rally, men, on the 17th Lancers*.' Someone immediately replied, 'It is the Russian Lancers, Sir.' Colonel Douglas shouted, 'Then fight for your lives, men.' Every man was now left to himself to take his own course and do his best—this being the last word of command we received till those who had escaped reformed on the ground we charged from.

---

* 'Retire upon the Portuguese, men' exclaimed the gallant Captain Benjamin Lutyens (wearing the Gold Medal for Egypt 1801), when in command of about the same number of the 11th just forty-four years before, when surrounded by French Cavalry in the Peninsula; he too mistaking the squadrons in his rear for friends—surrender never entered his mind. When he discovered they were the enemy, wheeling about, he charged them breaking through the first line. But alas! as they came through broken, a line in the rear charged them; the consequence was every man was either killed, wounded or made prisoner, except one subaltern officer, Lieutenant W Smith, who was particularly well mounted.

It was for this piece of gallantry that the 11th got the soubriquet of 'Cherry Pickers'.'

Extract from *The Light Dragoon*. The writer of which I met in Calcutta in the year 1835, he then being on his way home to be discharged, having completed twenty-six years' service in the 11th. He was present at the above affair and was made prisoner; he was also present at Waterloo and Bhurtpoor. His name was George Farmer.

It was with great reluctance the men turned their backs on those they had so lately been pursuing but at last one or two turned, and then the remainder independently as best they could—all tellings off being lost—and started off at a gallop to break through the three squadrons of lancers that barred our way. All order now was lost. We no longer resembled the steady line we had done in passing over the same ground a few minutes before. The four officers, viz: Colonel Douglas, Captain Cook, Lieutenants Dunn and Palmer, and men being mixed up, but still keeping well together, so that we assumed an oval shape—the best horses in front. Many men whose horses had been wounded, others whose horses were fagged and could not keep up, were overtaken and killed, for the Russian Hussars were now pursuing us and shouting '*Bussu, bussu* English.' We were thus being driven on to the line of lancers in our front.

At this time I was riding on the right rear when, turning and looking over my right shoulder, I saw several Russian officers who were leading their squadrons close to me. I at once formed the right rear guard, expecting to be attacked. We were driven on till about 200 yards from the lancers, the Hussars then halted and, as it were, handed us over to the lancers who were waiting steadily for us, with their lances at the carry, instead of charging us as they should have done. This was the third time this day that I had seen the Russian cavalry remain halted when they should have charged.

I was now about fifty yards in front of their right squadron and on the right of our body so, drawing my reins a little shorter, taking a firmer grip of the saddle and clenching my teeth, I prepared to break through, saying to myself: I will go through here or fall—at the same time fixing my eyes on the part of the squadron I intended to try to break through. When but a short distance from them, and expecting the next moment to have a lance or two through me, to my astonishment they (the right

Squadron) went about, wheeled to the right, halted and fronted with the greatest precision as though they had been on parade, their lances still at the carry.

I now galloped along their front looking at them as though I had been inspecting them. When near the centre of the squadron, I heard the leader give a word of command. In a moment their lances came to the guard, and they galloped on to our flank. Then began a hand-to-hand fight, many of our men being killed and wounded. I, however, fought my way through them and was congratulating myself on my escape when the Russian artillery opened fire on us. I now felt my horse limp. Sergeant-Major Joseph, who was riding near me, said, 'Smith, your horse's leg is broken.' Feeling there was no time to be lost, I immediately dropped my reins, drew my feet out of the stirrups and jumped clear out of the saddle, my horse falling at the same moment on her near side. Without hesitation, I commenced running. Our men passed me galloping for their lives, some saying, 'Come along sergeant-major', but none could assist me it being every man for himself. Fearing I should get knocked down if I kept up the same track that the mounted men were going, I inclined to the left. In a moment I noticed that all the mounted men that had escaped, had passed me and were fast disappearing.

I was now about a mile from our position, so on I sped, sword in hand, still keeping well up the left side of the valley. I now found that I could not be far from a square of infantry, for the bullets showered around me, sometimes striking the ground and driving the dust over me. The ordeal was something frightful for I expected every moment to be struck.

Presently I heard galloping and, on looking round, I saw two Russian lancers about 50 yards in my rear and two men of my regiment about the same distance on my right rear. Feeling that they were in pursuit of me, I resolved to sell my life as dearly as possible. On looking round again, when I supposed they must be near me, still running as fast as I could, I saw them circle to the right and meet the two men. When close in front of them, I saw their lances go down. Both the men of the 11th must have been killed for, on questioning the prisoners closely the 12 months and a day afterwards (the day they returned to us) I found they were all taken before they reached that spot.

I now lost my breath and began to give up all hopes of escaping when the thought occurred to me that, by throwing myself down and pretending to be dead, I might recover myself. Then again, I thought, some of the infantry on my left might come and, on finding me alive, bayonet me, so I decided to keep on the move. I now walked a little distance and could occasionally hear a bullet pass close by me, so again commenced running.

After a little time, I saw one of the 17th Lancers in front of me. I sped on and, when I got near, I found that he was an officer and wore his forage cap, much to my surprise. When within a few yards of him, I said, 'This is warm work, Sir.' He looked over his right shoulder at me but made no reply—his face was covered in blood and he had a very wild appearance. This officer was Captain Morris, who led the 17th Lancers and behaved so gallantly.

I now inclined to my right towards the centre of the valley and, in another minute, lost sight of him. Had I followed him a little further, I should have seen him fall down by the dead body of Captain Nolan, the aide-de-camp that brought the order from Lord Raglan to Lord Lucan that the Light Brigade was to advance along the Causeway Heights and prevent the enemy removing our ship guns from the Redoubts. Instead of which, Lord Lucan ordered Lord Cardigan to attack the Russian battery in our front.

I found myself more in the centre of the valley, so halted and listened attentively for bullets, but not hearing any, I began to feel that I had escaped. So I returned my sword and took out of my haversack a little indiarubber bottle that had some rum in it and took a small quantity. I then surveyed the position I was in, and found that I was standing alone between the two armies—about three-quarters of a mile from the Russian battery that we had charged, and about quarter of a mile from our position. I then walked on, feeling thankful that I had escaped, when, on reaching the top of a little hillock, I suddenly came upon three Russians lying on the ground. The first was dead at my feet, the other two at a short distance from him and from each other, sitting up with their eyes fixed on me. I halted.

Seeing a carbine close by the side of the dead man, I seized it, brought it to full cock, presenting it first at one, then at the other. They both threw up their arms in an imploring attitude. When cocking the carbine, I saw there was no cap on it, so that presenting it at them was entirely bounce on my part, but I then put on a cap, still being ignorant as to whether the carbine was loaded or not. I then walked up to the one nearest to me and found that he was wounded in the body and unarmed. I then went to the other, whose left foot was shot off. These three men had been struck down by artillery and belonged to the Hussar Brigade.

Singularly enough, I found from the buttons of the one who had his foot shot off that he belonged to the 11th Russian Hussars. I pointed to the number on his buttons, then to my own, saying as I did so, 'English.' He evidently understood me by giving a nod of assent. A thought then struck me that I should like one of those Russian Hussar buttons to mark the singular coincidence so, stooping down, I took hold of one and by signs signified that I should like one. He took hold of one and tried to pull it off, but failed. He then hastily unbuttoned his jacket and, before I was aware of it, had partly got it off his shoulders with the intention of giving it to me. I immediately stooped down and pulled it over his breast again saying, 'No poor fellow. I won't take your jacket, most likely you will have to lie here all night.' Not wishing however to give up having the button, I drew my sword for the purpose of cutting the stitches when he, no doubt thinking I was going to kill him, raised his hands and eyes to heaven and uttered what must have been a prayer. I shook my head and carried my sword behind my back to reassure him. I then lent over him, took hold of one of his buttons, gently brought my sword forward and cut it off. The next day I cut a button off my own jacket and sewed the Russian button on in its place, where it still remains.

During the time I was with this Russian (some 4 or 5 minutes) three riderless horses came to me—they were wandering up the valley a little distance from each other. The first, seeing me and knowing the uniform, halted close to me. On looking round him, I found he was badly wounded, the blood flowing in several places, so I gave him a pat and said, 'Go on, poor fellow.' The second then came up, he too was wounded, so I said, 'Go on' and he followed after the other. When the third came, I found on looking round him that he was not wounded and that he belonged to the 4th Light Dragoons. I now picked up the carbine that I had placed on the ground while I cut the button off the Russian's jacket, and mounted. Then, looking round, bade him goodbye and rode quietly on.

The first of our people that I met with was the 'C' Troop RHA, they occupying the most advanced position. They were unlimbered and ready for action facing towards No. 2 Redoubt. It appears they had been engaged on the ridge with the enemy's artillery that were stationed there. We could not see them, as they had been on the side of the ridge farthest from us and did not at first know of the Charge, not having been ordered to co-operate with us. It was quite by chance they learnt that the Light Brigade had attacked. The captain, having ridden up to the crest to look into the outer valley hearing firing from that direction, saw to his dismay a part of the Light Brigade advancing down the valley, and the valley strewn with dead and wounded men and horses. But, strange to say, he received no order to engage the troops that were causing us such havoc. As I approached the left of the troop the commander, Captain Brandling*, rode out and met me.

---

* 'When Captain Brandling returned to his troop, after looking into the outer valley, he exclaimed, holding his hand in the air and letting it fall on the front of the saddle, 'My God!' there's a bad business over there; they've sent the Light Brigade into the heart of the enemy's position. They'll never get back; they're being shot down right and left.'

'C' Troop RHA now took up a position facing the opening between two of the Redoubts. While there, a sergeant-major of the 11th Hussars came out from the opening between the Redoubts and made for the troop. On his arrival at the guns Brandling said to him, 'Who on earth gave the order sergeant-major?' 'Oh, sir, God knows! We heard "Come on! Come on!" called out. My horse was shot when I was down at the bottom of the plain; this is a loose horse of another regiment I am on, and this a Russian loaded carbine I have been defending myself with against some lancers, who attacked and knocked me about.'

His story was quite true as regards the horse and the carbine and his jacket bore evidence of the struggle he had undergone, for the wadding was all sticking out through the rents made by the lances. He also said the Russian infantry were hidden in enormous masses at the foot of the hills on the other side of No. 2 Redoubt and all about there. This was the last man observed by 'C' Troop returning from the Light Cavalry Charge, and how he crossed the bottom of the outer plain amongst the Russians and got out where he did, is known only to himself.'

Extracts from *Coruna to Sebastopol* by Colonel F A Whinyates, late Royal Horse Artillery, pp138-140.

Some little distance on their left rear was the 'I' Troop RHA, they too were ready for action. As I rode through them, I was saluted by many that knew me, with, 'We are glad to see you back again, sergeant-major.' But I, burning with indignation at what had happened, only replied 'Someone will have to answer for this day's work.' Feeling that, if we had been commanded by some intelligent private soldier who had been a few years in the service and had taken notice of his drill, the affair would not have turned out as it did. We had lost our guns, we had taken the enemy's, but had been compelled to leave them behind for the want of timely support.

At a short distance on the right rear of the 'I' Troop RHA was the remnant of my regiment in line and, on their right again, the 4th Light Dragoons. So I rode round to the rear of the 4th where I met with a sergeant-major and handed the horse over, which I saw given to one of their dismounted men. I then returned. As I neared the rear of my regiment I heard them numbering off and someone said, 'Number off, sergeant-major,' so I called out, 'Sixty-three,' as sixty-two was the last number I heard. Thus it is evident that the 11th was the last regiment, and I the last man, that returned up the valley.

I then formed up with about half a dozen dismounted men in the rear. Colonel Douglas now came round and ordered me to march the dismounted men down to the encampment, mount them on any spare horses I could find and bring them back. On arriving at the encampment, I found that all the horses left there had been wounded by the Cossacks who, after pursuing the Turks, had ridden into our encampment. Of the four horses of my troop left, belonging to men now in hospital, one was missing, the other three had received severe sword cuts—one across the head, another across the back, the other a terrific gash on the near quarter a foot in length and several inches deep. I cannot help thinking that, if we had retired with skirmishers and a detachment had been left for the protection of the camp, this brutality might have been prevented and the lives of numbers of the Turks might have been saved.

So, being unable to procure horses, I decided on remaining. Going to my tent, which was lying on the ground like the rest, I found near by it my comrade the orderly room clerk. He shook hands with me saying, 'How glad I am you have escaped George.' I told him I had lost my horse and how fearfully the regiment had been cut up. He then said, 'What is this on your busby and jacket?' On picking it off, I found it to be small pieces of flesh that had flown over me when Private Young's arm was shot off.

I now sat down and the feelings that came over me are not easy to describe. I was moved to tears when I thought of the havoc I had witnessed, and that I had lost my beautiful horse. She was a light bay, nearly thoroughbred; I became her master three years before.

It was now about 12 noon and I had eaten nothing since the day before, so my comrade made me some tea which was very acceptable. We then strolled together over the ground in front of the encampment, where the affray of which I have before spoken, between the Heavy Cavalry and the enemy took place. Close to my tent lay one of the 12th Russian Hussars dead and, not far off, several others. There was also a young fair-haired Russian officer badly wounded and six or seven of his men also wounded, sitting huddled together—for as yet our people had had no time to attend to the prisoners. These prisoners belonged to the 11th and 12th Russian Hussars.

As dusk drew on, the remnant of the 11th returned to camp. I them assembled the men of my troop and called the roll. One half were missing (six being killed), ten wounded and two were made prisoners. Three of the ten lost their right arms, and one his left (he died three days afterwards). Another lost his left leg and he died at Scutari. Of the two prisoners, one died in Russia of his wounds, and the other returned having lost a leg. Twenty-four horses were killed, and five so severely wounded that two had to be destroyed. Captain Cook was wounded and had his horse killed, and Cornet Houghton was mortally wounded.

Thus ended a day of disaster, which might have been avoided if more forethought and discretion had been observed. It had been expected and was well known that the Russians were preparing to attack us for, only two nights before, we stood to our horses the whole night in the plain, about halfway between Canrobert's Hill and our encampment, but still no preparation was made. I believe that, had a few battalions of English or French infantry been posted in the Redoubts to support the Turks, and more of our artillery brought into action, and the cavalry properly commanded, the day would have ended very differently. General Leprandi might well ask our prisoners if we were 'drunk.'

In retiring after Canrobert's Hill was taken, we were not covered by skirmishers; had we been, numbers of our allies (the Turks) would have been saved. Then we retired through our encampment and left it without any protection. This encouraged the Cossack skirmishers to gallop into it and mutilate our spare horses that were fastened up to the picket ropes. Again, when the body of Russian Cavalry passed over the Causeway Heights and became engaged with the Heavy Cavalry, we were held as spectators of the fight. Then again the 'I' Troop of Horse Artillery that was contiguous to the Light Brigade, (from want of timely warning and the nature of the ground which partially hid them), had only time to fire one round, and that over high ground towards the Russian Cavalry, previous to that cavalry crossing over the ridge to attack our Heavies. This troop of horse artillery was not again made use of during the day, although it was specially attached to the cavalry under the orders of Lord Lucan.

The other troop, 'C', of horse artillery hurried down by themselves from before Sebastopol. The captain, having independant authority, at once took the initiative and came into action twice in support of the Heavy Cavalry charge, doing good service. This troop afterwards, during our charge, advanced by the ridge and fired vigorously in the direction of No. 2 Redoubt, but this last was the only artillery assistance the Light Brigade received during their combat. And the world would ask: who was answerable for all this? The same man that ordered Lord Cardigan with 670 men to charge an army in position and then left them to their fate when he had at his command eight squadrons of Heavy Cavalry and two troops of Horse Artillery, besides a division of infantry with field batteries close in his rear. True, that he advanced two regiments of this brigade a short distance down the valley; but why did he not follow on? What did this avail us, for as soon as he came under fire, he began to retire—as the following extract will show:

> I looked up to try to measure the distance when, to my dismay, I saw the Scot Greys, who had come part of the way down the valley to our support where they were halted and were now about 500 yards from me, in the act of 'retiring at a trot.' I thought there was no chance now, when our supports were retiring at a trot at that distance ahead of us. On my arrival at the spot whereon the Greys had been formed previous to retiring, it appeared quite plain that the battery on the slope had got their range, shelling them and wounding many men. There was a man standing by himself whom they had left behind. As I came along, he heard me and calling out, said, 'Is that an Englishman?' I replied, 'Yes' and, on going to him, found he had been wounded by a piece of shell just between the eyes, which had blinded him. He had bled very much and was still bleeding. I had a handkerchief in my breast, which I bound round his wound, and taking him by the arm, led him along.

Extract from *Reflections of One of the Light Brigade* by Albert Mitchell, late Sergeant 13th Light Dragoons p86

(The fact of Sergeant Mitchell belonging to the first line and having his horse killed before arriving at the guns he would consequently be one of the first to return up the valley).

It was not unlike leaving the forlorn hope, after storming a town, to fight their way out again instead of pushing on the support. We cut their Army completely in two, taking their principal battery and driving their cavalry far to the rear. What more could 670 men do? A glorious affair might have been made of it, had our infantry been pushed along the Causeway Heights with the Heavy Cavalry, and the French infantry with the Chasseurs d'Afrique along the Fedioukine Hills. The enemy was so panic-stricken that I feel convinced the greater part of this army of 24,000 would have been annihilated or taken prisoners—they having only two small bridges to retreat over: the Traktir and the Aqueduct.

Never, I should say, was such an opportunity lost. As soon as it was dark, we retired about quarter of a mile and took up a position near the Chersonesskij Heights. About midnight, we again retired and took up a position on the hillside, about a mile to the rear of our original position. The order was, 'No fires to be lit. No noise to be made.' This was indeed a sorry night. Scarcely any had had more than a little biscuit and a drachm of rum since the day before. It was spent by us standing in groups talking over the sad misadventures of the day.

PART SIX

26th October 1854–26th January 1855

After the Charge

Thursday 26th October 1854 During the morning we took up a position in rear of the Heavy Cavalry and encamped. An inspection of the horses now took place. Those that were considered incurable from the wounds they had received were selected to be shot. It was a sad sight to see these noble animals—many that had brought their masters safe out of battle—led from the encampment and placed by the side of a ditch, then to be shot by the farriers. I now had but 18 horses fit for duty, so re-arranged the mounting of the troop. I took a horse that had belonged to a sergeant.

During the time this was going on, the Russians were attacking our troops on the Inkerman Heights, which consisted of the 2nd Division under the command of Sir De Lacy Evans. We could distinctly hear the cannonade and musketry. They were soon repulsed with a loss of 270 killed and wounded, and 80 prisoners, including two officers. Captain Fellows and Sergeant-Major Joy (17th Lancers) were sent by Lord Raglan with a flag of truce to General Leprandi, to ask permission for us to go down the valley to bury our dead. Having no white flag, an officer lent a tablecloth which was fastened to a lance pole. We all looked anxiously after them as they disappeared in the Russian lines. After some time they returned with General Leprandi's answer: that they (the Russians) were Christians as well as ourselves, and that they would bury our dead. They likewise went over the following day to get the names of the prisoners, there being one officer and about 40 non-commissioned officers and men taken. The next day they took over some things for the officer.

In my tent were four sergeants. Some time after dark on the evening of the 26th, when all was quiet in camp and the last of the four had fallen asleep, I found myself sitting fully dressed with my feet to the tent pole, looking at a candle that was burning (stuck in the muzzle of the Russian carbine which I had substituted for a candlestick, tied to the tent pole), and thinking seriously of all that had happened. Just as I was about to blow it out, I heard someone call out 'Lights out. Turn out.' I immediately put on my busby and sword, sprang up and awakened those around me, then saw to the tents of my men, aroused them, and ordered them to turn out.

Both encampments were now in the greatest uproar. Officers and non-commissioned officers calling out to their men to make haste, for the noise of galloping horses became more distinct every minute. The French battery that commanded the plain opened fire and our outlying piquet, consisting of the the Heavy Cavalry, came galloping into camp. By this time I was mounted, as were many of the men. Others, in the darkness and confusion, came out of their tents withou their jackets. I called out, 'Get on your horses men, as you are, and draw your swords. Here they are!' at the same time drawing my sword. Colonel Douglas at this moment passed me. The enemy, as we supposed, now rushed into the encampment. We were not long, however, in discovering they were but rideress horses, fully equipped, about 100 in number, all grey. Some had their master's swords hanging by the belts on the saddles. One sergeant-major of the Heavy Cavalry found the part of the sword belt that fastens round the waist filled with gold roubles.

The next morning the sergeant-majors were ordered to send

in returns of the number of horses they required to mount their men. I received seven of these grey horses, and told my men off to them. We were obliged to tie them up well away from our horses, for they tried to kick and bite them. They gave us great trouble. I suppose this arose from our uniform and language being different from what they had been accustomed. My farrier, on looking at the shoeing, both to his astonishment and mine, found a shoe on one of them that he had made. The fact was the Russian farriers had taken the shoes either off our dead horses, or out of the shoe cases, and made use of them. Each of our horses carried two pairs of new shoes, marked with his number, in the shoe cases attached to the saddle. A horse belonging to the 4th Light Dragoons returned with them. His master, Trumpeter Lovelock, was killed in the charge: it is said he led the Russian horses into our encampment. This horse survived the winter and came home with the regiment. He was made a great pet of and lived for many years afterwards.

A few days after this, there being no cavalry at the front to support the infantry, we (the Light Brigade) marched about three miles and took up a position in rear of the right of our Army, not far from the windmill near the Inkerman Heights, and sent out piquets to the right and right front, this being considered the most exposed part, as it afterwards proved.

Friday 3rd November 1854 From a letter written home, I take the following:

> Mr Palmer commands the regiment; he is a young Lieutenant. All the officers are either dead, wounded or sick, such is the state of things with us. I have had no officer in my troop for some time: Captain Cook and Cornet Houghton were wounded on the 25th October and Lieutenant Dunn has since been sick. The troop left Dublin 74 men and 62 horses. All that I can now muster is about 40 men present, (many of whom are sick) and 24 horses.

They are scarcely able to carry us, through exposure and lack of forage—we have such a difficulty in getting it up from Balaclava. There was a heavy cannonade all last night. We have to be constantly on the alert, always dressed and horses saddled, ready to turn out at a moment's notice.

Sunday 5th November 1854 Just before daybreak, we were standing to our horses ready to mount when, on a sudden, a heavy cannonade opened directly in our front. We at once mounted ready to advance. We, the 11th, like the other regiments of the brigade, were now reduced to one weak squadron. Some of the men were mounted on the Russian grey horses. The only officers on parade were Colonel Douglas, Captain Ennis, Lieutenant Palmer and Adjutant Yates, so, there being only two troop officers, Colonel Douglas ordered me to command the left troop. The battle had now commenced in right earnest, for the cannonade and rolls of musketry were incessant. I cannot express my feelings of pride and satisfaction on finding myself about to lead in what appeared then to be the commencement of a great battle.

We had not advanced far when Lieutenant Dunn came galloping round the flank of the squadron saying, 'I will take this troop, sergeant-major.' I then took my place as serrefile. As we passed a battery of artillery, the Duke of Cambridge came galloping back, calling out to the captain to advance. In a minute they were mounted and hurried past us, and were soon in action.

We now came under fire, the cannonballs reaching us. It was now one of the men, who had turned round looking to the rear, called out, 'There goes Joey.' All within hearing turned to look when, in the distance, could be seen the adjutant galloping back towards the encampment. This caused great amusement and laughter—he had only been with us a month and had made himself thoroughly obnoxious to everyone. When those that had escaped at Balaclava were galloping back for their lives to the original position, he met them at the top of the valley, calling out, 'Walk your horses. What are you galloping for? What are you afraid of?' Colonel Douglas said, 'Now Mr Yates, these men are not afraid of anything.' He, it will be remembered, remained behind when the brigade was ordered to attack.

The Chasseurs d'Afrique now went past us at a gallop and passed over the brow of the hill. We halted about 200 yards from the top. The enemy must have known we were there, for they dropped their cannonballs just over the brow of the hill so that they passed through us about breast high. One struck a horse's head knocking it to pieces, then took off Sergeant Breese's arm, taking the three bars and leaving the crown. It then struck Private Wright, who was riding a Russian horse, full in the chest, passing through him. He fell out of the saddle close to my horse's feet. His horse then galloped away and we never saw it again.

Shortly after a man reined back out of the ranks saying, 'sergeant-major, I have lost the use of my arm.' His left arm was hanging down by his side, a cannonball had passed close by it. I ordered him to return his sword and go to the rear. Another cannonball struck a man's leg just above the knee, taking it clean off, and passing through his horse.

On our left front at this time, three of our guns were in possession of the Russians—I was expecting we should be ordered to retake them. They remained in possession of the enemy about twenty minutes, our infantry then advanced and retook them.

Lord Paget had up to this time commanded us. Lord Cardigan

now galloped up and took command. He at once ordered us to retire and take up a position a few hundred yards to rear. The battle all this time was raging close in our front; the wounded infantry frequently passing through us, some saying they thought we should be beaten. One poor fellow of the Guards, face blackened with powder, blood coming through his great-coat, staggered up to us and leant against my horse for support. I gave him some rum out of my little flask, which revived him. He then went on towards his own hospital tent.

Private Molloy, who was orderly to one of the infantry generals of division, told me afterwards that the general ordered him, if the battle went 'gainst us, to go to his hut, take possession of all his papers, gallop down to Balaclava, get on board the first ship he could and bring them home to England. Our generals at one time so feared we should be beaten, that they ordered the colours of all the regiments to be collected and, in the event of a disaster, to be taken down to Balaclava and put on board ship.

The new position we had taken up was out of fire. It was now that Colonel Douglas called out the adjutant, seeing he had just returned. He galloped out to the front. The colonel the addressed him saying, 'Where have you been Mr Yates?' He replied, 'I have been to the camp.' 'Now Mr Yates,' said the colonel, 'This is the second time this has happened. If ever it happens again, I will report you to the general.'

Several French regiments now passed us: one was Algerines. We cheered them on—they were soon in action. About midday the Russians began to retreat. The battle was then virtually won, although there was more or less firing for many hours afterwards, and we returned to camp.

Monday 6th November 1854 We now began to realise what a great and glorious battle had been won. We heard that the Russians attacked us with about 70,000 men and were everwhere defeated and driven back into Sebastopol, with the loss of nearly 12,000 men in killed, wounded and prisoners. Our loss in killed and wounded was over 2,500.

Soon after we had turned in, I heard that a number of Russian wounded had been brought in and placed in a farmyard not far from the windmill, about quarter of a mile from our encampment, so I went to see them. Sad indeed was the sight. They were placed in rows, all round and down the centre of the yard on the bare ground. They had lain there all night, many were dead, others horribly wounded dying, some few sitting up. I do not think their wounds had been attended to, or provisions given them. There were about a hundred. One poor fellow was so peculiarly struck that I cannot help describing it. He was lying on his back, the sockets where his eyes had been were filled with blood. A bullet had entered on one side, passing under the bridge of the nose and so destroying both eyes. I felt deeply for these unfortunate creatures.

On my way back to camp, it struck me that some biscuit, if I could get some, would be acceptable to those that were not badly wounded and could eat, so I enlisted the help of Trumpeter Keates, who at once offered to assist me. We got a sack and went round the tents. I appealed to the men. They rapidly gave all they could spare which amounted to a sack nearly full—as much as Keates could carry. I never saw men more grateful than were these poor fellows, as I gave to each a double handful in their caps which they took off as I came to them.

In the afternoon the burying of the dead was being carried out, but I did not care again to witness the sight, after what I saw at the Alma. As then, the duty of burying all the dead devolved on us as we held the ground the battle was fought on. The Russian general, Prince Menschikoff refused to assist, stating this as a reason: a flag of truce having been sent, asking for the Russians to bury their own dead.

Wednesday 8th November 1854 We were much pleased this morning on receiving an order to hand the Russian horses over to the artillery. I had now more of our own horses than I required many of the men being sick—diarrhoea becoming very prevalent in consequence of insufficient and badly cooked food. Salt beef was issued every other day which it was impossible to eat, for there was no water or time to soak it before cooking; then the coffee was issued green, as it had been all the campaign so far. Had the coffee been issued ready for use, tinned meat with carrots such as was issued on board ship when I went to India nearly 20 years before, and a piece of waterproof sheeting for each man to lie on to keep him from the damp ground, I am convinced thousands of lives would have been saved.

The only mode we had of preparing the green coffee was as follows: the lid of a camp kettle being greased with a piece of pork fat, or any fat at hand, the green coffee was then put in, placed on a fire and moved about to prevent it burning. When sufficiently roasted, it was put in a piece of cloth, placed on a stone, then crushed and beaten with another stone till it was small enough. The coffee, no doubt was the choicest from Turkey and, when the above mode was properly carried out, it was excellent—but this seldom happened.

Friday 10th November 1854 This evening, a reinforcement of French and English infantry joined, which has cheered us up, for we hold at this moment a most critical position, being surrounded on three sides by an enemy far superior in numbers, with a numerous artillery and their cavalry numbering 7 to

1 of ours. On our side, there are precipices and the waves of the Black Sea dashing against them. If we had been beaten at Inkerman, we should have been made prisoners or driven into the sea.

Saturday 11th November 1854 Last night it rained in torrents. Whe we turned out this morning as usual an hour before daylight to saddle our horses, we found them standing nearly up to their knees in mud (this having been a ploughed field) and the rain dripping off them. We are in a deplorable state: some of the men nearly lost their boots, they being sucked off their feet.

Today for the first time since we left Ireland (we having had no vegetables since then), one pound of potatoes per man has been issued, for which 2¼d is to be paid. It having rained all day and the fires being repeatedly put out, it was 5 o'clock before the cooks could get the salt beef and potatoes boiled. Breakfast we got none, except a little rum in some cold water, and biscuit.

Sunday 12th November 1854 Sergeant Guttridge has been sent to Balaclava with the mule cart and a party to get our valises from on board ship, many of the men not having a shirt to their backs, and some being almost without boots. Never did 'Prince Albert's Own' turn out in such a plight as we did this morning. The horses and saddles were smothered in mud, some of the horses had been rolling, so that we scarcely knew them. My boots being completely worn out, I gave Sergeant Guttridge sufficient money, telling him not to mind the price but bring me a pair if he could possibly get them. I likewise commissioned him, as did the other two non-commissioned officers in my tent, to bring some bottled beer. [It was 2s a bottle in Balaclava at this time].

I have generally now to command a troop, there seldom being

more than two duty officers on parade besides the colonel and adjutant.

The nights are getting so cold that we can scarcely sleep, having but one blanket each and our cloaks. For weeks after we landed every man slept ready dressed. My jacket that was new when we left home is now nearly worn out and in rags and I have not had my overalls off since we landed, nor a change of any underclothing these seven weeks. Water has generally been too precious and too difficult to get at, to be used for washing, so that we have seldom had an opportunity of washing our faces. The little leather buckets bound with copper bands that we carried for watering our horses were very useful. One day I had just finished having a good wash near a spring at the entrance of the Windmill Ravine, when two young infantry officers came up to me, saying how much obliged they would be to me if I would lend them the bucket, which they looked at with longing eyes. As I could not wait, I told them if they would promise to bring it to my encampment I would lend it. They readily did so, and true to their word, about an hour after I got back I saw them enquiring for me.

About 8pm the cannonade on both sides was very heavy. Long after dark we were sitting anxiously waiting for Guttridge, when at last to our delight he opened the tent door. The first thing, he handed me a pair of boots, such boots that I became the envy of everyone who saw them. Then, in was bought the dozen of beer, three bottles each. Corkscrews we had none, but we soon found out a substitute: a sharp click or two with the back of a sword would nearly in every case take the top of the bottle clean off. We were not long in disposing of two bottles each. It was then proposed that the other bottle be left till morning, then again it was argued that before morning we might be somewhere else and lose our beer. We then agreed to finish the other bottle. By doing so we followed the example of the soldiers on board ship, a story my grandfather told me:

> The captain said, 'Soldiers, will you have your plum-pudding tomorrow, Christmas day, instead of today?'
> —Oh no, captain, we will have it today, tomorrow we may all be at the bottom.'

The passing of the horses close in front of my tent door disclosed the bodies of some of the Russian soldiers that were killed in the attack on Sir De Lacy's Division on the 26th October. I found that several of the horses were absolutely standing on dead bodies. I had them covered over and passed away on the picket ropes, though it was still very dreadful, for within four or five yards from where I slept were dead bodies not more than a foot underground.

Monday 13th November 1854 The misery this morning was very great, both amongst men and horses—the horses had now changed so much in appearance that we scarcely knew them. Some of the men called my attention to a horse fastened up amongst ours, saying, 'Sergeant-major, here is a horse that does not belong to us.' I did not recognise him, so ordered one of the men to lift up his near forefoot. On seeing the letter and number I at once knew who he belonged to, turning round, there stood his master. I said, 'You are a pretty fellow not to know your own horse.' He excused himself by saying, 'Really, sergeant-major he is so altered I did not know him.' The fact was they had eaten one another's manes off, and their eyes had become so small, through starvation and cold.

My boots now became a great attraction. I tucked my overalls inside, Russian fashion—they nearly came up to my knees. Little did I know at this time who they had belonged to, for it was not till the following Summer that I was accidentally looking inside, when I discovered the name of the officer that had the forethought as to provide himself with such boots before leaving home. He was the only officer of cavalry that was killed at Inkerman: Cornet Cleveland, 17th Lancers.

The colonel was one of the first to remark on the boots, saying, 'Where did you get those boots sergeant-major?' I replied, 'Sergeant Guttridge bought them in Balaclava yesterday, colonel.'
'Send for Sergeant Guttridge.'

On being interrogated by the colonel, he said he met with a man in Balaclava who offered them for sale, but he did not know the man and did not see any other boots for sale. Several men standing in a group, as I passed one of the adjoining regiments, sprang up to attention with their eyes fixed on the boots. I wished I could wear them without attracting so much attention.

Tuesday 14th November 1854 Some little time after we had turned in I was lying down in the tent, as were the others, waiting for the coffee (warm, dirty water and sugar would be the proper name for it) when all of a sudden, without any warning, came a mighty rush of wind accompanied with driving rain. Over went the tent and our things began to blow away. After securing mine (except an air pillow that had been a great comfort to me, which I never saw again) I was afraid the tent would be blown away, so picked up a large stone and threw it on it. On looking round I felt somewhat disconcerted for I noticed there were only one or two other down in the encampment. In another minute or two they began to turn over one after another and it became almost laughable to see both men and officers crawling from beneath the wet canvas.

The wind had now increased to a hurricane, for it was impossible to stand up and it rained in torrents. Some of the men crawled beneath the wet tents as they lay on the ground, others huddled together rolling themselves up in their wet cloaks and blankets. I could not help laughing for the scene was most ludicrous. Breakfast we got none for the camp kettles were all blown off the fires; dinner we got none for the storm continued till nearly dark. All this time we could do nothing—we were perfectly helpless.

We now began to put up the tents—this was the time a piece of waterproof sheeting would have been of use, and meat in tins that could have been eaten cold. This was the misery we had to endure: the wet, cold and hunger, nowhere to lie but on the wet muddy ground, with everything sopping wet and a long night before us. The poor fellows in hospital tents, many in a dying state, were exposed to all this misery, their tents having been blown over same as ours so that they lay in torrents of rain all day. Many succumbed during the night.

The regimental sergeant-major's was the only tent that remained up during the day—and that was held up by the sheer strength of himself, the farrier-major and Sergeant Horn, the paymaster's clerk. Meeting me at dusk, he kindly asked me where I was going to sleep, at the same time offering me a place in his tent (the ground being dry) so I gladly accepted it. My man Sampson brought me a little hay which I sprinkled on the ground. I was afraid to make use of either my blanket or cloak, they being quite wet; my jacket and overalls were somewhat wet and my boots covered with mud, so I lay down and sprinkled some of the hay over me but was so cold all night that I could not sleep.

This was a wretched night for tens of thousands.

Wednesday 15th November 1854 The turn out this morning was a sorry affair. I could not mount all my horses, some of the men had lost their boots, many were sick. We were men and horses certainly, but beyond that I cannot say much. If a troop could have been suddenly dropped into the camp fresh from England they could have annihilated the whole brigade.

Private Powell of my troop came to me during the morning, saying he had something to shew me in his tent. I went with him to find a nice little sheep, one of a flock that had escaped from Sebastapol the day before. He said, 'I will send you a leg when I kill it,' and sure enough in the evening he bought me a leg.

During the morning I went over to the hospital tents to see my men that were sick. Poor Dan Smith was in a dying state, he said, 'Ah, sergeant-major, the grapes are the cause of this.' No man, I think, ate more grapes than I did, but I always took care to swallow neither stones nor skins so I felt they did me good rather than harm.

We now received an order to move our encampment a few hundred yards off to firmer ground. On assembling my men I had only five, and there were 23 horses to be removed, so when all was ready they took four each and I took three. They required but little leading—being half-dead they followed us like dogs. It was piteous to see what cold and starvation had brought these poor animals to, that had been so beautiful and full of life.

Thursday 16th November 1854 This morning things looked somewhat better than they had done the last few days, the ground was firmer, but still I had only a few men on parade. As I was hoping to have a good dinner off the leg of mutton, and arranging about the cooking of it, the colonel's orderly came, saying, 'The colonel wants you, sergeant-major.' I at once went to his tent. I cannot describe what I felt, in fact I thought my ears had deceived me when he said, 'I am going to send you to Constantinople, sergeant-major, to bring up our baggage and to purchase anything that will be of use to us, as we are to remain here the winter. You are to embark at once. Go to the paymaster and get what money you require, then to the officers and find out what they want.'

I was not long in doing all this after I had first ordered my man to saddle our horses, as he was to go with me to Balaclava to bring my horse back. In less than half an hour I was clear out of sight of the camp on my way to Balaclava. On arriving there I soon found the ship that was to convey us, there being a sergeant-major from each of the ten cavalry regiments there on the same errand. On board the ship there were between three and four hundred sick and wounded men. We applied to the captain for berths, but he told us that every part of the ship was taken up with the sick and wounded and that we must do the best we could, so, soon after dark I lay down on deck, rolled up in my cloak and blanket and soon fell asleep. Sometime during the night I was awoke by something being placed against my feet, I rose up a little and saw that it was the lifeless body of one of the sick or wounded men rolled up in his blanket. Not knowing where to go if I left there, I pulled the cape of my cloak over my head and after a time fell asleep again.

In the morning there was a pile of dead on deck, sewn up in their blankets and placed one on top of another to be committed to the deep when we got out to sea. Just as we were about to weigh anchor, we were attracted by the sound of a band. On looking towards the mouth of the harbour we saw a steamer and as it neared us we found it contained an infantry regiment with their band playing, the officers standing on the poop and the men covering the other part of the relief in their bright scarlet coatees. They little thought as they passed us what a freight we had. If they could have stopped and looked between decks their ardour would have been somewhat cooled—they were cheering in response to those on shore.

During the day I went between decks. What a scene of misery and suffering. Sick and wounded men, most of them without any kind of bedding except their one dirty camp blanket, placed side by side on every available part of the main and lower deck. They all belonged to the infantry—the wounded were principally those that had fought at Inkerman, some were without legs, others without arms and wounded in every conceivable way. I returned to deck sick at heart, but thankful to think how mercifully I had been preserved, never in better health, never better clothed, for I had now changed everything: new pelisse, new trousers, boots well cleaned and worn over them—I looked as though I had just been imported from England. This was the advantage we and the 8th Hussars had over all the other regiments in the army, for when our dress jackets were worn out, we were able to fall back on our pelisses, they being made to fit, to be worn in winter. We did not make a quick passage across the Black Sea, the sea being rough and the wind against us, which was most unfortunate for the poor fellows on board. Many of them died and were committed to the deep, in some cases their very names unknown they were in such a deplorable state.

Wednesday 22nd November 1854 We cast anchor off Scutari. I, in company with the other sergeant-majors, at once disembarked, reported ourselves at the barracks and were told off to a large upper room, a kind of attic. Beds we were not provided with, so had to put up with a quantity of straw that was on the floor—this was clover to what we had been accustomed to.

During the day, on passing through one of the corridors of the hospital, I met with Private Foster, Cornet Houghton's servant. He told me his master was dying so I went with him to the room he was in alone. Poor young fellow, he was lying on his back with death depicted in his face. He recognised me and asked what I had come to Scutari for. I told him. Foster lifted up a piece of lint on his forehead, disclosing a hole about the size of a shilling where a piece of shell had struck him. He died shortly afterwards. I at once took an inventory of his effects, which I took back to the regiment and sold by auction. I then visited the ward that contained the men of the 11th that were wounded at Balaclava and advanced each of the men of my troop 10s. They were very pleased to see me, as was I to find they were all doing well, except Private Purvis who died a few days afterwards, having lost a leg. On asking the sergeant whose arm was struck off at Inkerman, how he was, he said his arm had been amputated a second time, and that he suffered greatly and feared he should not live he had such a dreadful diarrhoea. Having heard that dutch cheese was an excellent thing for diarrhoea, I went out to the bazaar and bought one. He eat a large piece at once, the next day he was much better, after that he improved daily and was quite well as far as his health was concerned. Before I left Scutari, he often thanked me, saying the cheese saved his life.

There was a great mortality amongst our sick and wounded at Scutari during the latter end of November and the beginning of December. I heard that as many as 86 died in one day.

We, the sergeant-majors, having no duties to perform, and having made arrangements for the embarkation of our baggage, when we should be told off to a ship that was to take us back, were quite at liberty to go where we liked. Small steamers and kiosks were constantly passing from Scutari to Constantinople, so I went over and was not long in finding my friend Mr Brown. His duties could not have been very arduous for we spent days together. He could speak the language and knew Constantinople well, every place of interest we went to see, he being employed in the mint was able to show me everything there—all the process of making gold and silver coin. One of the head engineers told me they were preparing designs for medals to be given by the Sultan to the allied Armies.

One day we went to see the Sultan's new palace. Nearly ready for occupation it was built close to the banks of the Bospherous, from which a broad flight of marble steps led up to the main entrance. The rooms were spacious, lofty and beautifully decorated, the floors were inlaid with wood of different colours and so arranged in patterns, that on entering a room at first sight it had the appearance of a magnificent carpet. Each room had a different design. The flights of stairs to the upper rooms were of marble, broad and very beautiful. Here was the bathroom—almost too magnificent for description—it was lofty, circular, the roof dome-shaped, held by golden girders and beautifully wrought. The baths were cut out of solid blocks of rare marble—one very beautiful had all the appearance of amber. The view from the windows was exceedingly grand, kiosks flitting about like butterflies on the beautiful clear blue waters of the Bosphorous, then the Pacha's mansions studded on the opposite shore. It was a sight not to be forgotten.

Another day we went to one of the first bath establishments in Constantinople. The process occupied about two hours, during which we had sundry cups of coffee and pipes of tobacco.

I made the acquaintance of the sergeant in charge of the Russian prisoners and was taken by him round the wards that contained them. One he pointed out to me as the officer that was detected in killing our wounded at Inkerman.

The great Turkish cemetery was not far from the Scutari hospital. In wandering through this vast labyrinth of tombs, overhung with cyprus trees, their dark foliage imparting to it a most sombre appearance, this, with the death-like stillness that prevailed (there only being a solitary Turk occasionally met with) inspired me with most solemn feelings. The tombstones were much of the same pattern, but of various sizes, and it appeared, when once placed, they were not again touched as hundreds lay on the ground and others partially down.

Saturday 2nd December 1854 Yesterday the 34th Regiment passed here for Sebastopol, today the 90th Regiment and 600 men that have recovered from sickness and wounds have embarked to follow them. All the available steamers have been ordered to Marseilles for French troops.

Monday 4th December 1854 When in Constantinople today, I met the captain of the *Asia,* the ship I came out in, and all his crew with him. He told me his ship was wrecked close to Sebastopol on 14th November in the great storm, but that all the crew were saved. Many were the enquiries they made about different men. Some I told them had been killed, others died, many wounded and that nearly all the horses were dead. They expressed their sorrow in various ways; many said they were glad they were not soldiers, and I felt equally glad that I was not a sailor.

The weather was generally fine and mild, so that I had every opportunity of strolling about the country and through the bazaars and seeing everything worthy of note. One day I was attracted by two Turkish soldiers. They were very young and walking hand in hand. One accidentally looked into a shop window (it was the European part of the city) when he saw something that appeared to surprise or rather shock him very much, for he instantly turned away and whispered to his companion. His companion then went back and looked, instantly turning away and holding his head down. They then conversed, had another peep or two and passed on. I crossed over the road to see what it could be that had appeared to shock them so much, when I found it was a naked doll.

One afternoon I amused myself by watching the Pacha's wives pass over the bridge, guarded by eunuchs. There were usually four ladies in each carriage, their faces, except their eyes, being covered with thin gauze veils. From what I could see of them they were very pretty—some particularly so. The eunuchs were Africans of immense stature, mounted and carrying terrific swords at their sides.

The sundry good dinners I now got, frequently dining at restaurants in Constantinople, did not agree with me. After the starvation, the fact was, I was scarcely even satisfied, always looking for something to eat. The consequence was I began to get sick and had a slight touch of the jaundice, so went to one of the doctors and got some medicine, and began to heartily wish the time would come when we should be told off to a ship to take us back. At length the day came that I learnt the name of the ship we were to return in. I at once had all my baggage put on board, took a bunk and with my bottle of medicine was glad to get into it two days before we set sail. In a few days I was quite well again. The passage was a long and rough one, the wind being unfavourable nearly all the way.

Monday 1st January 1855 We dropped anchor in Balaclava Harbour. I at once disembarked and went up to camp, which was a mile and a half off, and reported myself to the colonel. He told me Bull had received a commission and that he had appointed me regimental sergeant-major in his stead. Also that he had recommended Troop Sergeant-Major Silver for the 5th November commission and that he had no doubt but that there would be a commission for me before long.

Silver was senior to me, and at this time was on his way home sick.

Besides the baggage we left at Scutari, I took back for the

use of the Regiment £6 worth of chrome yellow and pipe clay to clean up with, also six small Turkish stoves (value 4s 6d each) in which charcoal could be burned, to warm the tents and cook on. These I sold to the officers; also a number of Dutch cheeses, tobacco, pipes, candles etc, all of which were most readily purchased by the officers and non-commissioned officers, so that I became a kind of general dealer and salesman, for it was my duty to sell by auction all the effects of the deceased officers and hand the proceeds over to the major of the regiment after deducting five percent commission.

I now learned what had happened during my absence at Constantinople. It appeared the march from the hind encampment where I left them close to Inkerman was a most fearful affair, many of the horses dropping down dead on the road. The commissariat had been unable to bring up forage from Balaclava in consequence of the bad state of the roads. For a week they got but one pound of oats a day, so that my horse and several others of my troop died in the lines of sheer starvation. Others ate their ropes, wandered away and were lost. Death had done it's work amongst the men too, and Lord Cardigan had returned home on sick leave. All the horses the regiment could muster were between 60 and 70. Scarcely a morning now passes but we find one or more frozen to death, the frost being very severe and the snow frequently knee deep. Thaws too came on very suddenly, which were far worse than frost, for we then got wet-footed, being ankle deep in mud. One of our poor horses I saw lying in the mud, half covered, unable to get up. Before it died it was frozen into the ground. The cooks having no shelter, skinned some of the dead horses, and with boughs and the skins made a covering to get under, and to protect the fires from the rain and snow. Fresh meat at this time was issued but once a week, the other days salt beef or pork. I ate but little of it, for hundreds of men were laid up with the scurvey.

The country between Balaclava and the front was literally covered with dead horses. The commissariat animals were now all dead, so that all our available horses were employed day by day taking provisions for the infantry which lay near Sebastapol, and bringing back their sick and wounded to Balaclava to be sent to Scutari. Sad indeed it was to see long strings of poor wounded men, bowed nearly double, mounted on wretched horses scarcely able to carry them, clinging to the saddles, the horses being led by their masters—and this for five long miles across a desolate hilly country, often covered with snow and the bleak north wind blowing. Many of these poor fellows were in rags, almost shoeless, frostbitten, wounded and sick. I believe some died on the road. These were the men who had been doing trench duty and repulsing sorties, for scarcely a night now passed without a sortie.

It was bitter suffering too for our men, as they had first to go to Balaclava and load the horses with provisions, then go to the front and deliver them to the infantry, then go to the hospitals and secure the poor infantry fellows on the saddles the best way they could, then carefully lead them by the best roads they could find to Balaclava. This sometimes took from morning to night and they got nothing till they returned except a little biscuit they carried in their haversacks. It was a common occurence for these men to come to me carrying their saddles to report that their horses had fallen down dead, or that they had left them on the road dying. Wild dogs prowled about the encampment living on the dead horses as they remained unburied. The saddles, as the horses died, were placed in a heap in the centre of the encampment, frozen together and covered with snow. Covering for them we had none—any more than for our unfortunate horses.

If ever an army was in a deplorable plight it was ours during the months of December and January, but I do not think there was any feeling of blame to our commander for the cruel sufferings the army was enduring. I, and all that I conversed with on the subject attributed it entirely to circumstances. Circumstances brought us where we were, and there we must remain. Retreat was impossible, the position we had taken up was against us, the elements were against us. The wreck of the *Prince* screw-steamer on the 14th November in the great storm just outside Balaclava Harbour, was in a great measure the cause of our misery, for she had brought out from England a complete suit of winter clothing and a pair of blankets for every man in the army. The regiment at this time was most deficient in officers, there being only two available and sometimes only one to perform orderly officer's duty, so that I took a turn with them in performing this duty. This took me every second or third day to Balaclava with a party to draw our forage.

Monday 16th January 1855 I am happy to inform you that I never was in better health, with the exception of a slight cough which I have sometimes at night when the wind is high, which makes the tent flap about and causes a draught inside. In my tent are three more non-commissioned officers. We have dug out the ground about two feet deep in the centre round the tent pole and have our beds on the part all round which is not dug away. This enables us to sit down as though we were sitting on bedsteads. Then we have a closed stove, sunk, with the pipe running under the ground, then coming to the surface about two feet from the tent which carries off the fumes of the charcoal or wood. By this means the tent is made warm and comfortable without any fear of letting it on fire.

Rain is our greatest discomfort. Few tents can resist it on the weather side for the wind drives it through the canvas. It is rather unpleasant to have water dripping on me when in bed. Sometimes I find the canvas swagged down with the weight of snow only a few inches from my face, but this makes the tent warmer at night for it keeps out the wind.

On the whole the army does not suffer so much from the cold as it did, for within the last week each man has been completed with the following articles, viz: 1 fur or pea coat, 2 flannel vests, 2 pairs worsted drawers, 2 pairs socks, 1 pair gloves, 1 comforter, 1 extra blanket and a pair of Turkish boots with felt socks given by the Sultan. Several large cans of preserved potatoes too, have been given to each regiment. This being the second issue of vegetables since leaving home. Fresh meat we get but once a week. Although the weather is so severe, we do not lose so many men as we did in the hot weather, the cholera having now abated. Numbers of men have been frostbitten and two of ours have lost some of their toes.

The ground being covered with snow enables us to see distinctly the Cossack piquet and vidette on Canrobert's Hill. Immense entrenchments have been made between us and them and are defended by several French and Turkish regiments. It is generally thought that the Light Brigade will be sent home shortly, for what use are we now! Nearly all our horses are dead and those that are left are quite unfit for duty.

Monday 22nd January 1855 Since I last wrote the snow has all disappeared except on the distant hills. Today all hands are employed in burying dead horses, that are now to be met with in every direction. Hundreds have been buried around us, some with barely sufficient earth to cover them and one often stumbles over a head or the legs of one sticking out of the ground. At present no stench arises, but next summer it will be impossible for anyone to live near this place. We have nearly completed a large cutting in the ground about nine feet deep, which is to be covered over with boards to contain the remainder of our unfortunate troop horses.

What gay fellows our Allies the French are. At this moment

the band of the 20th Regiment encamped on a hill close to us, are playing delightfully. They appear quite at home, although wading through mud like ourselves. This is not unlike living in a brick field, in the part where they mix the clay—when one places his foot on the ground he is not sure he will raise it again with a boot on. I have often seen men go up to their horses with boots on and come away without.

Our prospect at times is dismal enough, but after all we are better off than either the French or the Turks, the former have very small tents that they have to crawl into and cannot sit up in them (they complain bitterly of this) whilst the Turks have tents like ours, but they are wretchedly clothed and fed and I am sorry to say both our men and the French treat them very badly. They daily come through our camp begging and picking up anything that may be thrown away by our men, such as old boots and shoes (for many of them are nearly bare-footed) bits of biscuit and lumps of salt beef. Not half the salt beef that was issued was ever cooked by our men. Taking all things into consideration I should say that no army has ever suffered so much as this except Napoleon's on their retreat from Russia.

Tuesday 23rd January 1855 There was a sharp frost during the night, but this morning is beautiful, ground quite hard, air clear and not too cold. I have been to Balaclava this afternoon with our foraging party, the roads were almost impassable, a thaw having come on when the sun got up. The place was all bustle and confusion unloading the shipping. Such motley groups were there to be met with, the like I should say were never before seen, English, French and Turks intermixed making purchases.

Wednesday 24th January 1855 A sharp frost during the night, then a thaw came on.

Thursday 25th January 1855 Weather same as yesterday. Every hour brings a fresh report such as, 'Peace is proclaimed,' 'An attack is expected,' 'The Russians have received reinforcements,' 'Sebastapol is to be stormed tomorrow morning,' 'The Light Brigade is to be sent home.' These are the yarns we have spun in our ears so often that we take no notice of them now, but heartily wish the first and last were about to be realised.

Friday 26th January 1855 We have been busy today putting up the first wooden hut we have received, which is to be used as our hospital. Scarcely a day has passed lately without losing one or more horses. We have now but nine at headquarters fit for duty and 19 with the infantry divisions in front on letter duty, the remainder to about 50 are sick and lame.

PART SEVEN

1855–56

Winter in the Crimea—Discharge from the Army—Return to Old England

Sunday 4th February 1855 It rained the greater part of last night, so that our poor horses stood nearly up to their knees in mud and water without any covering whatever, then the most severe frost we have yet experienced set in this morning.

We found but one man for outlying piquet. When he came to my tent to be paraded, before I handed him over to the brigade major, it was piteous to see him sitting on a wet frozen saddle, muffled up, looking perfectly helpless and the poor horse without mane or tail, eyes nearly closed, fore and hind feet nearly close together with lumps of ice hanging on his legs. It was a sad sight and in this condition he was shortly afterwards placed in the centre of the Balaclava Plain as a vidette. I was so struck with his utterly helpless and wretched appearance, that I was tempted to take a sketch of him and his horse as he stood in front of my tent door, a copy of which was sent home to the London Illustrated news, but it never appeared. (They had not the courage to reproduce it, but they in their camp scenes represented horses with flowing manes and tails and looking quite frisky, much to our amusement). So are facts misrepresented. Perhaps it is as well in such cases.

Having heard that a transport had come into harbour, the steward being a friend of mine, I went down to see him. On leaving he loaded me with bread, butter, eggs, jam, marmalade etc, so that I could scarcely get back to camp without assistance. For his kindness, the following day I sent him a Russian officer's sword with a gold sword knot attached, that I bought from one of our men who had picked it up when returning up the valley after the charge.

The Navies, of whom 250 arrived from England a short time since, have commenced the road from Balaclava to the Heights. When this is completed, it will be a great boon to the army, for all the shot, shell and provisions will be sent by it.

Wednesday 7th February 1855 Our prospects are beginning to brighten. The day is beautifully fine and altogether the weather is much milder than it has been. The French band is playing delightfully on the hillside, while the regiment below are making a road from Balaclava. We have now got the few horses under cover that have survived the cold and starvation they have had to endure. Both they and the men are beginning to improve in appearance.

Thursday 8th February 1855 The cannonade in front was very heavy last night. A few nights since the Russians made a sortie in force, but were repulsed by the Zonaves.

The saddler sergeant, with assistants, has been busy packing up the spare saddlery to take to Scutari to repair and fit to remount horses as they come out from England.

A report has just reached us, that those that were engaged at Balaclava on the 25th October are to receive a clasp.

Sunday 11th February 1855 It rained all last night and still continues, so you may be sure what a mess we are in. The

(Note: Unfortunately this was not carried out. Numbers received the clasp who, though present in camp, were not mounted on this occasion and this led to endless trouble many years afterwards).

insides of the tents are nearly as bad as the outside, for every time one comes in, he brings in nearly as much mud as would make a brick. A comfortably carpeted room would appear very strange to me now, but I live in hopes of being in one some day or other.

4pm The rain and sleet is falling very fast. A poor fellow of ours, Private Powell (belonging to the letter party close to Green Hill Battery) who had come to Balaclava for corn and left here about an hour ago, on his way back (riding one horse and leading another) has just returned without the corn, saying that the poor animal sank under the load. We have given him another horse to replace the one knocked up, but he has a six mile journey before him and is now completely saturated and covered with sleet. This is the kind of thing that kills our men. We have replaced several horses for the letter parties lately, all that we have now left at headquarters fit for duty, are five.

The Russians are making batteries and entrenchments on the hills opposite to Balaclava.

Monday 12th February 1855 It froze all last night, but is now thawing again so we are in as bad a mess as ever. Our saddler sergeant leaves here today for Scutari with all our spare saddlery.

Tuesday 13th February 1855 Lord Lucan has been ordered home.

Wednesday 14th February 1855 On looking out of my tent door, the various scenes are really amusing. On a distant hill, opposite to Balaclava, stands a Cossack vidette. Not far off the Russians are throwing up breastworks, making batteries and placing guns. Whole regiments of French infantry are making a road from Balaclava, their band playing, some digging roots to make fires for cooking, while our Heavy Cavalry exercise their horses, they having more left than us. (The few we have left get exercise enough in going to Balaclava for their own forage—and those that are sick). Farriers are busily at work at their forge carts, making shoes and shoeing horses, strings of bat ponies are bringing from Balaclava all kind of things, some laden with biscuit, others warm clothing, some with planks etc, for huts and so on. Then may be seen companies of infantry plodding their way through the mud from the front to Balaclava to get their muskets exchanged for Menie rifles; then again, the hill side behind our encampment is studded with men wearing crimson overalls picking up stones. Anyone not accustomed to the camp would naturally enquire, 'what are those men doing?' He would be told, those are 'Prince Albert's Own' picking up stones to pave the stables that contained the remainder of their poor unfortunate horses.

2pm It rains in torrents. I have just asked in a poor French corporal of the 20th Regiment to take shelter. He was passing and appeared very ill so we gave him some grog. Our paymaster's clerk can speak French, so through him he told us that they never get vegetables—in consequence of which the scurvey is very prevalent amongst them. The English papers say they are much better off than us. It is a mistake altogether, they are not so well off in any respect as we are.

6pm It is astonishing how our men bear up against the misery and privations they have to endure, for they are at this moment singing, *England, dear old England.*

Friday 16th February 1855 We had a court-martial parade this morning, afterwards the colonel read a very nice address to the regiment from Prince Albert, accompanying which was a present of two pounds of tobacco and two pipes for each man. The Guards and the Rifles have received a like present from His Royal Highness.

Monday 19th February 1855 *11pm* About an hour since we received an order to mount every effective horse, the men to carry two days rations and two feeds of corn. They have just marched off to form with the remainder of the cavalry and join a division assembling near Kadikoi, under the command of Sir Colin Campbell, and proceed in the direction of Tchorgoun to surprise and capture, if possible, a body of Russians sustained there. All the 11th could turn out for this duty was the sergeant, one corporal, one trumpeter and one farrier—four in all. Captain Ennis and one subaltern went with them.

Tuesday 20th February 1855 It rained and snowed for several hours after they left last night, then a keen frost set in. The sleet now drifts along so that it is almost impossible to face it. Everyone is pitying our poor fellows.

11pm Our men have just returned, having suffered dreadfully; their moustaches and beards had icicles hanging to them. They had only advanced a few miles, but it was impossible to go further, the cold was so intense. Our men wore their sheepskin caps, those that we had served out lately, which protected their ears. (Numbers of those who wore helmets and shakos had their ears frostbitten and are now in hospital). They only saw about 150 Cossacks who retired as soon as they advanced.

Sunday 25th February 1855 We have just erected a hut which the non-commissioned officers are to have.

A few days since, amongst other articles I received, was a pair of socks, in the inside of one I found the following letter:

> My dear fellow countrymen,
>
> I can no longer resist telling you, tho' it may do little good, how truly grieved and distressed are the women of England to read, day after day, of your dreadful sufferings

in the camp before Sebastopol. Words cannot express our deep sympathy for you all; suffering too with such sad diseases and agonising wounds—and there is not one woman amongst us who would not gladly give up everything she has to promote your comfort.

I do think, however, a speedy change is at hand, whereby efficient arrangements will be made for your receiving the warm clothing and other things already sent out. Wise men are now being chosen to advise our beloved Queen in this dreadful war. Be assured we never lie down at night or rise in the morning without offering our earnest prayers that God would bless and comfort you and that wisdom may be given to your commanders, as well as good common sense to guide them.

Then again we never sit by our own warm fires without thinking of your continued sufferings, with wet cold feet and we long to give up our seats and to crowd you all into our houses this severe weather; then when taking our warm breakfast, dinner and tea we think with pain of your unroasted coffee, your half-cooked salt pork, your hard biscuit; in fact night and day you are in our thoughts and your sad state makes us quite miserable. I know some ladies, connections of my own, who daily weep when the paper comes in detailing your suffering and exposure in the trenches. If it were possible for us to do anything we would gladly do it for your comfort.

But we entreat of you to keep up your spirits, relief is at hand, put your trust in the Almighty, commend yourself to him and be assured of the unceasing prayers and sympathies of your sincere friends.

The women of England

31st January 1855.

Monday 26th February 1855 Last night we moved into our new quarters. It is many a long day since I was so comfortable as I am now. I have got a corner about eight feet square and have had some boards put up to form a kind of bedstead. All the sergeant-majors and sergeants are in with me.

Wednesday 7th March 1855 A great change has taken place in the weather. For many days past it has been beautifully fine, so that we are getting on well with the erection of huts for the men. A mess hut has also been erected for the officers.

There is a report this morning that the Emperor Nicholas is dead, so that we are all hoping peace will be proclaimed.

Friday 9th March 1855 The navies have erected two lime kilns near Balaclava, so that the grave-yards may be covered with it, as it is feared that when the hot weather sets in, the place will become very unhealthy. There is a field between Kadikoi and Balaclava where some four or five thousand Turks have been buried for nearly all that landed with us are now dead. They have been so badly cared for by their government that they would have all been starved, had not our commissariat, by Lord Raglan's order, issued them rations.

Saturday 17th March 1855 Yesterday the colonel sent me to visit a party of ours consisting of a sergeant and four privates who are stationed in the ravine near the Green Hill Battery, in an excavation in the hillside called the Ovens. Their horses live in the cave with them, but although they are so close to Sebastopol, they are quite safe from the shot and shell till they leave their abode. When outside, they are not sure a moment about being knocked over, as hundreds of shot and shells have fallen in the ravine; it is so covered with these missiles that I dismounted and led my horse, not feeling it safe to ride.

The inside of the cave was very comfortable. They find an orderly mounted for the Green Hill Battery every night. Before leaving I went up to the battery and could distinctly see the Russians in their batteries just opposite, as well as Sebastapol and the harbour. They can send their shot and shell half a mile beyond this battery, but one is quite safe whilst in it.

Tuesday 20th March 1855 Yesterday afternoon several Cossacks were knocked over by a shell, for coming too close to Balaclava. I saw the shell burst, for we allow them to look at Balaclava and our railway, but if they come beyond a certain point, bang goes a shell amongst them.

Wednesday 21st March 1855 About one hundred prisoners have passed here today on their way to Balaclava to be sent to Scutari. The seige operations are being pushed with all vigour these last few days, and the cannonade and musketry have been incessant.

Thursday 22nd March 1855 I was awoke several times last night by the cannonade and it continued till long after daylight this morning. At intervals we could hear the musketry, although so far off. We hear the garrison of Sebastopol is very much reduced. A few days ago they sent out a flag of truce requesting two days to allow them to bury their dead, but Lord Raglan would not grant it. We are beginning to think that Sebastopol will be ours before long.

Friday 23rd March 1855 The weather has been beautifully fine lately. The men go about without their jackets—it is more like the month of May or June than March.

Sunday 1st April 1855 On muster parade this morning, the colonel called me to the front of the regiment and presented me with the Victoria Medal, which carries an annuity of £20, and read the Queen's Warrant. He then addressed me saying he was highly pleased with my conduct during the whole campaign. You may be sure how highly gratified I was. On one side of the medal are the words, 'For distinguished conduct in the field.' The ribbon is very pretty, being of red and blue.

Wednesday 4th April 1855 Yesterday we sent 38 men to Constantinople, (every cavalry regiment has sent about the same number). They are to bring up horses that have been purchased in Spain and other parts, and some from England, to re-mount us, so that in another month we shall be ready for the field again.

Thursday 5th April 1855 The railway is completed as far as Lord Raglan's quarters and is at work day and night. Our batteries are now well supplied with shot and shell. We, as well as the French, have many batteries that have not yet opened fire, but in a few days it is expected the bombardment will commence in right earnest and we are to open fire from all the batteries at once. We have nearly 500 guns in position.

Friday 6th April 1855 We hear that a strong body of Turkish cavalry disembarked early this morning and have marched to the front.

1pm I have just ascertained that the strong body of Turkish cavalry that passed here this morning was our 71st Regiment, mounted on bat ponies, going to the front to construct two new batteries, and are to return this evening by the rail.

Saturday 7th April 1855 A sad misfortune occured last evening, as the 71st were returning to Balaclava. In running down the incline, the breaks became useless, not being strong enough. The consequence was they went at a terrific speed, some of the trucks ran off the line and the men were pitched out. One of the 71st and one navvy being killed and a number of men seriously wounded.

Sunday 8th April 1855 We hear that Omar Pasha and 14,000 Turks have landed at Kamiesch and are to be encamped on the plateau about a mile from here.

Monday 9th April 1855 Our batteries opened in right earnest about 5am, the roar has been terrific ever since. The Russians did not expect it, for the rain has been falling in torrents since 8 o'clock last night.

I am happy to say that of late our men have improved much in health and appearance. Some are getting quite stout.

Friday 13th April 1855 The bombardment has continued without intermission, day and night since last Monday. The enemy still keep up a fire although rather weaker than it was. A number of our artillery men and sailors have been killed and several of our guns disabled.

We hear that our 3rd and 4th Divisions and twelve thousand French are under orders to storm, but when is not yet known. The ladders, planks, etc, are all ready in the advanced trenches.

A part of the 10th Hussars from India disembarked at Balaclava today.

Sunday 15th April 1855 It rained all last night, the mud is something frightful today.

Tuesday 17th April 1855 About 500 of the 10th Hussars disembarked today (the remainder are expected shortly) and have encamped close to us. The regiment is between 600 and

700 strong and mounted on beautiful Arab horses. We are quite in the shade, having in the Crimea but 128 men and 62 horses. The 12th Lancers are on their way from India and are expected shortly and it is generally thought we shall be sent home on their arrival.

Colonel Palby, 10th Hussars, has taken command of the cavalry division.

Thursday 19th April 1855 A strong division under the command of Omar Pasha marched early this morning in the direction of the Tchernaya river, to ascertain the position and strength of the enemy in that neighbourhood. The division consisted of 12 battalions of Turkish infantry, a regiment of French cavalry and battery of artillery, 2 squadrons of English Heavy Cavalry, 2 squadrons of the 10th Hussars and a troop of horse artillery. Near the village of Tchorgoun were stationed two regiments of infantry and a few guns. Omar Pasha, having satisfied himself as to the position and strength of the enemy, ordered the division to retire.

The fighting in the trenches is now very severe. Scarcely a night passes without a sortie in force, numbers of our people as well as the enemy being killed. The storming has again been postponed.

Saturday 28th April 1855 There has been very little firing the last few days, the seige appears once more at a standstill. When everything was in readiness to storm, General Canrobert refused to allow his troops to take part, as he and his generals considered it impracticable.

Thursday 3rd May 1855 This afternoon an expedition sailed from Balaclava Harbour and Kamiesch Bay under the command of Sir George Brown, consisting of about 3000

English and 8000 French of all arms. Their destination has been kept a secret.

Saturday 5th May 1855 The expedition which sailed on the 3rd inst. has just returned. We hear that General Canrobert would not allow the French contingent to proceed. (Their destination was Kerč').

Tuesday 8th May 1855 The first contingent of the Sardinian army under the command of General La Marmora, consisting of 5000 infantry, has arrived at Balaclava. There are 9000 more at Constantinople who are expected in the course of a few day.

The weather has been very bad lately, almost perpetual rain, so that the country is in a frightful state and nearly as bad as in the winter. The Sardinians are to remain on board ship till the weather clears up.

Monday 14th May 1855 Detachments have arrived from England for the 4th Light Dragoons, 8th Hussars and 17th Lancers and we hear there is a detachment for the 11th on their passage out, so after all the Light Brigade is to be made up here.

A part of the 12th Lancers from India landed a few days since. The Sardinians have now all arrived and are encamped on the plateau about half a mile from us. Three of their infantry regiments passed through our camp this morning, they are particularly smart, fine looking fellows. They wore broad rimmed hats with plumes of black cock's feathers.

The cannon roared fearfully all last night, and our parallels still creep, on slow and sure. An old general said the other day, it would have to be taken by the pick and shovel.

Saturday 19th May 1855 There is a report that General Canrobert has resigned the command of the French army and that General Pelissier has succeeded him, which we are all very pleased to hear, for we think that Sebastopol would have been ours 'ere this if he had not been in command.

Monday 21st May 1855 Yesterday afternoon I took a stroll through the Sardinian lines. The strength of their army is 17,500, the gun carriages, waggons, commissariat carts, lancer's flags and clothing are all light blue. They have small tents, same as the French, the Lancer's tents were fastened to their lance poles stuck in the ground, the flags waving over them which had a very pretty effect. Their horses were picketed between the rows of tents. The men appear in the prime of life and are very smart fellows; I met three sergeants of the 4th Infantry who spoke English—one of the three exceedingly well. He told me he commenced learning it as soon as they knew they were to join the army.

Tuesday 22nd May 1855 Another expedition has sailed for Kerč', consisting of 16,000 English, French and Turks, under the command of Sir George Brown.

A detachment of recruits for the 11th, mounted and fully equipped, consisting of 6 men and 11 horses, disembarked today. They were drawn for by the officers in command of troops according to the number they required to equalise the troops.

Wednesday 23rd May 1855 A division of the French army marched past here this morning and have taken up a position along the Fedioukine Hills as far as the Traktir Bridge. A division of the Turkish army under the command of Omar Pasha have encamped along the Causeway Heights and the Sardinian army have encamped in the neighbourhood of Kamara, so that we now occupy the same ground that we did on the morning of the 25th October, the day of Balaclava, the Russians having had possession of it since then. The 10th Hussars and 12th Lancers accompanied these divisions. The Russians surrendered the ground without any fighting.

The cannonade in front was very heavy all last night.

The weather is now exceedingly hot. Fortunately a suit for each man has been issued today, consisting of tunic and trousers made of a material something like brown holland.

Thursday 24th May 1855 This being Her Majesty's birthday, a review of the cavalry and field batteries took place. The cavalry mustered 2000 horses. Lord Raglan ordered an extra ration of rum to be issued to each man to drink the Queen's health.

Another detachment for the 11th, consisting of 27 men and 49 horses, disembarked today.

Friday 25th May 1855 More for the 11th disembarked, consisting of 2 officers, 33 men and 50 horses, so that during the past four days, 66 men and 110 horses have joined. We are busy enough distributing them and re-arranging the mounting of the men.

I have now got a horse, not having had one to call my own for the last six months, so, after all, it appears we are to be made up here, but it is like building a house on sand. The men are all recruits and not half drilled, and the horses are no better.

We have now left that came out with the Regiment, 135 non-commissioned officers and men and 37 horses—total strength 201 men and 147 horses.

Monday 28th May 1855 *11am* The enclosed flowers I picked about an hour ago on the very ground where the Russian guns were placed that we charged in the never to be forgotten 25th October. The whole valley is now covered with flowers and the larks are singing delightfully. I thought, when riding quietly over the ground by myself, on my new horse, how very different it was now to when I was last here. Then the ground was strewn with men and horses, dead and dying; the cannon roared and the shells burst amongst us with terrific crashes, spreading around death and destruction. Now, all is still as the grave, except occasionally the report of a distant gun fired by the Russians from the heights near McKenzie's Farm upon our advanced piquets. A mound here and there indicate the spot where the remains of those rest who fell on that memorable occasion. The skeletons of horses lie in every direction, only half buried by the Russians. I brought back to camp a Russian 12 pound shot and piece of shell that I picked up in the centre of the valley.

Tuesday 29th May 1855 We have had a field day in marching order. All our recruits and new horses were present; we had mounted 101. The remainder of the horses are sick.

Wednesday 30th May 1855 We have been very busy today drilling the new recruits. I am afraid some of them would stand a poor chance should we meet the Russians shortly.

Thursday 31st May 1855 I have had a most delightful ride by myself as far as the Tchernaya; it is but a small river and can be forded in any part. Before reaching it I had to pass over the the Aqueduct bridge—the same that I saw the Cossack fall from on the 25th October.

The French carabineers were on vidette along the banks of the Tchernaya on our side and their 1st Foot formed a chain of sentries close in their rear. The Sardinian riflemen were on a hill across the river on the right of all. In front, on a range of hills, the Russian videttes were posted. I could see them distinctly.

Friday 1st June 1855 We hear the French have taken 170 head of cattle from the Russians and that the Sardinians have taken a Cossack piquet consisting of about 40 men.

Saturday 2nd June 1855 This morning the whole of the English cavalry, mustering 19 squadrons, turned out in marching order under the command of Colonel Palby, performed a few manoeuvres, then marched past, the band of the 12th Lancers playing, (this is the only cavlary band in the Crimea).

I am happy to say we the 11th have very few sick just now. The Sardinians have been most unfortunate since landing. Although encamped on fresh ground, beautifully situated, we hear they have lost already 200 men and have double that number in hospital. The 10th Hussars and 12th Lancers have also lost a number of men.

Wednesday 6th June 1855 This afternoon all the batteries, both English and French commenced a furious cannonade which was kept up all through the night.

Thursday 7th June 1855 The cannonade still continues and we hear that every preparation has been made for a general assault.

Friday 8th June 1855 It appears the assault took place about 7pm yesterday and that our people and the French succeeded in capturing some of the most advanced works, so that we are now about to close to Sebastopol. We hear that between 3000 and 4000 English and French were killed and wounded.

Monday 17th June 1855 At daylight this morning all the batteries of the Allies once more opened fire, which has continued throughout the day. Tomorrow a general assault is to be made.

Tuesday 18th June 1855 I am sorry to say that the assault on the Malakov and Redan has been a failure, and that both the English and French have sustained serious losses.

Wednesday 19th June 1855 Today, a suspension of arms has taken place to enable the enemy as well as the English and French to bury their dead.

Thursday 20th June 1855 This morning, for the first time since leaving home, the troops turned out for squad drill under the adjutant. We had on parade about 130, all the recruits being present. After we had been at drill some little time practising increasing and diminishing the front, Colonel Douglas rode up to see how his new adjutant was getting on. To his surprise and mortification he found out he was no good at drill. The fact was he was making all sorts of mistakes in his instructions, and we were doing nothing but the most simple rudiments. After looking on some little time and correcting the mistakes he was making, he said, in the hearing of all present, 'It appears to me Mr Yates that I shall have to drill the regiment myself.' He then galloped away appearing much annoyed. Mr Yates took care not to give the colonel another opportunity of seeing him drill in the Crimea, for the following day he went in the sick report and shortly afterwards was invalided home. Consequently his duties again evolved on me, as in the Charge of Balaclava.

When the Board of Medical Officers had decided that he should be sent home, Colonel Douglas sent for me to his hut and said, 'The adjutant is going home so that his duty in a great measure, will devolve on you. I hope you will do all you can to get the regiment in as good order as possible, and persevere with getting the recruits on, for we may have to meet the enemy shortly.' I promised him that I would do all that lay in my power and he then said he would recommend me for a commission.

It now became my duty to drill the regiment, some mornings at riding school drill, then squad drill, other mornings field evolutions on the inner valley of Balaclava. The colonel sometimes attended and appeared satisfied with what I did. At this time I was receiving sixpence a day field allowance, the same as the youngest and most inexperienced private soldier in the army, whereas the officers received field allowance according to the rank they held, field officers 4s, captains 3s, subalterns 2s 6d.

Saturday 29th June 1855 It was with deep sorrow we heard this morning that our much respected commander, Lord Raglan, departed this life about 9 o'clock last night. All feel deeply this sad bereavement as he was much beloved by all ranks. General Simpson has taken command of the army.

Wednesday 3rd July 1855 This afternoon the remains of our late commander were conveyed to Kamiesch to be put on board ship to be sent home. The coffin was placed on a gun carriage belonging to the 'C' Troop RHA, drawn by 8 horses. General simpson, General Pelissier, General La Marmora and Omar Pasha accompanied it, besides detachments from every regiment in the three armies.

Saturday 20th July 1855 A squadron of ours, composed of all the old soldiers under the command of Major Peel, marched today in company with several other squadrons of the Light Brigade to the valley of Baider about 19 miles from here.

I am very busy drilling the recruits, mounted in the morning and in the afternoon, sword drill.

Wednesday 24th July 1855 We hear that the squadron that marched to the valley of Baider a few days since, has scoured the country in all directions, but have only seen a few Cossacks. The Tartars remain in their villages and sell hay and cattle to our commissariat.

Tuesday 30th July 1855 Another detachment of 50 men and horses disembarked today under the command of Captain Miller and Lieutenant Annersley. We now muster 311 men and 228 horses and every other regiment that was here during the winter has been augmented in like manner so that we can now show a pretty good cavalry force. Unfortunately the recruits are too young and only half drilled.

I have ascertained from the sergeants of the detachments that have arrived from England that the slings used on board ship are made on the same principle that I recommended to the authorities and that it is impossible for a horse to fall with one on. Still not a word of credit has been given to me and I am beginning to think that Lord Lucan has introduced the invention to the authorities as his own.

Wednesday 31st July 1855 The seige drags slowly on. Nothing of importance has occured since the 18th of last month. The loss of life is now very great we are so close to the Redan and the French to Malakov. It is reported that another dash will be made about the beginning of the month.

Several Circassian Chiefs landed at Balaclava this morning and went past our camp at a gallop up to the English headquarters to offer their services to General Simpson.

Thursday 1st August 1855 It has rained in torrents all day, the huts not being waterproof it came in in every direction, which has caused us much uncomfort.

Friday 16th August 1855 We, the whole of the British cavalry, mustering 31 squadrons, with 3 troops of horse artillery, and 3 field batteries, turned out this morning an hour before daylight and paraded in the Balaclava plain, to support the French and Sardinians, who, from information received from their spies, expected to be attacked by the Russian army, 60,000 strong, situated in the neighbourhood of McKenzie's Farm.

As soon as we were formed in brigades we advanced over the Causeway Heights and took up a position in the north valley of Balaclava, the one we charged down on the 25th October. This brought us just behind the Fedioukine Hills where the French were posted, and in sight of the Sardinians, that were in position on the hill near the Aqueduct Bridge.

As we descended into the north valley the roar of the artillery of the three armies was terrific, and the rolls of musketry incessant. The position we were in prevented our seeing the fight between the French and Russians near the Traktir Bridge, but we could see the Sardinians. The scene became awfully grand. The Russians had 14 pieces of cannon placed on a hill and were pouring in a tremendous fire.

We could distinctly see the smoke from the Sardinian's rifles, as they were crawling up the hillside picking off the Russian gunners. The enemy came boldly on, (they were the Grenadiers of the Guard) crossing the Tchernaya, and the Aqueduct, but they were met by such an overwhelming fire from our brave allies that after several ineffectual attempts to capture the position they retired, having suffered fearful losses. The battle lasted about four hours. The 12th Lancers had several horses killed, being nearer the enemy than any other English cavalry regiment. Our Grey Battery fired about 12 shots per gun. No other English troops were engaged, they being kept in reserve.

11.30am We marched back to camp, the Russians then being in full retreat back to the McKenzie Farm heights.

3.30pm The regimental sergeant-major of the 10th Hussars gave me a call to know if I would accompany him for a side over the battlefield. So I got a pony and off we started. As we rode down the road leading to the Traktir bridge a cannonball from the Russian battery placed on the opposite heights whizzed past us, just over our heads and buried itself in the bank within a few yards of us. Hickman turned round to me and said, 'Will you go any further Smith?,' not liking to show the white feather, I replied, 'Yes,' never having had a presentiment that I should be killed. So on we rode.

As we neared the Traktir bridge, we began to meet with the lifeless bodies of the French, principally Zouaves, then nearer the bridge, Russians, one in the centre of the road on his elbows and knees, bareheaded, with his face buried in the dust, quite dead. I thought of the saying 'biting the dust.' He had a large hole in his forehead, from which quantities of blood had run, and a drain had been made in the dust by someone for the blood to run down. Not far off a Zouave and a Russian lay with their bayonets transfixed through each others bodies, both quite dead. I picked up a cap near one who was shot through the forehead—the bullet that killed him had passed through the peak and two other bullets had struck the cap in other parts. I brought the cap away to show how many narrow escapes the poor fellow had had before the fatal bullet struck him—he was one of the most advanced of the Russian skirmishers.

On arriving at the bridge where the Russians had come over with such determination, the scene was truly awful. They lay in heaps, here and there a Frenchman interspersed. How different were their countenances in death to the Russians: they looked manly and noble, some even wore a smile, whilst their enemies in most instances had a ferocity of aspect dreadful to behold. I particularly noticed close to the bridge a splendid hand. I also saw some fellow, a Zouave, and about two yards from him in line a private of the 27th French, and between these two a Russian, all lying on their backs quite dead. After passing over the bridge, we came to the French outlying piquet, standing in groups talking and smoking, whilst around and amongst them our enemies lay in dozens. They spoke to us and appeared delighted at the victory they had gained, pointing to the dead and dying Russians saying, 'Russ, Russ.'

On passing a little further on we came to several small fields, with deep ditches, some having water in them. Here they lay in hundreds, all Russians, particularly in the ditches, some partly in the water. The French ambulances were collecting the wounded. I stopped for a moment and saw them lift one poor fellow to place him on a stretcher on the side of a mule, but before they could get him placed he had breathed his last. So, laying him on the ground, they then picked up another, there being numbers about, some making signs for water. I heard one say, 'Hospital, hospital.' I made signs to him that he would soon be taken there.

The scene around me at this moment was heartrending, and I had the greatest difficulty in preventing myself crying like a child, my heart felt ready to burst. My thoughts were of how much the man who is the cause of all this suffering and death will have to answer for.

Near this spot I picked up a Russian drum, which I have now—it is made from brass with a large two-headed eagle embossed on the side (both heads were knocked in). I also brought away a grenadier's pouch and belt complete with the bayonet, ammunition and caps. The cannonball that passed close to us when riding down the road to the Traktir bridge must have been the last the Russians fired on the ambulance parties, for I did not observe any more firing. The Russian general, when written to the following day by General Pelissier, gave as a reason for this breach of humanity, that the French sentries had fired on the Russians when collecting their wounded.

The Russians lost, this day, in killed and wounded, over 8,000. The French found lying on the field, which they took into their hospitals, 38 officers and 1,626 men. The French lost, in killed and wounded 1,561 officers and men, and the Sardinians 200.

Saturday 17th August 1855 One hour before daylight this morning we were saddled and in readiness to turn out at a moment's notice, (2am is rather early rising, but nothing is a hardship or trouble when a man is willing and in the enjoyment of good health—and I thank God I never felt better).

Our squadron with those of the other regiments returned from Baider a few days since, the spoil they brought in was immense. Prince Woronzoff's mansion and chapel were ransacked, but the property belonging to the poor Tartars was not touched. I bought a priest's chasuble made of silver tissue, and beautifully embroidered with gold lace, from one of our sergeants for £2. I at once put it on and walked out of my tent to our parade ground. I was soon surrounded by the officers. Captain Cook who was going home on sick leave offered me £5 for it which I accepted, thinking it better to do so, than to run the risk of losing it, as we expected to leave our present position and advance inland.

Sunday 18th August 1855 The fire on the Redan has been kept up all night. It is reported that another assault will be made shortly. Two regiments of French with their bands playing have escorted about 400 Russian prisoners that were taken on the 16th August to Kamiesch for embarkation, the prisoners all being sent to Constantinople. We were ready to mount at 3am—it is a standing order now.

Monday 19th August 1855 As we were marching on the general parade ground for Divine Service this morning, an orderly came galloping up with an order for us to turn out immediately. The scene that ensured was really amusing. The different regiments instantly broke and ran off in all directions, every man to his horse. In a few minutes all were mounted and in their places. After a short time the dismiss sounded.

Tuesday 20th August 1855 Our brigade, which consists of the 8th, 10th and 11th Hussars and 17th Lancers, had a field day this morning under the command of Colonel Palby of the 10th Hussars. The 11th formed one squadron, Colonel Peel commanded, (Colonel Douglas being on leave at Constantinople since the beginning of the month). Only three young subalterns were present, the other officers, viz: Captains Cook and Miller, Lieutenant Palmer and Annersley and the 2nd Master, are going away sick, so that we are now worse off for officers than we were last winter, there being only four present fit for duty.

Our sergeant, Surgeon Ansell died on the 10th August of a putrid fever. I at once took an inventory of his effects, which I sold by auction in the centre of the encampment a few days afterwards (it being my duty to take possession of and sell by auction the effects of deceased officers, and after deducting a commission of five percent to hand over the balance to the major of the regiment). When I held up his dress jacket, none of the officers present would bid for it as a change of clothing had taken place, (tunics being substituted in place of dress jackets and pelisses), so I bid 15s. There being no advance I knocked it down to myself. The other articles were sold equally cheap, the officers not caring to possess the clothing of one who had died of such a terrible disease. Although Mr Ansell died in the centre of the encampment, his was the only case of the kind in the regiment during the campaign.

Wednesday 21st August 1855 *7am* We turned out before daylight, and have just returned. An attack was expected, but the Russians thought better of it. They got a lesson the other day they will not forget for some time.

Wednesday 28th August 1855 Last night we were aroused by a tremendous explosion, which we have just learned was a French magazine. It contained 15,000 pounds of gunpowder, blown up by a shell from the enemy. About 150 French soldiers were killed and wounded.

The siege works have progressed considerably lately. The French are now quite close to the Malakov, and the English as near the Redan as the nature of the ground will permit. Every preparation is being made for another assault.

Saturday 1st September 1855 We had a field day under Colonel Douglas this morning, there were only three lieutenants present. I performed the adjutant's duty, and the troop leaders were made up from the troop sergeant-majors. Colonel Douglas has received the Order of the Bath.

Yesterday I got permission from the colonel to leave the non-commissioned officer's hut, and have a tent for myself. He gave me boards sufficient to cover the floor. I have had it sunk two feet and shelves made all round, and a store put in, also a table that came from Prince Woronzoff's mansion: we have now got into the way of making the most of everything. I have made an oven of a preserved potato tin, sunken into the ground and a small space left underneath—it bakes beautifully.

Sunday 2nd September 1855 *8pm* We have just received an order to be mounted an hour before daybreak as a general engagement is expected (it being thought the Russian army will again attack the French and Sardinians). Our valises are to be left behind. Every sergeant-major and sergeant now carries a revolver, which they are busy loading—as well as issuing biscuits and filling water canteens.

Monday 3rd September 1855 The reveille sounded at 2am this morning. At 4am the whole of the cavalry were formed up on the plain and advanced about a mile towards the Tchernaya, where we remained in full view of the Russians, the French and Sardinians in battle array between us. Johnny Russ has not forgotten the 16th of last month, so he stopped at home and we returned to camp at 7am and had a second breakfast.

The weather had been much colder the last few days. I have just seen a man of ours who is orderly to General Simpson. He told me that yesterday the Sardinians took three Russian deserters to headquarters, who say that their army is in a fearful state from starvation. They had a most emaciated appearance—two were taken into hospital. All their water has to be brought a days' march from the Belbic. Although they are close to the Tcherneya and can see the French and Sardinians watering their horses and carrying water all day, it would be certain death for one of them to attempt to go near it. I think one of these fine mornings we shall find them in full retreat out of the Crimea. A strong squadron of the 10th Hussars embarked this morning for Kerč'.

We shall soon want another draught of recruits, for this morning we were obliged to leave in 40 horses that we could not mount. Last month we were very unfortunate, one officer died (Assistant Surgeon Ansell) and six left the Crimea for Scutari and England. Seven of the men also died, 24 were sent to

Scutari and 50 are now in hospital—they are nearly all recruits. The old campaigners stand their work and look well, but the recruits look very bad. This early rising (guards are being exposed to the sun nearly all day) is too much for boys. I compare war to an immense furnace that requires constant feeding.

We hear that a General Counsel of War composed of the Allied Generals has been sitting today to decide upon the plan of another assault on the Malakov and Redan. We are all anxiously hoping that we may be successful this time.

Wednesday 5th September 1855 This morning the whole of the English and French batteries opened fire simultaneously from 800 pieces of ordnance. The roar was terrific. Some time after dark one of their ships caught fire and burnt till midnight.

Friday 7th September 1855 The bombardment has continued without interruption since it commenced on the morning of the 5th August. Another line of battleships caught fire this afternoon; after dark the whole town and harbour were lit up by the conflagration.

The greatest excitement prevails in all the camps, as every preparation is now being made for the final assault. Each man is to carry two days rations cooked. Tomorrow we are to send a squadron, which, with some squadrons from other regiments, are to form a line of videttes between the attacking columns and the camps.

Saturday 8th September 1855 The cannonade still continues. We hear 12 noon is the time appointed for the general assault. We all sincerely hope this protracted struggle which has cost the lives of so many brave men will, this time, be crowned with success.

3pm We have just heard that the French have taken and hold the Malakov, but that the assaults on the Redan made by the English and on the Little Redan by the French have failed. During the night fires broke out in several parts of the town, so that the country was lit up by flames, and terrific explosions took place.

Sunday 9th September 1855 To our inexpressible joy we have just heard that the Russians evacuated the town during the night, so that Sebastopol is ours at last. In the afternoon I got leave from the colonel to go up to the front, so took a pony and started off. As I neared Sebastopol I met numbers of the French, as well as our people, who had been plundering. It was laughable to see them coming to camp laden with all manner of things; some with tables, others with chairs, and crockery of all kinds (one Frenchman had a piano on his back, and following him up the ravine an Englishman with a live pig). Others dressed as Russian officers and soldiers, some as priests, some wearing ladies bonnets and carrying parasols. The only Russian I saw besides a few dead lying about was one quite drunk lying on his back.

I bought as many things back to camp as I could carry; some I bought and some I had given to me. Among them were several pictures framed, a helmet and a new greatcoat belonging to the 26th Regiment of the Russian Imperial Guard—one of the regiments that defended the Redan.

Monday 10th September 1855 I have again been to the front in the hope of getting some more plunder, but could not get into the town. French sentries having been placed all round to prevent us English from entering, although I saw hundreds of the French coming out laden—two on stretchers severely hurt from an explosion. Several explosions took place while I remained. The town was on fire in several places and the Russian Fleet was either sunk or burnt to the water's edge.

The French police now have charge of the town. I was told that the sappers had discovered several mines with slow matches of various lengths burning. The Russians no doubt thought we should rush into the town and so be blown up in detail.

Many thousand French have marched from the front to reinforce the army on the Tchernaya. It is reported that the Russians are in full retreat; if so, no doubt we shall advance and try to cut them off. When at the front the other day, I heard the infantry say, 'No more trenches'

They appeared delighted at the thought.

Thursday 13th September 1855 General Windham has been appointed commandant of the part of Sebastopol known as the Karabelaia, where stands the barracks and dockyard. The French have the other part which principally contains the town. The 3rd Buffs and a portion of the artillery now garrison our part of Sebastopol. Passes can now be obtained from generals of division to enter the town. Two of our men were up today and went all over the town and into Fort Alexander.

Friday 14th September 1855 Sergeant-Major Guttridge and I have got a pass to go to Sebastopol tomorrow.

Saturday 15th September 1855 We started this morning making direct for the Redan, through the trenches and over the ground where so many of our brave countrymen had fallen in the two great assaults. Then over the ditch and through the embrasures. Several of the cannons had been dismounted and the parapets in many places were knocked to pieces by the terrific fire brought to bear on the place at the last bombardment. One of the guns had been rendered useless by one of our shots having struck it full in the muzzle and there stuck.

We have met with two of the 95th who had been in the assault and amongst those who had first entered the Redan, they pointed out the place they clung to until they were obliged to retire. Just in rear of the battery were constructed bomb-proof rooms underground, which would contain hundreds of men. The roofs were covered with masts of ships and immense beams. We went through one, but were glad to get outside again for the place was swarming with fleas. We then passed on to the barracks and went through many of the rooms; they were of immense size with raised benches running the whole length down the centre of the rooms. They were similar to our guard beds, only here were two rows with their heads to the centre. The rooms were heated by stoves in the passages. In the basement were rooms similar to those above. Here I found a Marine's jacket and Naval officer's cocked hat which I brought away.

The exterior was superior to any barracks I had ever seen in England, being built of white stone and beautifully situated overlooking the dockyard and harbour. The parade ground appeared to be made of concrete and in the centre was a very handsome cupola under which was a bell (possibly the same that was heard the night before the battle of Inkerman, taking the Russian soldiers to prayers). It was broken and the pieces lying about. I managed to secure a small piece of it. On the top of the cupola was a large cross fixed on a ball, which had been nearly cut in two by one of our cannonballs. This caused the cross to fall over and hang down. Several Turkish officers who had evidently come on the same errand as ourselves stood gazing at it.

When we next visited the dockyard, lying about were a great number of anchors. In one of the offices I found a manuscript book of orders for signaling, with various flags neatly drawn and painted. This, with a pair of compasses and some copper nails, I possessed myself of. We next strolled through the town. Most of the houses were completely destroyed by shot or fire. We then went into a church dedicated to St Paul. Only one or two shots had passed into it and everything had been removed from the interior, even to the very seats. There was nothing but bare walls and board. When standing on the raised part where the alter had been, I little thought that the whole of the Communion plate was buried underneath (this we learned afterwards when Sebastopol was given back to the Russians).

Thursday 20th September 1855 This is the anniversary of the Battle of the Alma. How different a day this is. That was beautifully fine, this is cold, miserable and muddy, for the rain fell in torrents last night. The weather lately has been altogether different from what it was this time last year. How fortunate we were to have had such beautiful weather, having no tents at that time.

The Heavy Cavalry are just giving three cheers on receipt of their medals. We had a parade this afternoon, every man present to receive his medal. The colonel first presented the officers with theirs, then the non-commissioned officers, afterwards the privates. He then said he should recommend us at present to wear the ribbon only, for fear anything might happen to us in the field, which advice most men will follow. I hope I may have the pleasure of wearing mine in Old England.

Saturday 22nd September 1855 The weather is still wet, consequently the ground is very muddy. It is reported the cavalry are to winter near Constantinople.

Sunday 14th October 1855 This morning Sergeant-Major Guttridge and I again got leave for the day, which we spent in looking over the Malakov and Redan. We first went through the French trenches, and into the Malakov. The ground was strewn with French and Russian caps, canteens, bayonets and bloody clothes. Those that fell are buried in the deep trenches, round this formidable work. The French flag waved triumphantly over the place and a strong French guard was stationed there. We remained about an hour, then went to the Redan by the same road the Russians did when they were driven out of the Malakov. Our infantry guarded the place and the colours of Old England waved over it. We did not venture into the town for the Russians were firing into it and the French and our people were returning the fire in good earnest.

Tuesday 16th October 1855 The 10th Hussars embarked yesterday, the 1st Royal Dragoons today, nearly all the other cavalry regiments have left. Just before marching the regimental sergeant-major of the 10th Hussars sent me a little Tartar chicken that he picked up in a village on the road to Baider, about three months ago. He was to have had it for dinner the day before marching, but neither he nor his man had the heart to kill it, it had been such a pet, living in the sergeant-major's tent, coming when he whistled for it and following him like a little dog. I was very pleased to have it. When evening approached it looked up at the tent pole for a place to perch, so I tied a stick across and it flew up. During the day it picked about in and around my tent, but did not attempt to go away.

Monday 22nd October 1855 The weather is still very fine, but the evenings and mornings are getting cold. This is a most delightful climate, for seven months out of the twelve, one might almost live out of doors.

Wednesday 7th November 1855 The Light Brigade have all left. A report is current today that the 11th is to remain here the winter and that all other cavalry regiments are to winter at Scutari and the neighbourhood, so in anticipation of this I am going to have a hut erected for myself, as we have an abundance of wood (all the huts of the 10th Hussars having fallen into our hands).

Friday 9th November 1855 It is now finally settled that the 11th is the only cavalry regiment to remain in the Crimea during the winter. This morning we relieved the detachment at headquarters and all the letter parties.

The following is a distribution:

	Offr	Sgt	Cpl	Pte	Horses
General Sir James Simpson (H.Q)	1	1	4	27	30
General Windham (Sebastopol)	1	1	4	3	3
2nd Master General (Balaclava)	1	1	1	3	4
Sir Hugh Rose (French Hussars 2nd)	1	1	1	1	1
Monastery	1	1	1	3	4
Kazach	1	1	1	8	9
Highland Division	1	1	1	4	5
Light Division	1	1	1	2	2
First Division	1	1	1	2	2
Second Division	1	1	1	2	2
Third Division	1	1	1	2	2
Fourth Division	1	1	1	2	2

Total strength of the regiments in the Crimea and at Scutari:

NCOs and men	372
Horses	275

The only officers now doing duty with the regiments, besides Colonel Peel who commands, are five subalterns. Colonel Douglas having gone home on leave, the remainder are away sick.

Sunday 11th November 1855 General Sir James Simpson having resigned, General Sir W Codrington has taken command of the army.

Sunday 25th November 1855 We have been very busy lately making every preparation for the coming winter so as to make ourselves and our horses as comfortable as possible, erecting huts, making and paving stables, digging drains to carry off the water in rainy weather and making roads. We shall be very differently off this winter than to last. We are not at all sorry at being left behind for we think we shall, on the whole, be far more comfortable than the regiments that have gone to Constantinople.

When the weather permits, I have the most backward recruits out at drill, mounted in the morning and sword drill in the evenings. A short time before the 10th Hussars embarked they sold a number of cast horses, amongst them was a little chestnut Arab which I bought for 7s. It had the mange at the time, but is now quite well. I would not take £10 for it. I have bought a plain saddle and bridle and keep it for my own private use.

I moved into my new hut last week; it is double boarded and covered with tarpaulin and is 16ft in length by 12ft in breadth. The farrier major made me a fireplace with hobs to put the kettle on and the chimney is built of bricks—I have often had a worse room when at home. The three carpenters, men of the regiments that built it, say it is worth £60. We had a house warming and I invited all the staff sergeants of the regiment to spend the evening with me.

Since the adjutant left in July last, everything has gone on smoothly and satisfactorily, the non-commissioned officers and men doing their duty from principle, the most ready obedience to all orders been shown by them at all times. Justice and firmness, I am convinced, will always go further with men than injustice and humbug—this is what destroys all *esprit de corps*.

We consider it fortunate that the lot fell to us to remain in the Crimea, it appeared that the 17th and 11th were the two regiments selected for this duty. The bearing, attention to duty, and good conduct of the 17th and our men must have been remarked by the authorities or this honour would not have been conferred upon us.

Saturday 1st December 1855 We have only had one night's frost so far. It is a much milder winter than last and we are much better prepared for it, the men all having plenty of good warm clothing and they wear their boots over their overalls, Russian style. The horses too are well sheltered and I do not think we shall lose one this winter. For my own part I never was happier in my life, or in such good health. This climate agrees with one well, the air is nearly always beautifully clear and I have no coughs or colds now as I often had when at home. We get bread four times a week, which is very good.

Colonel Peel had my name put in the regiment's orders the other evening to perform the duties of adjutant, although I may say that those duties have been principally performed by me for many months past. Lieutenant Harnet was appointed acting adjutant by Colonel Douglas when Mr Yates left.

Tuesday 25th December 1855 Sergeant-Major Guttridge (the armourer sergeant) and I, dined together today in my hut. We had an excellent dinner: goose, ashed mutton and a plum pudding made by the armourer sergeant's wife in Birmingham. The goose and two bottles of sherry, Colonel Peel kindly made me a present of. We cooked it beautifully in front of my fire. The officers gave the men dinners same as at home so that the 11th after all are very happy in their isolation.

It has been regular Christmas weather lately, the ground has been covered with snow and ice for the last ten days—any weather better than wet. The men and horses are all healthy and looking well.

The other day a great explosion took place in Sebastopol. We hear it was the dockyard being blown up by our engineers. They and the French are making preparations to blow up all the fortifications in Sebastopol including Fort Nicholas and Fort Alexander.

Monday 14th January 1856 During the past four weeks everything has gone on pleasantly with us. The men being well-clothed and housed do not feel the severity of the winter. The horses too are looking well. The little chick and her companion (a white one like herself, that I got to keep her company) are doing first rate for they lay a couple of eggs nearly every day, although the weather has been so severe.

Tuesday 15th January 1856 We have just heard to our intense horror that Mr Yates is on his passage out. Almost at the same time I learned that all men with over 20 year's service, who were ailing, are to be sent home, as the war is now considered virtually at an end (all firing on our part and that of the Russians having ceased for some time). Having at this time been nearly 23 years in the service, I determined it possible to avail myself of this order, dearly as I loved the service and my regiment. To come again in close contact with a man that had, as far as lay in his power, deprived me of the privileges of my predecessors and had imposed duties upon me that had never before been performed by my rank, and whose duties I had been doing for so many months, was more than I could endure—the very thought made me sick at heart. I could stand anything but pointed humbug, so that I became really indisposed and went into the sick report. This was the first time since leaving home that I had been a single day away from duty.

After being in the sick report a few days, the surgeon of the regiment brought the general doctor to see me. He ordered that I should be sent home. Accordingly on the 25th January I, in company with two more invalids of the 11th, embarked at Balaclava on board the steamer *Thames*. There are 220 invalids on board, about 120 of them have been wounded. Everything is beautifully arranged for our comfort and accommodation. In the afternoon we steamed out of the harbour.

During the passage to Constantinople I had a conversation with Mr Gloag our veterinary surgeon, who was going to Constantinople to inspect the Land Transport animals there. He expressed some surprise on learning that I was on my way home to be discharged. I told him that for certain reasons it was my determination at any sacrifice to leave the regiment. He very kindly offered to give me a letter of recommendation to Colonel McMuido, Director General, Land Transport Corps, London, from which the following is an extract:

> I beg to recommend Regimental Sergeant-Major Smith to your notice, as a highly active and intelligent non-commissioned officer. I think from his knowledge of cavalry duties he would make a valuable officer in the Land Transport Corps. It I had known that he had thought of leaving the regiment I would have recommended him to Colonel Weatherall. Colonel Douglas of the 11th Hussars is in England, and if you will refer to him respecting the capabilties and character of Regimental Sergeant-Major Smith, I am sure you will be very satisfied.

We made a quick passage across the Black Sea to Constantinople, where we cast anchor and remained a few hours. We next reached Malta where I went ashore, making several purchases, looking over the town and the beautiful Church of St John. After a pleasant passage of three weeks we cast anchor in Portsmouth Harbour on the 14th February 1856, at once disembarked and marched to Forehouse Barracks.

PART EIGHT

Appendices and Evidence from the Charge

APPENDIX 1

The Light Brigade

25th October 1854

The Earl of Cardigan Commanding

Regiments and Officers present in the Charge:

4th Light Dragoons

Lt Col Lord George Paget, Commanding
Major Halket (killed)
Captains: Low, Brown (wounded), Portal, Hutton (wounded)
Lieuts: Joliffe, Sparks (killed)
Cornets: Martin, King, Hunt

8th Hussars

Lt Col Shewell, Commanding
Major de Salis
Captains: Tomlinson, Lockwood (killed)
Lieuts: Seager (wounded), Clutterbuck (wounded), Phillips, Lord Viscount Fitzgibbon (killed)
Cornets: Henage, Clowes (wounded), Mussenden

11th Hussars

Lt Col Douglas, Commanding
Captain Cook (wounded)
Lieuts: Trevelyan (wounded), Dunn, Palmer
Cornet: Houghton (died of wounds)

13th Light Dragoons

Captain Oldham, Commanding (killed)
Captains: Goad (killed), Jenyns, Tremayne
Lieuts: Smith, Jervis
Cornets: Montgomery (killed), Chamberlayne

17th Lancers

Captain Morris, Commanding (wounded)
Captains: White (wounded), Winter (killed), Webb (died of wounds), Morgan
Lieuts: Thompson (killed), Sir William Gordon (wounded), Hartopp, Chadwick (wounded & taken prisoner)
Cornets: Sir George Wombwell, Cleveland

Present in the Charge:

Generals	1
Lieut-Cols	4
Majors	2
Captains	15
Lieutenants	15
Cornets	11
Sgt-Majors, Sgts, Cpls, Trumpeters, Farriers, Privates	628
TOTAL	676

(Strength of Squadrons 32 Files)

Total Loss:

Officers	21
NCOs and Men	257
Horses	335

Copy of Official Return dated 26th October 1854
(Signed) JBB Eastcourt, Adjutant General.

Names of Officers who commanded Regiments in the Charge, with the dates of their death:

Col Lord George Paget 4th Light Dragoons – 1879/80
Col Shewell 8th Hussars – 1859
Col Douglas 11th Hussars – 1871
Captain Oldham 13th Light Dragoons – Killed in the Charge
Captain Morris 17th Lancers – 1858 (India)
The Earl of Cardigan Commanding the Brigade – 1868

The Light Brigade

Return of Casualties 25th October 1854

4th Light Dragoons

Killed and Missing	2 Officers and 32 NCOs & Men
Wounded	2 Officers and 21 NCOs & Men
Total Loss:	4 Officers, 53 Men and 50 horses

8th Hussars

Killed and Missing	2 Officers and 26 NCOs & Men
Wounded	2 Officers and 17 NCOs & Men
Total Loss:	4 Officers, 43 Men and 38 horses

11th Hussars

Killed and Missing	1 Officer and 32 NCOs & Men
Wounded	2 Officers and 23 NCOs & Men
Total Loss:	3 Officers, 55 Men and 72 horses

13th Light Dragoons

Killed and Missing	3 Officers and 24 NCOs & Men
Wounded	14 NCOs & Men
Total Loss:	3 Officers, 38 Men and 76 horses

17th Lancers

Killed and Missing	3 Officers and 33 NCOs & Men
Wounded	4 Officers and 34 NCOs & Men
Total Loss:	7 Officers, 67 Men and 99 horses

TOTAL LOSS:	21 Officers, 257 N.C. Officers & Men and 335 horses

Copy of Official Return dated 26th October 1854
(Signed) JBB Eastcourt, Adjutant General

APPENDIX 2

11th PAO HUSSARS

Names of Killed, Wounded and Prisoners of War

25th October 1854

Killed:

Sgts:	J Jones, T Jordan
Ptes:	C Allured, J Brunton, R Bubb, C B Cooper, W Davis, J Elder, R Gwinnell, G Hoarne, J Jackman, J Larkin, R Lazzell, R Lovett, J McGeorge, D Parcell, A Russell, L Shoppee, J Shrive, J Stephenson, W J Wakelin, D Ward, W Wareham, G Wootton

(Killed at Inkerman: Pte J Wright)

Wounded:

Capts:	C A Cook
Lieuts:	H D Trevelyan
Cornets:	G P Houghton, (died of wounds)
Sgts:	W Bently, R Davies, J Kilrest, J Lawson (lost right arm)
Cpls:	E Hudson
Ptes:	G Turner (died of wounds), W Frith, T Roberts, J Glarister, S Milbourne, J Wilcox, N Jewell, C Cork, S Lancer, W N Pennington, R Young (lost right arm), J Purvis (died of wounds), T Greene, T Walker, J Bingham, R Martin (lost right arm), D Andrews, G Jowett, J Shurgold, J Strutt, J Flemming

Prisoners:

Cpls: J Williams (died of wounds)
Ptes: J Berry (died of wounds), W Hyde (died of wounds)
Returned: J Drydan (31 wounds), N Henry, H Parker,
W N Spring, W Sheppard (lost leg)

In the year 1881, 27 years after the Charge, I obtained Returns from 155 survivors; of that number 74 were wounded. The following Table will show the nature of those wounds, and will indicate the Regiments which more particularly came into contact with the Russian Lancers.

REGIMENTS	Sabre	Lance	Shot, Shell, Grape, Canister, Bullet	Wounded	Returns
4th Light Dragoons	2	—	7	9	29
8th Hussars	4	4	1	9	14
11th Hussars	7	9	6	22	45
13th Light Dragoons	1	1	13	15	32
17th Lancers	2	5	12	19	35
TOTAL	16	19	39	74	155

Average age of the 155 survivors at the time of the Charge:

REGIMENTS	No of Survivors	Total Age	Average Age
4th Light Dragoons	29	813	28
8th Hussars	14	340	24
11th Hussars	45	1126	25
13th Light Dragoons	32	840	27
17th Lancers	35	946	27
TOTAL	155	4065	26

Number under 20 years of age	8
Number between 20 and 30 years	110
Number between 30 and 40 years	34
Number between 40 and 50 years	3
TOTAL	155

(Signed) G. Loy Smith, late Regimental Sergeant-Major
11th Hussars.

APPENDIX 3

Russian Cavalry present at the Battle of Balaclava:

	Estimated strength
11th Hussars, or the Duke of Leuchtenberg's Regt Dress – Light blue with scarlet shakos	800
12th Hussars, or the Duke of Sax-Weimar's Regt Dress – Entirely Light Blue	800
The Combined Regiment of Lancers	600
Don Cossacks	400
TOTAL	2,600

These regiments were stationed in the Crimea. We saw them at the Buljanak and the Alma. At McKenzie's Farm several of the Hussars were taken prisoner, at the same time we took their baggage. I have in my possession an officer's shabrack, light blue, with the imperial initials of Nicholas 1st embroidered in gold at the points, but no number to indicate to which of the two Hussar regiments it belonged; also an officer's undress jacket belonging to the 12th Hussars, and a 12 pounder cannon-ball fired by the battery we charged. I have likewise some flowers that I gathered—on the very spot where the Russian guns stood—7 months after the Charge, and a carbine and button belonging to the 11th Hussars.

APPENDIX 4

To The Officers of the 11th PAO Hussars:

Gentlemen,

My object in drawing the accompanying plans and getting the evidence that circumstances have put me in a position to obtain, is, that the gallantry displayed by Colonel Douglas, the officers, non-commissioned officers and men that followed him in the Charge, shall be more particularly known and explained than it has ever been heretofore.

I should not have presumed to do this, had I not been perfectly clear as to what took place on that occasion. To this day I remember every little incident that came under my observation; not only that, I have all the letters I wrote home to bear me out in my assertions. At the time I had been 21 years in the service, had been present at field days on the plains of Meerut and Kānpur, and four seasons in Phoenix Park, and had often commanded a troop under the Earl of Cardigan. This experience enabled me to compass what was going on around me, then have free scope to ride about in rear of the regiment in the advance. The duties of adjutant having been desolved on me, this again gave me a greater opportunity of observing everything that passed, more so than those leading or riding in the ranks.

A few years ago a large picture was exhibited in the Royal Academy, representing Lord George Paget leading the 11th out of action. Seeing this picture finally decided me in taking this step, for I felt that Colonel Douglas was being deprived of the honour so justly due to him.

The evidence I shall now adduce will, I think, convince all impartial readers. First, that Colonel Douglas, and he alone, commanded us, that no word of command was given to the 11th by any other officer, that he carried every officer and man (that was not placed *Hors de Combat*) with him to the extreme end of the valley, and back to the original position.

His words of command frequently were, 'Follow Me Men,'—implicitly did the men obey him. Second, that the 11th *alone* pursued the Russian Hussar Brigade to the extreme end of the valley; that at the time the 11th was holding this brigade at bay, the remnants of the other regiments were in full retreat, pursued by the three squadrons of lancers on the other side of the valley. Third, that no regiment was engaged with the Hussar Brigade and the three squadrons of lancers on the right side of the valley but the 11th.

If, as has been represented, any portions of the other regiments had advanced beyond the guns they would have encountered no regular cavalry, the whole space in rear of them was quite clear, for within five or six minutes of the lst line coming in contact with the guns, I galloped across the great open space in rear of them, but met with none of our troops either advancing or retiring, nor yet the enemy.

Lord Paget in his Journal says, 'I met the 11th in full retreat pursued by the enemy, and gave the order "Halt Front," which they and the 4th did as if they had been on parade.' This word of command may have been given on the other side of the valley with the 8th Hussars, but most certainly not with us: common sense forbids it. The Hussar Brigade was close at our heels, till but a short distance from the lancers. To have halted then would have been sheer madness, for we should have been ridden over. Every man, from the time Colonel Douglas gave the order, (at the bottom of the valley when he found we were cut off), 'Then fight for your lives men,' till he arrived at the ground they charged from, galloped for his very life.

It is perfectly astonishing how little some men remember what occurred on that occasion, it was all a whirl to them. I have questioned many who simply remember nothing. Others have told the most extravagant stories, some have even said they carried gun spikes and spiked guns, when I knew well that only four non-commissioned officers in the whole brigade were possessed of them at the time. At the Battle of Alma, an aide-de-camp galloped up to the 11th and called out for the sergeant-majors and gave to each of them a gun spike, saying, 'These are all we have,' adding, 'you may have an opportunity of using them presently.' We, the 11th, being the first cavalry to ascend the heights. I never saw but one gun spike and that is now in my possession.

I never yet met with a non-commissioned officer or man of the 11th of whom Kinglake ever asked a question. I am of the opinion after reading from pages 336 to 346 of his 4th volume, that all the information he ever received as to the doings of the 11th at Balaclava, was from the youngest officer of the 11th present on that occasion, and that he took it for granted, without making further enquiry, that all Lord Paget said about his connection with the 11th was correct. He says nothing about the 11th being short of a troop leader, and Sergeant-Major Teevan commanding the troop of which he was troop sergeant-major, nor yet of the gallantry displayed by Lieutenant Dunn, for which he received the Victoria Cross.

There is nothing recorded in history to surpass the gallantry of Colonel Douglas and those under his command. When the third of a mile in rear of the guns, and a mile and a half from the English position, with no prospect of support, did he surrender? No. Like his predecessor Captain Benjamen Lutyens, he engaged the whole Russian cavalry, 30 to 1, breaking through them with the loss of only about 20 men.

As a proof of how little could have been known about our movements, I have at this moment before me a plan drawn by Captain Ennis 11th Hussars (and given to me by him) under the directions of the Earl of Cardigan, in which the 4th are represented inclining to the left across in rear of the 11th before arriving at the guns, and then actually on our left at the bottom of the valley close to the Aqueduct. Lord Paget does not even say he was there, but met us returning, yet in the plate in his Journal he represents the 4th on our right pursuing the Russian Hussar Brigade, when it is well known the 4th were in the battery at the time. Kinglake, again in Plate 6 represents the 11th close to the hill on the left of the gorge, whereas it was up the hill on the right that the 11th drove the Russian Hussar Brigade. This part of the plate is a misrepresentation of the affair altogether. No other regiment, or part of a regiment, was there at the time except the 11th. This I think I shall satisfactorily prove.

It is now 50 years since I joined the Eleventh. From that time up to the present it has always been my greatest pride to uphold and defend the honour of the regiment in which I spent so many happy years.

I am,
Gentlemen
Your most Obedient Servant
G. Loy Smith
Late Regimental Sergeant-Major 11th Hussars

March 27th 1883

The foregoing address 'To the Officers of the 11th Hussars,' with my narrative and the six plans of the Charge, I sent to the regiment when stationed in Leeds, to which I received the following letter from Lord Talbot:

Leeds, 5 April 1883

Dear Sir,

I am desired by Lieutenant-Colonel Balfe and the officers of the 11th Hussars to convey to you their very sincere thanks for the handsome and most interesting present you have given to the regiment.

We are all extremely pleased with your plans, which have been much admired and your interesting account has been considerably perused already.

Believe me, with many thanks,
Very truly yours

Edmund Talbot, Captain & Adjutant 11th Hussars

Mr G L Smith

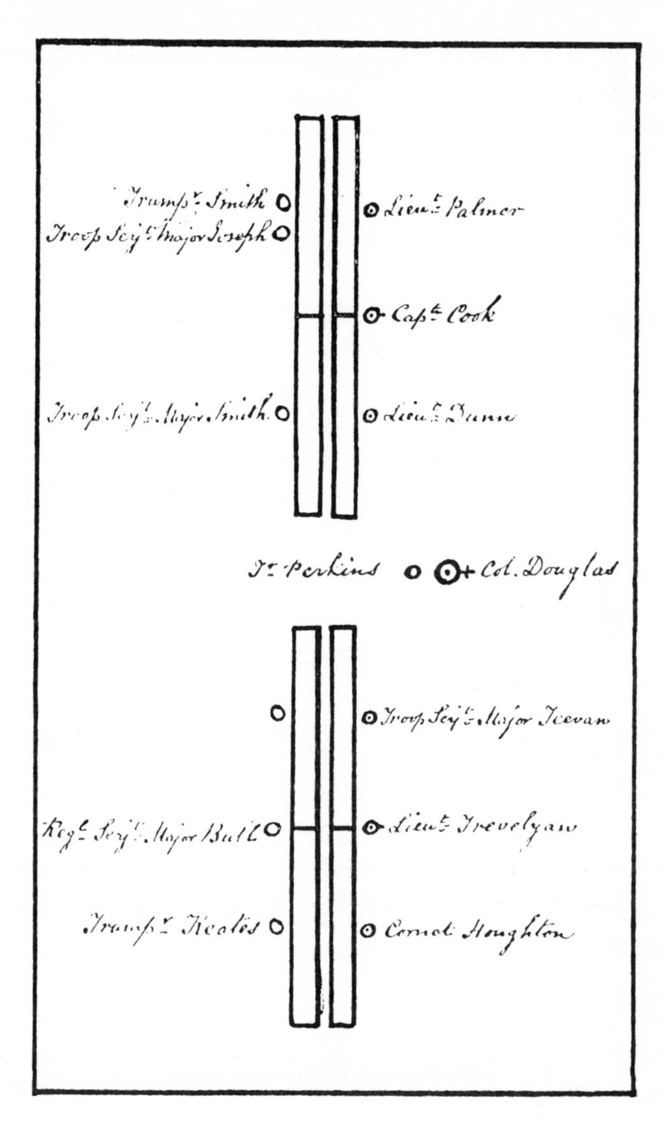

Plate 1

The 11th (P.A.O.) Hussars in Line. 25th October 1854.

Extent of Front 72 yards. Thirty-two files per squadron.
Before arriving at the guns, Lieutenant Trevelyan and Cornet Houghton had fallen back wounded. Regimental Sergeant-Major Bull, Trumpeter Keates and Smith had their horses killed; also about 50 non-commissioned officers and men riding in the ranks had been placed Hors de Combat.

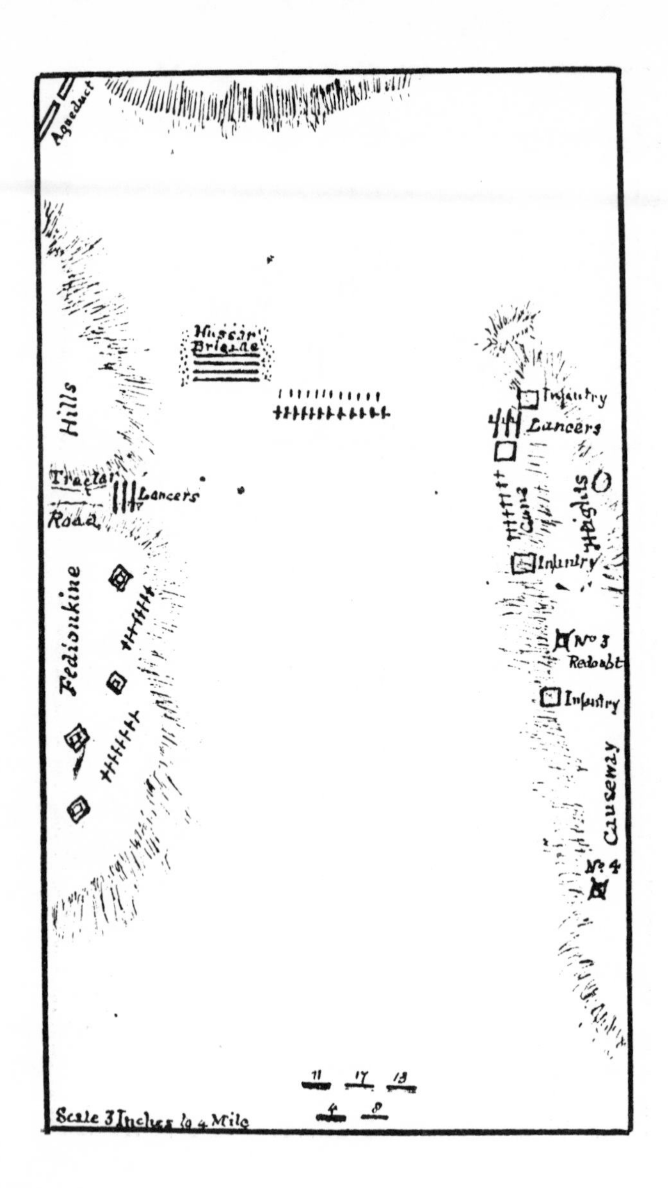

Plate 2

Length of valley, about two miles from the hill Lord Raglan stood on, just behind the Light Brigade, to the hill near the Aqueduct—Breadth from half a mile to three quarters.

Position of the Light Brigade just before the Charge.

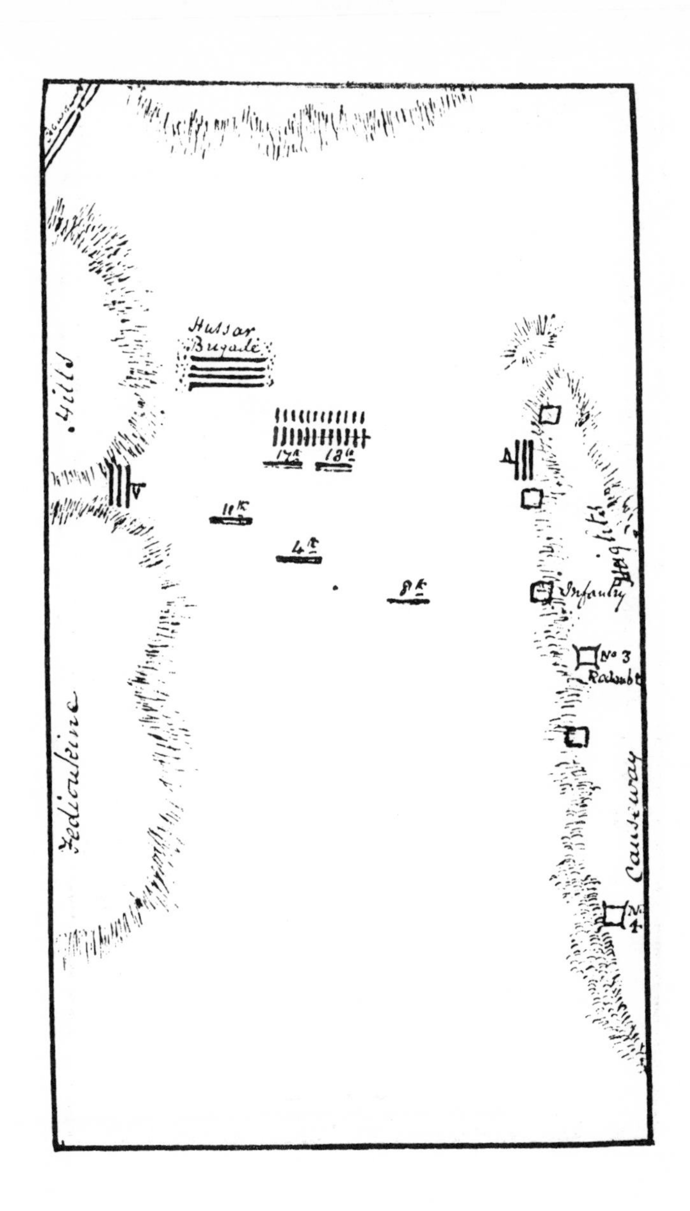

Plate 3

The 1st Line nearing the guns.

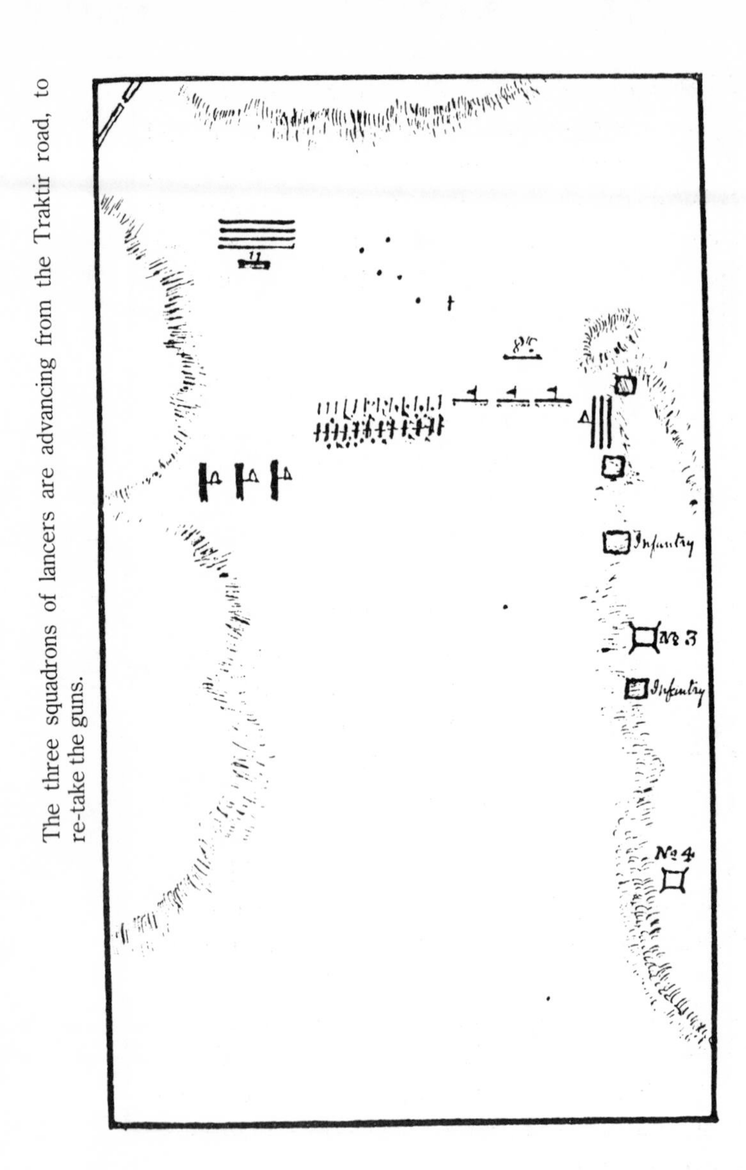

The three squadrons of lancers are advancing from the Traktir road, to re-take the guns.

Plate 4

The 4th are now in the 12 gun battery—the 8th have just wheeled about and are in the act of charging the three squadrons of lancers that had formed across their rear. The 11th are pursuing the Hussar Brigade. When the 8th had broken through the lancers, they were joined by the 4th and united together under the command of Lord George Paget and Colonel Shewell.

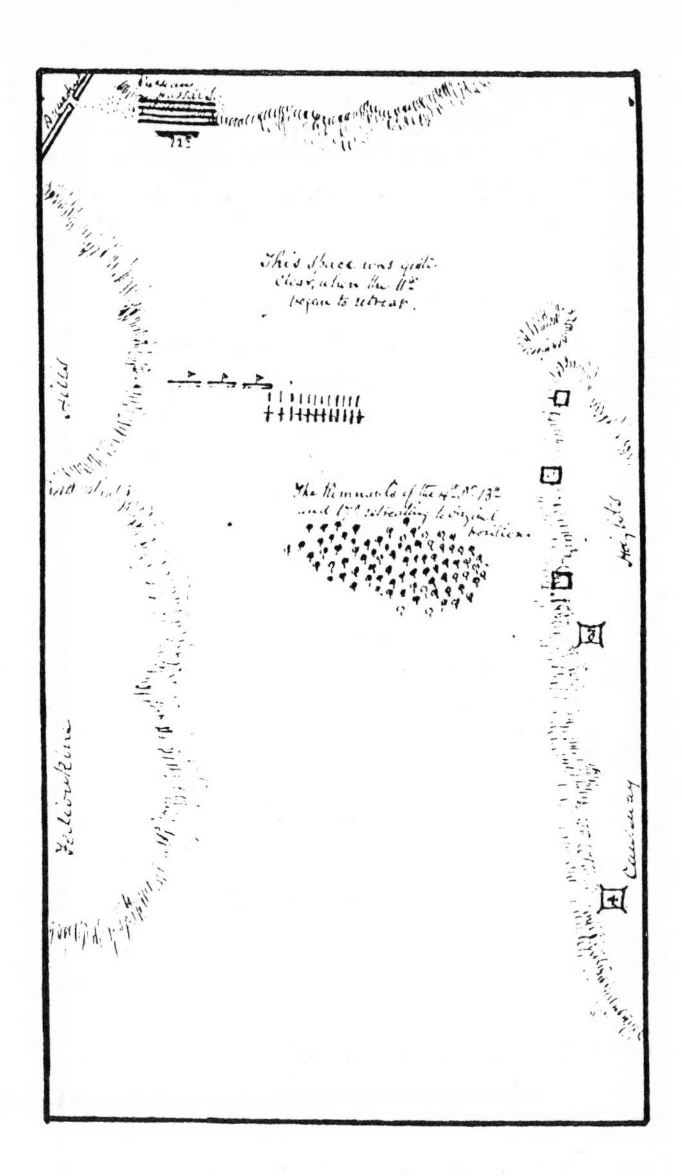

Plate 5

State of the battle at the time Colonel Douglas saw three squadrons of lancers form across his rear.

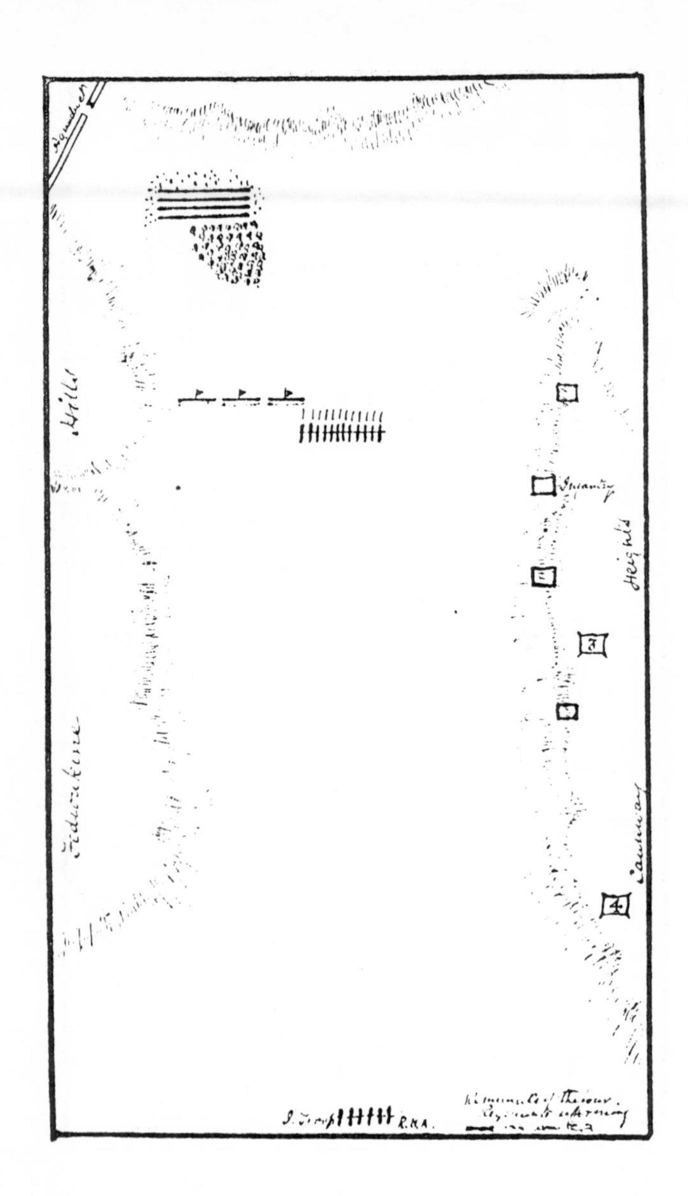

Plate 6

The 11th pursued by the Russian Hussar Brigade.

At this time the remnants of the other regiments had reached the ground from which they charged.

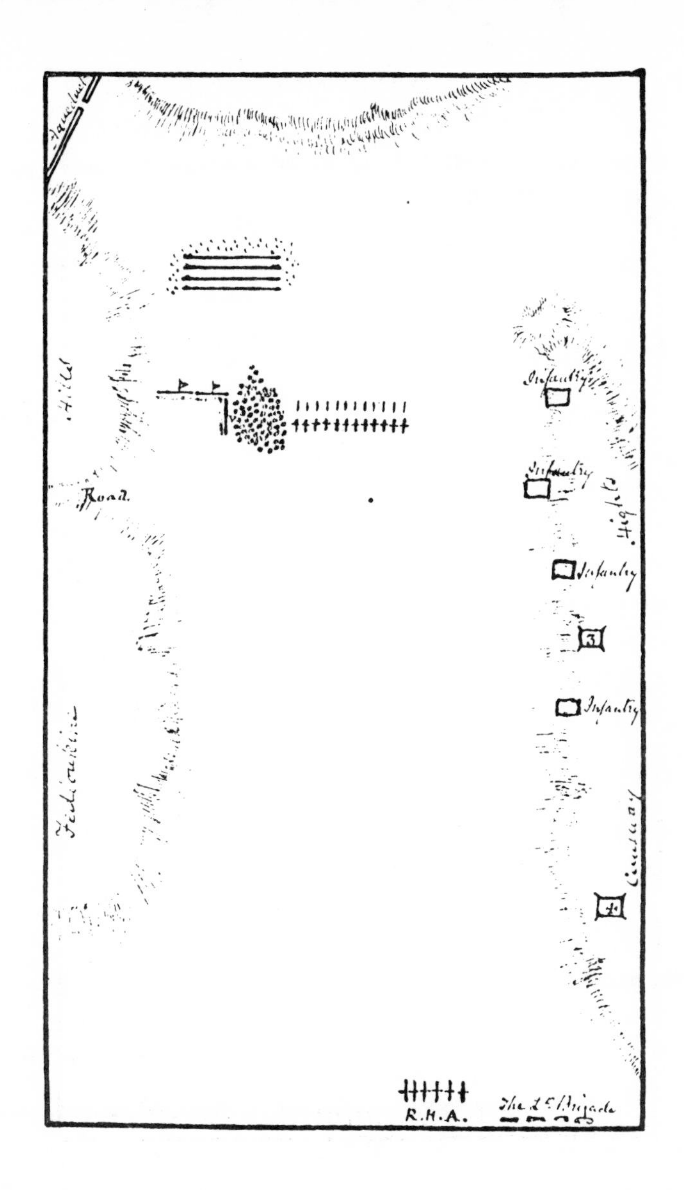

Plate 7

The 11th passing the Russian lancers.

APPENDIX 5

Field Marshal Lord Raglan to Duke of Newcastle
Received January 8th 1855
Before Sebastopol, December 16th 1854

My Lord Duke,

I regret to be under the necessity of forwarding to your Grace the copy of a letter which has been addressed to me by Lieutenant General the Earl of Lucan.

When I received it, I placed it in the hands of Brigadier General Airy, the Quartermaster General and requested him to suggest to his Lordship to withdraw the communication considering that it would not lead to his advantage in the slightest degree, but Lord Lucan having declined to take the step recommended, I have but one course to pursue—that of laying the letter before your Grace and submitting to you such observations upon it as I am bound, in justice to myself, to put you in possession of.

Lieutenant General the Earl of Lucan complains that, in my despatch to your Grace of the 28th October, I stated that, 'from some misconception of the instructions to advance, the Lieutenant General considered that he was bound to attack at all hazards'. His Lordship conceives this statement to be a grave charge, and an imputation reflecting seriously on his professional character, and he deems it incumbent upon him to state those facts which he cannot doubt must clear him from what he respectfully submits as altogether unmerited.

I have referred to my despatch and far from being willing to recall one word of it, I am prepared to declare that the

Lieutenant General misconceived the written instructions which called upon him to attack at all hazards, or to undertake the operation which led to such a brilliant display of gallantry on the part of the Light Brigade, and unhappily at the same time, occasioned such lamentable casualties in every regiment composing it.

In his Lordship's letter, he is wholly silent with respect to a previous order which had been sent him. He merely says that the cavalry was formed to support an intended movement of the infantry.

This previous order was in the following words, 'The cavalry to advance and take advantage of any opportunity to recover the heights. They will be supported by infantry which have been ordered to advance on two fronts.' This order did not seem to me to have been attended to and therefore it was that the instruction by Captain Nolan was forwarded to him. Lord Lucan must have read the first order with very little attention, for he now states that the cavalry was formed to support the infantry, whereas he was told by Brigadier General Airy, that, 'the cavalry was to advance and take advantage of any opportunity to recover the heights, and that they would be supported by infantry', and not that they were to support the infantry'; so little had he sought to do as he had been directed, that he had no men in advance of his main body, made no attempt to regain the heights and was so little informed of the position of the enemy that he asked Captain Nolan where and what he was to attack, as neither enemy nor guns were in sight?

This, your Grace will observe, is the Lieutenant General's own admission. The result of his inattention to the first order was that it never occurred to him that the second was connected with, and a repetition of the first. He viewed it only as a positive order to attack at all hazards (the word 'attack,' be it observed, was not made use of in General Airy's note), an unseen enemy whose position, numbers and composition he was wholly unacquainted with, and whom, in consequence of a previous order, he had taken no step whatever to watch.

I undoubtedly had no intention that he should make such an attack—there was nothing in the instruction to require it, and therefore, I conceived I was fully justified in stating to your Grace what was the exact truth, that the charge arose from the misconception of an order for the advance which Lord Lucan considered obliged him to attack at all hazards.

I wish I could say with his Lordship that, having decided against his conviction to make the movement, he did all he could to render it as little perilous as possible. This indeed, is far from being the case, in my judgement.

He was told that the Horse Artillery might accompany the cavalry, yet he did not bring it up; he was informed that the French cavalry was on his left, yet he did not invite their cooperation; he had the whole of the Heavy Cavalry at his disposal, yet he mentions having brought up only two regiments in support, and he omits all other precautions, either from want of due consideration or from the supposition that the unseen enemy was not in such great force as he apprehended (notwithstanding that he was warned of it by Lord Cardigan after the latter had received the order to attack).

I am much concerned, my Lord Duke, to have to submit these observations to your Grace. I entertain no wish to disparage the Earl of Lucan in your opinion or to cast a slur upon his professional reputation, but having been accused by his Lordship of having stated of him what was unmerited in my despatch I have felt obliged to enter into the subject and trouble your Grace at more length than I could have wished, in vindication of a report to your Grace in which I had strictly confined myself to that which I knew to be true, and had indulged in no observations whatever, or in any way grating to the feelings of his Lordship.

I have etc.

(Signed) Raglan

APPENDIX 6

Names of those to whom I am indebted for evidence in support of the correctness of the plans.

11TH HUSSARS
Lt Col Douglas
Troop Sgt-Major Joseph
Troop Sgt-Major Teevan
Sgt Bentley
Sgt Bonds
Sgt Guttridge
Sgt Lawson
Cpl Kilvert
Trumpeter Perkins
Pte Beeson
Pte Buckton
Pte Henry
Pte Holland
Pte Maule
Pte Parker
Pte Roberts
Pte Spring

ROYAL HORSE ARTILLERY
Troop Sgt-Major Norton
Sgt Lethbridge

4TH LIGHT DRAGOONS
Sgt Ferguson
Sgt Howes
Cpl Devlin
Cpl Grant
Pte Carroll
Pte Ford

8TH HUSSARS
Pte Bird
Pte Owen Glendwr

The following are extracts from Lord Paget's Journal:

Colonel Douglas
I did not cover the 17th Lancers, but was rather in echelon to them, thus:

17th Lancers
11th Hussars

The cavalry appeared to be in support of their guns, on their right rear.'

As to Lord Paget at any time rallying the 11th Hussars, *I cannot admit it.* Whatever was done in that way on the day of Balaclava, is fairly due to the officers and non-commissioned officers and discipline of the men of the regiment.'
(In marginal note Colonel Douglas writes, 'I dispute your rallying the 11th Hussars')

Troop Sergeant-Major J Joseph
I rode as a serrefile in rear of the left troop of the regiment in the Light Cavalry Charge. After passing the guns, I observed Troop Sergeant-Major Smith endeavouring to intercept the Russian artillery carrying off a field piece, but upon finding himself likely to be cut off, he returned to the regiment without effecting the object he was desirous of carrying out. I was at the extreme end of the valley when Colonel Douglas ordered us to save ourselves as we could, and bear witness to his noble actions in leading us so gallantly and coolly against the enemy's cavalry until we could proceed no further.

Troop Sergeant-Major Rourke Teevan
I was troop leader of the left troop of the right squadron in the Charge, and passed down to the extreme end of the valley in pursuit of the Russian cavalry. I was surrounded by the Russian lancers who had formed up to obstruct our return, but I passed through them, receiving a lance wound through my right thumb.

Sergeant W Bentley
I rode on the left of the first squadron. During the charge I was close to Colonel Douglas, who earnestly impressed upon us the necessity of keeping well together as we swept down the valley, encouraging the men by his own gallantry. After passing the guns which had been silenced, the colonel called upon us to

attack the cavalry which was drawn up in their rear, saying, 'Give them another charge.' We followed them as far as the valley would permit us, and came close upon them. The colonel then called upon us to retire and re-form upon the lancers in our rear. I drew his attention to the circumstance of their being Russian, and not our lancers, when we got his order 'Fight for your lives,' thereupon all retired. On passing them I was attacked by an officer and several of the men, and received a slight wound from a lance. I was pursued by them, and cut the officer across the face. Lieutenant Dunn came to my assistance. I saw him cleave one of them almost to the saddle and can bear witness to his admirable and gallant fortitude and determination. I did not see, or hear Lord Paget at any time give any word of command to the 11th, or any order to Colonel Douglas. We were not mixed up with any other regiment, we retired alone.

Sergeant Seth Bonds

I rode in the centre of the first squadron, consequently I was not far from Colonel Douglas. I heard no-one but him give any order to the 11th at any time during the Charge or retreat. I did not see Lord Paget at any time during the Charge, but when I arrived at the top of the valley, I saw him in conversation with Lord Lucan. I do not believe that any of the 11th remained at the guns. The only men with us when behind the guns were a few stragglers from the other regiments.

Sergeant G G Guttridge

I rode in the front rank on the extreme left of the regiment in the Charge. As we approached the battery, which was formed across the valley, the fire was most terrific. After passing the guns, I observed a Russian field piece, drawn by six horses, being taken away from its position, and Sergeant-Major Smith endeavouring to secure the assistance of a party to prevent it's being carried off. He followed after it, but finding himself alone and unsupported, and a party of Cossacks led by an officer intercepting him, he returned to his place. I witnessed him encouraging the men to bear up and show a good front, calling out, 'The better front we keep the better chance we shall all have.' His example had beneficial effect.

Sergeant J Lawson

I rode on the right of the second squadron, front rank, consequently was just behind Colonel Douglas during the entire advance, to the bottom of the valley, not far from the aqueduct. During that time I heard no-one give any order either to the 11th or Colonel Douglas, nor yet as we returned. I saw no other English regiment at the bottom of the valley except the 11th—we were entirely alone both going and returning. After passing the lancers my horse was killed and I lost my right arm.

Corporal J Hilrest

I feel certain that Lord Paget had nothing whatever to do with the 11th during the Charge. I neither heard nor saw him—the 11th was quite alone.

Trumpeter W Perkins

I was trumpeter to Colonel Douglas and rode close to him in the Charge and retreat, till my horse was killed after passing the lancers. When halted about a hundred yards in right rear of the guns, I heard Colonel Douglas call out, 'What are we to do now Lord Paget.' He replied, 'Where is Lord Cardigan,' and galloped away. I neither saw nor heard him again. The 11th alone pursued the Russian Hussars to the bottom of the valley. When surrounded, Colonel Douglas ordered us to rally on the 17th Lancers. I immediately sounded the 'Rally.' We were then close face to face with the Russian cavalry. When engaged with the lancers I saw Lieutenant Dunn, with one stroke of his sword, sever a Russian Lancer's head all but off.

Private B Beeson

I rode in the centre of the right squadron. During the Charge I neither saw nor heard Lord Paget give any word of command to the 11th, nor did I hear him give any order to Colonel Douglas.

Private J Buckton

I rode within a few files of the right of the regiment in the rear rank—several men on my right were killed in the advance. We passed close by the guns (I do not think any men remained behind) we then halted about one hundred yards in rear. After closing in, Colonel Douglas ordered us to give them another charge, we then pursued the Russian cavalry to the bottom of the valley. No other regiment was with us, I only saw a straggler or two (one belonged to the 17th, he rode near me). I did not see Lord Paget, nor yet did I hear any word of command given except by Colonel Douglas.

Private N Henry

My horse was killed just before arriving at the guns. On recovering myself I saw Lord Paget leading the 4th but did not see him afterwards. Seeing my regiment a little distance beyond the guns, halted, I ran to them, when I was directed by Sergeant-Major Smith to a riderless horse in the ranks, which I mounted. We then pursued the cavalry in our front to the bottom of the valley not far from the Aqueduct bridge. No other regiment was with us or near us, and no word of command was given except by Colonel Douglas. After passing the lancers that were formed across the valley to intercept our retreat my second horse was killed and I was taken prisoner.

Private M Holland

I rode in the front rank of the right troop of the regiment. I heard no word of command given by anyone except Colonel Douglas, either going down the valley or returning. I did not see Lord Paget at any time during the Charge.

Private G Maule

I rode about the 5th file from the right of the regiment; we passed close by the right of the guns. I saw none of our men remain behind with them. I did not see Lord Paget at any time during the Charge or retreat. When at the bottom of the valley, we, the 11th, were quite alone. A few stragglers joined us as we returned.

Private H Parker

I rode on the left of the rear rank of the lst Squadron, covering Sergeant Bentley. I was not many yards from Colonel Douglas during the Charge and retreat. None of the 11th remained at the guns for Colonel Douglas frequently called out, 'Follow me men, and use the point.' When we halted a short distance on the right rear of the guns, I heard Colonel Douglas call out, 'What are we to do now Lord Paget?,' he replied, 'Where is Lord Cardigan?' and galloped away. I did not see him again.

Colonel Douglas immediately gave the order for us to charge the Russian cavalry in our front, which consisted of Hussars and Cossacks. They retreated and did not halt till we got to the bottom of the valley, not far from the Aqueduct (no other English regiment was near us or in sight at this time).

The other regiments must have retired, for three squadrons of lancers formed across our rear; as we approached them their right squadron was thrown back, after passing them, the artillery opened fire on us, when my horse was killed and I was made prisoner. During the afternoon General Leprandi visited the prisoners and through an interpreter asked me many questions. He then told me that I belonged to a brave regiment.

Private T Roberts

I feel certain that Lord Paget had nothing whatever to do with the 11th during the Charge. The 11th was quite alone.

Private M H Spring

I rode in the centre of the 2nd Squadron front rank. When halted, after passing the guns, I heard Colonel Douglas call out, 'What are we to do now Lord Paget?,' he replied, 'Where is Lord Cardigan?'

I did not see Lord Paget either then or at any subsequent period. We pursued the Russian cavalry to the bottom of the valley. When returning after passing the lancers my horse was killed and I was made prisoner. Colonel Douglas was the only officer we received any order from, he alone commanded us.

Troop Sergeant-Major W Norton, J Troop RHA

When the Light Brigade returned, my troop was standing prepared for action at the top of the valley where they charged from. I saw Lord Paget return with the remnants of the 4th and 8th, the 13th and 17th, much broken, retired before them.

We now looked eagerly for the 11th fearing they were cut off as none but wounded and unhorsed men had returned. After 8 to 10 minutes we saw them breaking through the Russian line, they came up the valley headed by Colonel Douglas and galloped passed the right flank of the troop, forming up on our right rear—we cheered them as they passed us, I noticed they retired in a compact body, about 60 in number (I did not observe that there were any men of other regiments with them). Some little time after this Sergeant-Major Smith returned alone. As he rode through us, I congratulated him on his escape.

Sergeant Lethbridge, J troop RHA

I commanded the left gun of the troop and saw the Light Brigade return from the Charge. The 11th came back alone some little time after the other regiments and we cheered them as they passed. They formed up on our right rear.

Sergeant R Ferguson, 4th Light Dragoons

I rode in the centre of the 1st Squadron. During the advance I saw the 11th Hussars on our left front, but saw nothing more of them after we arrived at the guns (the 4th was completely broken up). After taking possession of the battery, and disabling as many of the gunners and drivers as we came in contact with, some of us passed a little beyond, but there being no troops there, and an alarm being given that the Russian lancers were intercepting us, we began to retire, passing along their front as best we could, all order being lost. They appeared to come from the Traktir Road—it was in front of the guns we passed them, *not* in rear. I saw Lord Paget at this time, he retired with us. We had no gun spikes, I never saw one. At the time I had been 13 years in the service.

Sergeant J Howes, 4th Light Dragoons

I was the left hand man of the regiment. When we reached the end of the Charge, I found myself amongst the Russian guns—a few of my troop, including our Troop Sergeant-Major Herbert (who was killed) surrounded one of the guns. He dismounted with the intention of cutting the traces. We killed all the men belonging to the said gun, and I went to the leading horses and turned their heads round with the view of bringing the gun away, but finding it impossible, I left them. I did not at this time see either Lord Paget or Colonel Douglas. We now received the order to retire. The next thing I recollect, we were cutting our way through the lancers. I received a slight sword cut on the ear. A Russian horse now came galloping along side me which I brought back, and sold the next day for £5. I have the pistol, the only relic I have kept out of the kit I found on the horse.

Corporal J Devlin, 4th Light Dragoons

We were well in hand on arriving at the guns. After seizing them the portion of the brigade then there was rallied by Lord George Paget. Finding our position untenable we rode back over the same ground.

Corporal R Grant, 4th Light Dragoons

When we charged into the guns I dismounted and could have used some gun spikes had I had them, but unfortunately none had been issued. I never saw a gun spike. We then disabled as many of the gunners and drivers as we could, to prevent them taking away the guns, feeling they were ours. After some little time I found myself in the rear almost alone, the greater portion of my regiment having retreated. Seeing the 11th coming up the valley pursued by the Russian Hussars, I galloped towards them. In tacking on to their rear, a sergeant of the Hussars galloped at me and tried to cut me down, but I defended myself. I did not see Lord Paget at this time, in fact I had not seen him since the moment we were approaching the guns. At the time I had been 19 years in the service.

Private P Carroll, 4th Light Dragoons

When we commenced to retreat my horse was killed and I was wounded with grape shot just in front of the guns. After running some little distance Lord Paget and Colonel Shewell passed me riding together, they appeared to be speaking to each other.

Private J Ford, 4th Light Dragoons says

My horse was killed about 150 yards from the guns. Whilst entangled with my dead horse, Lord Cardigan passed me galloping to the rear. As we advanced, many of the 17th Lancers passed us returning. On recovering myself, I began to retire but could not run having been hurt in the fall. I had not proceeded far when the men of my regiment, and the 8th Hussars that has escaped, passed me galloping back up the valley.

Private W Bird, 8th Hussars

I remember distinctly seeing Lord Paget after we halted on the left rear of the guns. His words are most vividly impressed on my memory. He shouted, 'Shewell, have you seen the General?' He replied, 'No.' At this moment it was discovered that the Russian lancers had formed across our rear to cut us off. We immediately wheeled about and charged them. In the *mêlée* their artillery opened fire on us, when my horse was killed and I was made prisoner.

Private R Owen Glendwr, 8th Hussars

My horse was killed just before arriving on the left front of the guns. I caught a riderless horse of the 13th Light Dragoons, mounted and overtook my regiment before they wheeled about to charge the lancers that had intercepted us. After charging through them, my second horse was severely wounded. I was then surrounded by lancers and taken prisoner, but they leaving me that they might continue the pursuit of my regiment. I was enabled to catch another riderless horse belonging to the 4th Light Dragoons, which I mounted. Looking round to see which course I had better take, being at this time in the rear of the guns, I saw the 11th Hussars down the valley, galloping towards me, pursued by a strong body of Russian cavalry. I galloped towards, joined and returned with them. They were quite alone with the exception of a few stragglers like myself. I saw no other regiment near them. On arriving at the top of the valley I saw Lord George Paget talking to the staff.

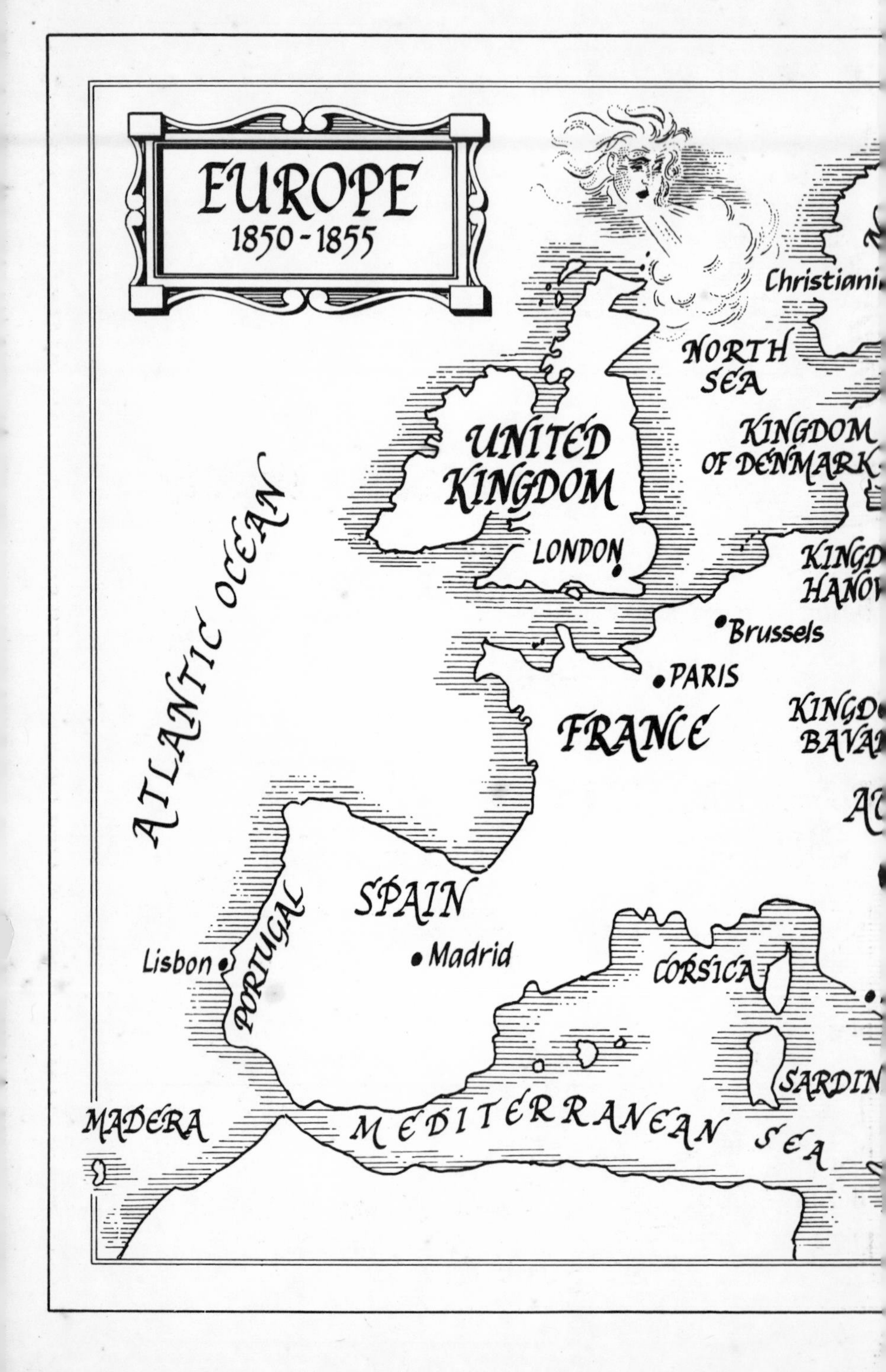
EUROPE
1850 - 1855
NORTH SEA
KINGDOM OF DENMARK
UNITED KINGDOM
LONDON
Brussels
PARIS
FRANCE
ATLANTIC OCEAN
SPAIN
PORTUGAL
Lisbon
Madrid
CORSICA
MADERA
MEDITERRANEAN SEA